TYPE 2 DIABETES

COOKBOOK FOR BEGINNERS

1300 Days of Healthy and Delicious Recipes to help you Achieve a Better Lifestyle

© Copyright 2022 - All rights reserved.

The content contained within this book may not be reproduced, duplicated or transmitted without direct written permission from the author or the publisher.

Under no circumstances will any blame or legal responsibility be held against the publisher, or author, for any damages, reparation, or monetary loss due to the information contained within this book. Either directly or indirectly.

Legal Notice:

This book is copyright protected. This book is only for personal use. You cannot amend, distribute, sell, use, quote or paraphrase any part, or the content within this book, without the consent of the author or publisher.

Disclaimer Notice:

Please note the information contained within this document is for educational and entertainment purposes only. All effort has been executed to present accurate, up to date, and reliable, complete information. No warranties of any kind are declared or implied. Readers acknowledge that the author is not engaging in the rendering of legal, financial, medical or professional advice. The content within this book has been derived from various sources. Please consult a licensed professional before attempting any techniques outlined in this book.

By reading this document, the reader agrees that under no circumstances is the author responsible for any losses, direct or indirect, which are incurred as a result of the use of information contained within this document, including, but not limited to, errors, omissions, or inaccuracies.

Table Of Contents

WHY I DECIDED TO WRITE THIS BOOK 8

INTRODUCTION 10

CHAPTER 1: TYPE 1 AND TYPE 2 DIABETES 12
- TYPES OF DIABETES 12
- WHAT'S THE DIFFERENCE? 12
- FOOD TO EAT 13
- FOODS TO AVOID 14

CHAPTER 2: HOW TO DEAL WITH DIABETES 18
- HOW TO LIVE WITH DIABETES? 18
- WHAT FOODS SHOULD BE IN A DIABETIC DIET PLAN? 19

CHAPTER 3: DIETARY REQUIREMENTS FOR TYPE-2 DIABETES... 20
- PROTEIN 20
- FATS 20
- CARBOHYDRATES 21
- FIBER 22

CHAPTER 4: TIPS AND TRICKS FOR DIABETIC RECIPES 24

CHAPTER 5: COOKING TRICKS, TIPS, AND TIMESAVERS 26
- DIFFERENT TYPES OF COOKING FOR DIABETIC RECIPES 26
- TIPS ON COOKING WITH DIABETES 26

CHAPTER 6: BREAKFAST 28
1. Whole-Grain Breakfast Cookies 28
2. Blueberry Breakfast Cake 28
3. Whole-Grain Pancakes 29
4. Buckwheat Grouts Breakfast Bowl 29
5. Peach Muesli Bake 30
6. Steel-Cut Oatmeal Bowl With Fruit and Nuts 30
7. Whole-Grain Dutch Baby Pancake 30
8. Mushroom, Zucchini, and Onion Frittata 31
9. Spinach and Cheese Quiche 31
10. Spicy Jalapeno Popper Deviled Eggs 32
11. Lovely Porridge 32
12. Salty Macadamia Chocolate Smoothie 32
13. Basil and Tomato Baked Eggs 33
14. Cinnamon and Coconut Porridge 33
15. An Omelet of Swiss Chard 33
16. Cheesy Low-Carb Omelet 34
17. Yogurt and Kale Smoothie 34
18. Bacon and Chicken Garlic Wrap 34
19. Grilled Chicken Platter 35
20. Parsley Chicken Breast 35
21. Mustard Chicken 35
22. Balsamic Chicken 36
23. Greek Chicken Breast 36
24. Chipotle Lettuce Chicken 36
25. Stylish Chicken-Bacon Wrap 37
26. Healthy Cottage Cheese Pancakes 37
27. Avocado Lemon Toast 37
28. Healthy Baked Eggs 38
29. Quick Low-Carb Oatmeal 38
30. Tofu and Vegetable Scramble 39
31. Breakfast Smoothie Bowl With Fresh Berries 39
32. Chia and Coconut Pudding 39
33. Tomato and Zucchini Sauté 40
34. Steamed Kale With Mediterranean Dressing 40
35. Healthy Carrot Muffins 41

CHAPTER 7: MEAT 42
36. Fried Pork Chops 42
37. Pork on a Blanket 42
38. Chicken Thighs 42
39. Tasty Harissa Chicken 43
40. Pork Rind 43
41. Ginger Chili Broccoli 43
42. Pork Tenderloin 44
43. Chicken Soup 44
44. Roasted Pork 44
45. Marinated Loin Potatoes 45
46. Homemade Flamingos 45
47. Meatloaf Reboot 45
48. Tasty Chicken Tenders 46
49. Creamy Mushroom Pork Chops 46
50. Pork and Sweet Potato Mash 46
51. Lamb Roast 47
52. Burgundy Lamb Shanks 47
53. Fruity Pork Roast 48
54. Pork Carnitas 48
55. Spiced Lamb Shoulder With Carrots 48
56. Pineapple Pork Tacos 49
57. Lamb Tagine 49
58. Barbecue Pulled Pork 50
59. Zoodles Carbonara 50
60. Pork and Apple Skillet 50
61. Vegetable Beef Soup 51
62. Open-Faced Pub-Style Bison Burgers 51
63. Broccoli Beef Stir-Fry 52
64. Beef and Pepper Fajita Bowls 52
65. Lamb Kofta Meatballs With Cucumber Quick-Pickled Salad 53
66. Turkey Scaloppini 53
67. Ground Turkey Taco Skillet 54
68. Turkey Meatloaf Meatballs 54
69. Citrus Pork Tenderloin 55
70. Beef and Sweet Potato Stew 55
71. Pork Diane 55
72. Pork Souvlakia With Tzatziki Sauce 56
73. Beef, Tomato, and Pepper Tortillas 57
74. Classic Stroganoff 57
75. Ritzy Beef Stew 57

#	Recipe	Page
76.	Slow Cooked Beef and Vegetables Roast	58
77.	Easy Lime Lamb Cutlets	58
78.	Sumptuous Lamb and Pomegranate Salad	59
79.	Pork Fillet on Lentils	60
80.	Turkey Rolls	60
81.	Turkey Escalope Pan	60
82.	Schnitzel With Chinese Cabbage	61
83.	Lemon Chicken With Basil	61
84.	Mississippi Style Pot Roast	62
85.	Pesto Chicken	62
86.	Chicken and Tofu	62
87.	Chicken and Peanut Stir-Fry	62
88.	Honey Mustard Chicken	63
89.	Lemon Garlic Turkey	63
90.	Chicken and Spinach	64
91.	Greek Chicken Lettuce Wraps	64
92.	Lemon Chicken With Kale	65
93.	Pumpkin, Bean, and Chicken Enchiladas	65
94.	Mu Shu Chicken	65
95.	Stove-Top Chicken, Macaroni, and Cheese	66
96.	Chicken Sausage Omelets With Spinach	66
97.	Chicken-Broccoli Salad With Buttermilk Dressing	67
98.	Country-Style Wedge Salad with Turkey	67
99.	Turkey Kabob Pitas	68
100.	Chicken Broth—Easy Slow-Cooker Method	68
101.	Oven-Fried Chicken Thighs	69
102.	Another Healthy "Fried" Chicken	69
103.	Buttermilk Ranch Chicken Salad	69
104.	Pineapple-Orange Grilled Chicken Breasts	70
105.	Herbed Chicken and Brown Rice	70
106.	Walnut Chicken	71
107.	Easy Chicken Paprika	71
108.	Chicken and Broccoli Casserole	71
109.	Chicken and Green Bean Stovetop Casserole	72
110.	Chicken and Asparagus in White Wine Sauce	72
111.	Chicken Kalamata	73
112.	Chicken Breasts in Balsamic Vinegar Sauce	73
113.	Easy Herbed Chicken	74
114.	Tomato and Pepper Steak	74
115.	Mexican Meatloaf	74
116.	Provencal Chuck	75
117.	Shredded Chili Beef	75
118.	Asian Beef and Broccoli	75
119.	Beef Bourguignon	76
120.	Chili Flank Steak	76
121.	Beef and Peas	76
122.	Classic Steak	77
123.	Satay Beef	77
124.	Roasted Chicken Breasts	77
125.	Sticky Chicken	78
126.	Stuffed Greek-Style Chicken Breasts	78

CHAPTER 8: SEAFOOD 80

#	Recipe	Page
127.	Cheesy Salmon Fillets	80
128.	Salmon With Asparagus	80
129.	Shrimp in Garlic Butter	81
130.	Baked Salmon With Garlic Parmesan Topping	81
131.	Baked Seafood Casserole	82
132.	BBQ Oysters With Bacon	82
133.	Blackened Shrimp	83
134.	Cajun Catfish	83
135.	Cajun Flounder and Tomatoes	83
136.	Cajun Shrimp and Roasted Vegetables	84
137.	Cilantro Lime Grilled Shrimp	84
138.	Coconut Shrimp	84
139.	Crab Cakes	85
140.	Crab Frittata	85
141.	Crispy Baked Flounder With Green Beans	86
142.	Crockpot Fish and Tomatoes	86
143.	Crunchy Lemon Shrimp	86
144.	Dill Smoked Salmon Over Noodles	87
145.	Fisherman's Pie	87
146.	Garlic Shrimp With Sun-Dried Tomatoes	88
147.	Tuna Sweet Corn Casserole	88
148.	Lemon Pepper Salmon	88
149.	Green Salmon Florentine	89
150.	Seared Scallops With Orange Sauce	89
151.	Cod Fillet With Quinoa and Asparagus	90
152.	Red Cabbage and Mushroom Pot Stickers	90
153.	Grilled Shrimp Skewers	91
154.	Tuna Salad	91
155.	Herring and Veggies Soup	92
156.	Salmon Soup	92
157.	Salmon and Shrimp Stew	93
158.	Salmon Curry	93
159.	Salmon With Bell Peppers	94
160.	Shrimp Salad	94
161.	Shrimp and Veggies Curry	95
162.	Shrimp With Zucchini	95
163.	Shrimp With Broccoli	95
164.	Montreal Style Salmon	96
165.	Cracker Crusted Cod	96
166.	Phyllo Vegetable Triangles	97
167.	Salmon Chowder	97
168.	Mustard-Crusted Sole	98
169.	Lemony Salmon	98
170.	Shrimp With Green Beans	99
171.	Crab Curry	99
172.	Mixed Chowder	99
173.	Mussels in Tomato Sauce	99
174.	Citrus Salmon	100
175.	Herbed Salmon	100
176.	Salmon in Green Sauce	100
177.	Braised Shrimp	101
178.	Shrimp Coconut Curry	101
179.	Trout Bake	102
180.	Sardine Curry	102
181.	Swordfish Steak	102
182.	Lemon Sole	102
183.	Grilled Tuna Steaks	103

#	Title	Page
184.	Red Clam Sauce and Pasta	103
185.	Salmon Milano	103
186.	Shrimp and Artichoke Skillet	104
187.	Tuna Carbonara	104
188.	Mediterranean Fish Fillets	104
189.	Alaskan Crab Omelette	105
190.	Fish Pie	105
191.	BBQ Prawn Gremolata	106
192.	White Fish Kebabs	106
193.	Tuna Nicoise	107
194.	Tuna-Stuffed Tomatoes	107
195.	Smoked Salmon Salad	108
196.	Baked Salmon With Zucchini Noodles	108
197.	Keralan Fish	109
198.	Shrimp With Spinach	109
199.	Scallops With Broccoli	109
200.	Salmon With Veggies	110
201.	Shrimp and Endives	110
202.	Baked Fish Fillets	110
203.	Salmon Cakes	111
204.	Grilled Split Lobster	111
205.	Fish Bone Broth	112
206.	Garlic Butter Shrimp	112
207.	Grilled Shrimp	112
208.	Garlic Ghee Pan-Fried Cod	113
209.	Mussel and Potato Stew	113
210.	Mustard Salmon With Herbs	113
211.	Nutty Coconut Fish	114
212.	Olive Oil Poached Tuna	114
213.	One-Pot Tuna Casserole	115
214.	Bacon-Wrapped Salmon	115
215.	Bagna Cauda	115
216.	Salmon Tikka	115
217.	Almond and Parmesan Crusted Tilapia	116
218.	Golden Turmeric Fish	116

CHAPTER 9: SALAD 118

#	Title	Page
219.	Thai Quinoa Salad	118
220.	Green Goddess Bowl and Avocado Cumin Dressing	118
221.	Sweet and Savory Salad	119
222.	Kale Pesto's Pasta	119
223.	Beet Salad With Basil Dressing	119
224.	Basic Salad With Olive Oil Dressing	120
225.	Spinach and Orange Salad With Oil Drizzle	120
226.	Fruit Salad With Coconut-Lime Dressing	120
227.	Cranberry and Brussels Sprouts With Dressing	120
228.	Parsnip, Carrot, and Kale Salad With Dressing	121
229.	Tomato Toasts	121
230.	Every Day Salad	121
231.	Super-Seedy Salad With Tahini Dressing	122
232.	Vegetable Salad	122
233.	Greek Salad	122
234.	Alkaline Spring Salad	123
235.	Fresh Tuna Salad	123
236.	Roasted Portobello Salad	123
237.	Shredded Chicken Salad	124
238.	Broccoli Salad	124
239.	Cherry Tomato Salad	124
240.	Ground Turkey Salad	125
241.	Asian Cucumber Salad	125
242.	Cauliflower Tofu Salad	125
243.	Scallop Caesar Salad	126
244.	Chicken Avocado Salad	126
245.	California Wraps	127
246.	Chicken Salad in Cucumber Cups	127
247.	Sunflower Seeds and Arugula Garden Salad	127
248.	Supreme Caesar Salad	127
249.	Tabbouleh-Arabian Salad	128

CHAPTER 10: SOUP 130

#	Title	Page
250.	Fresh Garden Vegetable Soup	130
251.	Raw Some Gazpacho Soup	130
252.	Alkaline Carrot Soup With Fresh Mushrooms	131
253.	Swiss Cauliflower-Emmenthal-Soup	131
254.	Chilled Parsley-Gazpacho With Lime and Cucumber	131
255.	Chilled Avocado Tomato Soup	132
256.	Pumpkin and White Bean Soup With Sage	132
257.	Alkaline Carrot Soup With Millet	132
258.	Alkaline Pumpkin Tomato Soup	133
259.	Alkaline Pumpkin Coconut Soup	133
260.	Cold Cauliflower-Coconut Soup	134
261.	Raw Avocado-Broccoli Soup With Cashew Nuts	134
262.	White Bean Soup	134
263.	Kale Cauliflower Soup	135
264.	Healthy Broccoli Asparagus Soup	135
265.	Creamy Asparagus Soup	136
266.	Quick Broccoli Soup	136
267.	Green Lentil Soup	136
268.	Squash Soup	137
269.	Tomato Soup	137
270.	Basil Zucchini Soup	137
271.	Summer Vegetable Soup	138
272.	Almond-Red Bell Pepper Dip	138
273.	Spicy Carrot Soup	138
274.	Zucchini Soup	139
275.	Kidney Bean Stew	139
276.	Cabbage Soup	139
277.	Pumpkin Spice Soup	139
278.	Cream of Tomato Soup	140
279.	Shiitake Soup	140
280.	Spicy Pepper Soup	140
281.	Zoodle Won-Ton Soup	140

CHAPTER 11: DESSERT 142

#	Title	Page
282.	Chocolate Crunch Bars	142
283.	Homemade Protein Bar	142
284.	Shortbread Cookies	142
285.	Coconut Chip Cookies	143
286.	Peanut Butter Bars	143
287.	Zucchini Bread Pancakes	143

288.	Berry Sorbet	144
289.	Quinoa Porridge	144
290.	Apple Quinoa	144
291.	Kamut Porridge	145
292.	Hot Kamut With Peaches, Walnuts, and Coconut	145
293.	Overnight "Oats"	145
294.	Blueberry Cupcakes	146
295.	Brazil Nut Cheese	146
296.	Slow Cooker Peaches	146
297.	Pumpkin Custard	147
298.	Blueberry Lemon Custard Cake	147
299.	Sugar-Free Carrot Cake	148
300.	Sugar-Free Chocolate Molten Lava Cake	148

CHAPTER 12: MEAL PLAN 150

1-Week Fast Easy Diet Plan 150
4-Week Diet Plan 150

CONCLUSION 154

APPENDIX MEASUREMENT CONVERSION CHART 155

Volume 155
Weight 155
Metric Cups Conversion 155
Oven Temperatures 156
Weight 156

Why I Decided to Write This Book

When I was diagnosed with type 2 diabetes, it took a huge toll on my life. I had to step back from running for a few months and rely solely on what the medical professionals told me. It was as well one of the hardest moments of my life, but in hindsight, it wasn't as bad as I thought it would be.

I had always been in great shape, and eating healthy was second nature to me. I didn't give in and go on a diet of fad meals or start taking medications that would help with my condition. I started by slowly changing my bad habits into good habits, something that was sustainable for the rest of my life, not just until my condition got better.

I learned a lot about this disease over a year or so. And now I have decided to put all that information into an e-book so anyone diagnosed with type 2 diabetes can benefit from what I learned.

But first, I want to let you know that this book is not meant for type 1 diabetics. This book is strictly for people with type 2 diabetes, which is a completely different condition than type 1 diabetes.

Type 1 diabetes is caused by a lack of insulin and can only be managed by injecting insulin. The diet plan I describe in this book does not allow for injecting insulin, and therefore will not work for people with type 1. The diet plan works with the body's capacity to produce more insulin once the digestive process starts working optimally.

The diet I am talking about has nothing to do with taking medications or getting shots of insulin. This diet can only be implemented by eating like a normal human being. Restricting calories and food types in the diet will eventually lead to the body's own insulin production increasing.

Of course, it would be great to be able to take shots of insulin, but that is not an option. There are several reasons why taking insulin is not an easy choice for anyone with diabetes. It's expensive and it doesn't do all that much for people with type 2 diabetes, especially when you consider how much weight you would have to lose for that amount of insulin to help you. As I mentioned before, I don't recommend taking medications. So, we are left with a diet.

The problem is that most people are used to eating a particular way and changing that way of eating is one of the hardest things to do. You have to start thinking about what you eat and how long it takes for your digestive system to process each food before it gets used by your body. It sounds simple, but the truth is, most people don't know anything about their digestive systems so they don't know exactly how long certain foods take to digest properly. It took me a few months before I understood food digestion in great detail.

It takes a lot of motivation, will power, and determination to start implementing changes in your diet. That's why I am so glad that I now know my way around this condition. And because I know how hard it is to implement the changes in your diet, I have put all the information you need in this book that will help you get started as soon as possible.

Please note that I am not a health professional. I am an information junkie and so, I have done research on the latest and most important information about type 2 diabetes or metabolic syndrome. This book is meant to give you a basic understanding of this condition, but if you need more information or have specific questions, always consult your doctor.

Let's get started.

Introduction

Type 2 diabetes is a form of diabetes that occurs when the body doesn't produce enough insulin or becomes insensitive to it, which prevents the body from properly using sugar. It develops with age, consistently overweight and diet-rich western lifestyle, inactivity, and sometimes genetic predisposition. Type 2 diabetes is responsible for more than 90% of all diabetes cases in adults. Type 1 has been known as insulin-dependent diabetes since these people are unable to make their own insulin because they lack the necessary pancreatic cell growth factors. An estimated 24 million Americans have some form of type 1 or type 2 diabetes according to World Health Organization statistics from 2012.

Type 2 diabetes is a public health disease with rising cases of obesity, aging, inactivity, and genes as the main causes.

Diabetes is usually diagnosed by blood glucose tests taken at least twice a month for people with type 1 diabetes and once every few months for those with type 2. The conditions are monitored by taking blood samples. If the results are not within normal limits, medications may be prescribed to control symptoms, lower blood glucose levels, and reduce the risk of complications such as heart disease and neuropathy (nerve damage).

Type 2 diabetes, also known as Type II diabetes or non-insulin-dependent diabetes, is a metabolic disorder that occurs when the body does not produce enough insulin or becomes resistant to insulin. This type of diabetes accounts for 90–95% of cases in adults. In this situation, the pancreas will begin to secrete more insulin to compensate for the lack of cell sensitivity to it; however, the cells become less and less responsive to the continued presence of insulin. Eventually, if untreated, the pancreas will be unable to produce enough insulin, and blood sugars will rise above normal levels.

This form is primarily caused by obesity and genetics.

CHAPTER 1:

Type 1 and Type 2 Diabetes

Diabetes is a common disease that leads to metabolic disorders of carbohydrates and water balance. As a result of that, pancreatic functions are impaired. It is the pancreas that produces an important hormone called insulin. Insulin regulates the level of blood sugar that is supplied with food. Without it, the body cannot convert sugar into glucose, and sugar starts accumulating in the body of a person with the disease.

Apart from the pancreas disorders, the water balance is impaired as well. As a result of that, the tissues do not retain water, and the kidneys excrete much fluid.

So what happens when a person has diabetes?

When the condition develops, the body produces too little insulin. At the same time, the level of blood sugar increases, and the cells become starved for glucose, which is the primary source of energy.

Types of Diabetes

There are two types of diabetes:

- **Type 1 diabetes.** This condition is also known as insulin-dependent. It usually affects young people under 40. People with type 1 diabetes will need to take insulin injections for the rest of their lives because their body produces antibodies that destroy the beta-cells which produce the hormone.

- **Type 2 diabetes.** This happens as a result of the lack of sensitivity of the pancreas cells towards insulin because of the excess nutrients. People with excess weight are the most susceptible to the disease.

What's the Difference?

	TYPE 1	TYPE 2
Who it affects	Represent up to 5–10% of all cases of diabetes. It was once called "juvenile-onset" diabetes because it was thought to develop most often in children and young adults. We now know it can occur in people of any age, including older adults.	Accounts for 90–95% of all diagnosed cases of diabetes. It used to be called "adult-onset" diabetes, but it is now known that even children—mainly if they're overweight—can develop type 2 diabetes.
What happens	The pancreas makes little if any insulin.	The pancreas doesn't produce enough insulin or the body doesn't respond properly to the insulin that is produced.

Risk factors	Less well-defined, but autoimmune, genetic, and environmental factors are believed to be involved.	Older age, obesity, family history of diabetes, physical inactivity, and race/ethnicity.
Treatment	Individualized meal plans, insulin therapy (usually several injections a day), self-monitoring glucose testing several times a day, regular physical activity, and a healthy diet.	A healthy diet, weight loss (if overweight), regular exercise, and monitoring blood glucose levels. Some people can manage blood sugar through diet and exercise alone. However, diabetes tends to be a progressive disease, so oral medications and possibly insulin may be needed at some point.

Food to Eat

Vegetables

Fresh vegetables never cause harm to anyone. So, adding a meal full of vegetables is the best shot for all diabetic patients. But not all vegetables contain the same amount of macronutrients. Some vegetables contain a high amount of carbohydrates, so those are not suitable for a diabetic diet. We need to use vegetables that contain a low amount of carbohydrates.

- Cauliflower
- Spinach
- Tomatoes
- Broccoli
- Lemons
- Artichoke
- Garlic
- Asparagus
- Spring onions
- Onions
- Ginger, etc.

Meat

Meat is not on the red list for the diabetic diet. It is fine to have some meat now and then for diabetic patients. However certain meat types are better than others. For instance, red meat is not a preferable option for such patients. They should consume white meat more often whether it's seafood or poultry. Healthy options in meat are:

- All fish, i.e., salmon, halibut, trout, cod, sardine, etc.
- Scallops
- Mussels
- Shrimp
- Oysters, etc.

Fruits

Not all fruits are good for diabetes. To know if the fruit is suitable for this diet, it is important to note its sugar content. Some fruits contain a high amount of sugars in the form of sucrose and fructose, and those should be readily avoided. Here is the list of popularly used fruits that can be taken on the diabetic diet:

- Peaches
- Nectarines
- Avocados
- Apples
- Berries
- Grapefruit
- Kiwi fruit
- Bananas
- Cherries
- Grapes
- Orange
- Pears
- Plums
- Strawberries

Nuts and Seeds

Nuts and seeds are perhaps the most enriched edibles, and they contain such a mix of macronutrients that can never harm anyone.

So diabetic patients can take the nuts and seeds in their diet without any fear of a glucose spike.

- Pistachios
- Sunflower seeds
- Walnuts
- Peanuts
- Pecans
- Pumpkin seeds
- Almonds
- Sesame seeds etc.

Grains

Diabetic patients should also be selective while choosing the right grains for their diet. The idea is to keep the amount of starch as minimum as possible. That is why you won't see any white rice in the list rather it is replaced with more fibrous brown rice.

- Quinoa
- Oats
- Multigrain
- Whole grains
- Brown rice
- Millet
- Barley
- Sorghum
- Tapioca

Fats

Fat intake is the most debated topic as far as the diabetic diet is concerned. As there are diets like ketogenic, which are loaded with fats and still proved effective for diabetic patients. The key is the absence of carbohydrates. In any other situation, fats are as harmful to diabetics as any normal person. Switching to unsaturated fats is a better option.

- Sesame oil
- Olive oil
- Canola oil
- Grapeseed oil
- Other vegetable oils
- Fats extracted from plant sources

Dairy

Any dairy product which directly or indirectly causes a glucose rise in the blood should not be taken on this diet. other than those, all products are good to use. These items include:

- Skimmed milk
- Low-fat cheese
- Yogurt
- Trans fat-free margarine or butter

Sugar Alternatives

Since ordinary sugars or sweeteners are strictly forbidden on a diabetic diet. There are artificial varieties that can add sweetness without raising the level of carbohydrates in the meal. These substitutes are:

- Stevia
- Xylitol
- Natvia
- Swerve
- Monk fruit
- Erythritol

Make sure to substitute them with extra care. The sweetness of each sweetener is entirely different from the table sugar, so add each by the intensity of their flavor. Stevia is the sweetest of them, and it should be used with more care. In place of 1 cup of sugar, a tsp. Stevia is enough all other sweeteners are more or less similar to sugar in their intensity of sweetness.

Foods to Avoid

Knowing a general scheme of diet helps a lot, but it is equally important to be well familiar with the items which have to be avoided.

With this list, you can make your diet 100% sugar-free. Many other food items can cause some harm to a diabetic patient as the sugars do. So, let's discuss them in some detail here.

Sugars

Sugar is a big NO-GO for a diabetic diet. Once you are diabetic, you would need to say goodbye to all the natural sweeteners which are loaded with carbohydrates. They contain polysaccharides that readily break into glucose after getting into our bodies. And the list does not only include table sugars but other items like honey and molasses should also be avoided.

- White sugar
- Brown sugar
- Confectionary sugar
- Honey
- Molasses
- Granulated sugar

Your mind and your body, will not accept the abrupt change. It is recommended to go for a gradual change. It means start substituting it with low carb substitutes in a small amount, day by day.

High-Fat Dairy Products

Once you are diabetic, you may get susceptible to many other fatal diseases including cardiovascular ones. That is why experts strictly recommend avoiding high-fat food products, especially dairy items. The high amount of fat can make your body insulin resistant. So even when you take insulin, it won't be of any use as the body will not work on it.

Saturated Animal Fats

Saturated animal fats are not good for anyone, whether diabetic or normal. So, better avoid using them in general. Whenever you are cooking meat, try to trim off all the excess fat. Cooking oils made out of these saturated fats should be avoided. Keep yourself away from any animal-origin fats.

High-Carb Vegetables

As discussed above, vegetables with more starch are not suitable for diabetes. These veggies can increase the carbohydrate levels of food. So, omit these from the recipes and enjoy the rest of the less starchy vegetables. Some of the high carb vegetables are:

- Potatoes
- Sweet potatoes
- Yams, etc.

Cholesterol Rich Ingredients

Bad cholesterol or High-Density Lipoprotein tends to deposit in different parts of the body. That is why food items having high bad cholesterol are not good for diabetes. Such items should be replaced with the ones with low cholesterol.

High-Sodium Products

Sodium is related to hypertension and blood pressure. Since diabetes is already the result of a hormonal imbalance in the body, in the presence of excess sodium—another imbalance—a fluid imbalance may occur which a diabetic body cannot tolerate. It adds up to the already present complications of the disease. So, avoid using food items with a high amount of sodium. Mainly store packed items, processed foods, and salt all contain sodium, and one should avoid them all. Use only the "unsalted" variety of food products, whether it's butter, margarine, nuts, or other items.

Sugary Drinks

Cola drinks or other similar beverages are filled with sugars. If you had seen different video presentations showing the amount of sugar present in a single bottle of soda, you would know how dangerous those are for diabetic patients. They can drastically increase the amount of blood glucose levels within 30 minutes of drinking. Fortunately, there are many sugar-free varieties available in the drinks which are suitable for diabetic patients.

Sugar Syrups and Toppings
Several syrups available in the markets are made out of nothing but sugar. Maple syrup is one good example. For a diabetic diet, the patient should avoid such sugary syrups and also stay away from the sugar-rich toppings available in the stores. If you want to use them at all, trust yourself and prepare them at home with a sugar-free recipe.

Sweet Chocolate and Candies
For diabetic patients, sugar-free chocolates or candies are the best way out. Other processed chocolate bars and candies are extremely damaging to their health, and all of these should be avoided. You can try and prepare healthy bars and candies at home with sugar-free recipes.

Alcohol
Alcohol tends to reduce the rate of our metabolism and take away our appetite, which can render a diabetic patient into a very life-threatening condition. Alcohol in a very small amount cannot harm the patient, but the regular or constant intake of alcohol is bad for health and glucose levels.

CHAPTER 2:

How to Deal With Diabetes

Diabetes is a serious condition that causes lifelong health complications. Diabetes affects nearly 78 million people in the US alone and is one of the leading causes of blindness, kidney failure, and limb amputation. But there are many things you can do to deal with diabetes.
The following are some of the most important ways to help you with diabetes:
- Watch what you eat. Avoid trans fats, saturated fats, sugar, and junk food.
- Exercise regularly. The more active you are between meals, the better your blood sugar level will be.
- Stay away from cigarettes and alcohol as they both contribute to elevated blood sugar levels in the body.
- Don't drink too much caffeine (tea, coffee, etc). Caffeine blocks the body's ability to regulate its fat and carbohydrate metabolism. Caffeine also disrupts sleep patterns and can cause anxiety when consumed in excess.
- Don't use medications unless absolutely necessary as they can affect your blood sugar levels. Be sure to tell your doctor and pharmacist of any supplements you may be taking.
- Get adequate sleep each night and try to avoid stress if at all possible.
- Avoid diuretics, water pills, and other medications that dehydrate the body.

If you suffer from any of the following symptoms then it is in your best interest to schedule a diabetes screening with your doctor as soon as possible: frequent urination, fatigue, rapid weight gain, blurred vision, tingling in hands or feet, excessive thirst (especially at night), cuts or sores that are slow to heal and unusual feelings of hunger or weakness.
Keep in mind that the risk factors for diabetes mellitus—Type 2 are: persistent high blood sugar, high blood pressure, overweight, and obesity.
Diabetes has been known to affect many persons worldwide. According to a study in 2015, about 28.1 million adults and nearly 586,000 children had diabetes. This is 2.8% of the U.S. population. The CDC also says another 86.4 million adults and 8.6 million children, or about 10.6% of the U.S. population, have prediabetes.

How to Live With Diabetes?

Persons with diabetes need to have a doctor who can advise them on how to care for their condition. Persons with diabetes can control their blood glucose levels by taking medications, watching what they eat, and being physically active. When someone is diagnosed with diabetes, particularly Type 2 diabetes, they are immediately advised to:
- Start on a healthy diet and get a lot of exercises.
- Know their target blood glucose levels and keep these levels within the blood.
- Get their blood glucose levels tested regularly. This will allow for good self-regulation of your blood glucose levels, and it will help your body become more efficient at managing glucose levels on its own.

It is important to have a healthy diet for diabetics and they need to pay extra attention to it. Unhealthy food is rich in both fat and carbohydrates and unhealthy eaters tend to eat a low fiber diet. Transfats, cholesterol, and saturated fats, all can promote insulin resistance, boosting blood glucose levels.

What Foods Should Be in a Diabetic Diet Plan?

As diabetics, the diet plan should be properly supplemented with the right types and amounts of foods and some activities that can help you be healthy. Several foods are recommended to take in like green vegetables, juices, whole grains, lean meats, and fruits. We should consume the recommended amount of food if we are diabetics.

A diabetic diet plan is also important. People with diabetes usually take insulin to control their blood glucose levels, so it is important to understand how insulin interacts with food. This interaction between certain foods (carbohydrates) and insulin can make it harder for the body to control blood glucose levels.

Lifestyle change. It can be hard for you to adapt to this change, but it is the only way that you would be able to fit dietary requirements that, hopefully, you can retain for the rest of your life.

As you start this journey on diabetic meal preparation, you are committing to a healthier lifestyle and doing it for the rest of your life. The lifestyle changes that people with diabetes have to undergo are not a joke, they call it a lifestyle change because it means you have to undergo permanent changes for the rest of your life.

CHAPTER 3:

Dietary Requirements for Type-2 Diabetes

Understanding what is in your food and how it can affect your blood sugar levels can seem like a daunting task. But it's important to first learn which foods are mostly carbohydrates, mostly protein, and mostly fat so you can learn the best foods to choose, the appropriate amounts, and the best times to eat them. Having a good grasp of diabetes nutrition basics will help you make the best decisions in any setting and you will be surprised to discover that it's a lot less complicated than it may seem.

Food is one of the oldest forms of medicine, and that is especially true when it comes to living with diabetes. Taking control of what you eat will have immediate benefits to your health.

Think of your body like a car: You want to fill it up with quality fuel to make sure it runs optimally. If you have type 2 diabetes, feeding your body with healthy nutrients will help control blood sugar, aid with weight management, decrease your risk of complications, and promote overall health. So here is a crash course in nutrition.

Carbohydrates, proteins, and fats are the 3 macronutrients your body needs. Carbohydrates possess the most significant impact on blood sugar levels. Fats and protein have little or no effect on blood sugar.

Protein

Protein is used for building and repairing tissues, as well as making enzymes, hormones, and other body chemicals. It can also help make you feel fuller and more satisfied at meals. Research has shown that the body uses protein best when you space your intake throughout the day, rather than eating a large amount just once a day.

Protein comes from animal products, including meat, poultry, eggs, dairy, fish, seafood, and protein powder. Vegan sources of protein include soy products (such as tofu, tempeh, and edamame), seitan, legumes (beans, nuts, peas, and lentils), and seeds—and again, some protein powders.

Recommendations for healthy protein choices:
- Choose fish and seafood over red meat.
- Remove the skin from poultry.
- Choose lean or low-fat cuts of red meat. Limit or avoid fatty luncheon meats like salami, bologna, and hot dogs.

Fats

Fats are essential for maintaining cell membranes and facilitating vitamin absorption, as well as other functions. Eating fat at meals can also help promote feelings of fullness. There are four major kinds of fat: monounsaturated, polyunsaturated, saturated, and trans fats. Generally speaking, you should choose the unsaturated types, limit saturated fats, and avoid trans fats.

Unsaturated fats, which are found in the Mediterranean diet, may actually reduce the risk of cardiovascular disease and improve glucose metabolism. A diet high in saturated fat is linked to elevated LDL (bad) cholesterol levels. There is some conflicting research on whether or not saturated fat increases the risk of heart disease. At this time, though, most experts still recommend that saturated fat intake be limited.

Recommendations for healthy fat choices:
- Avoid trans fats, which are present in stick margarine and many processed snack foods. Read the ingredient list on food labels for processed snack foods.
- Limit your intake of saturated fats, which are found in full-fat dairy, butter, well-marbled meat, and chicken fat and skin.
- Choose monounsaturated and polyunsaturated fats, which are found in olive oil, canola oil, and other vegetable oils; nuts and nut butter; seeds; avocado; and olives.
- Include omega-3 fats (a type of polyunsaturated fat) in your diet. They have numerous health benefits and are found in fatty fish such as salmon, trout, sardines, anchovies, and herring. Plant forms of omega-3 fats are found in flaxseeds, chia seeds, walnuts, canola oil, and leafy greens.

Carbohydrates

Carbohydrates are your body's main source of energy. They are found in almost all foods, including the following:

Fruits

Fruits provide fiber, vitamins, minerals, and other nutrients that promote good health. Fruits contain more carbohydrates than most vegetables, so be careful with portion sizes.

Recommendations for healthy fruit choices:
- Choose fresh fruit over dried fruit and juice.
- If you buy frozen or canned fruit, choose those without added sugar.

Nonstarchy Vegetables

Think leafy greens, broccoli, cauliflower, peppers, asparagus, artichokes, tomatoes, and eggplant. These nonstarchy vegetables are low in calories and high in fiber, vitamins, minerals, and other nutrients that promote good health. They contain only a third as many carbohydrates as fruits, dairy, grains, beans, and starchy vegetables.

Recommendations for healthy vegetable choices:
- Choose various vegetables, of all colors of the rainbow, to obtain a variety of nutrients.
- Buy fresh vegetables or frozen (with no added sauce). If you buy canned, look for low-sodium.
- Buy 100% vegetable juice, with no added fruit juice or sweeteners.

Grains, Beans, and Starchy Vegetables

Refined grains, such as white rice and white bread, have been processed to remove the bran, germ, and endosperm.

They contain fewer nutrients and less fiber than whole grains. Beans and lentils are high in fiber and protein, as well as carbohydrates. Certain vegetables, such as corn, peas, and winter squash, are considered starchy because they contain more carbohydrates than nonstarchy vegetables. These vegetables are good sources of vitamins, minerals, fiber, and other nutrients that are important for good health.

Recommendations for healthy choices:
- At least half of all the grains you eat should be whole, not refined. Examples of whole-grain foods include whole-wheat bread, brown rice, quinoa, farro, millet, bulgur, wild rice, oatmeal, wheat berries, and barley.
- Include beans in your diet. Soak and cook them yourself, or buy them canned, drain out the liquid, and rinse.
- Buy starchy fresh vegetables or frozen (with no added sauce). If you buy canned, look for low-sodium.

Dairy

These are milk-based products and include milk, cheese, yogurt, and Cottage cheese. Dairy products contain many nutrients, including calcium, protein, potassium, and vitamin D. Ideally, look for a brand that is fortified with calcium and vitamin D. Almond milk, cashew milk, soy milk, and hemp milk can all be good non-dairy milk substitutes, as can leafy greens and tofu processed with calcium. All of these choices are very low in carbohydrates.

Recommendations for healthy dairy choices:
- Choose non-fat or low-fat dairy products or non-dairy milk substitutes that are fortified with calcium and vitamin D.
- If you do choose full-fat dairy, keep portions moderate.
- Plain Greek yogurt, with 0% or 2% fat, contains half the amount of carbohydrate and double the protein of regular milk and yogurt.

Fiber

Fiber is the indigestible part of plants. It's found in vegetables, fruit, whole grains, legumes, and nuts. Although most of it doesn't get digested, fiber does a lot of good things in the body. It contributes to digestive health and helps keep you feeling full longer. The soluble fiber (it absorbs water to form a gel) found in foods such as beans, lentils, and nonstarchy vegetables helps lower cholesterol and regulate blood sugar.

Recommendations to increase your fiber intake:
- Eat plenty of vegetables every day.
- Eat several servings of fruit a day.
- Choose whole grains over refined grains.
- Include beans and lentils in your diet.

Sodium

Sodium is a mineral that helps maintain your electrolyte balance, as well as perform other functions in the body. However, excessive amounts may increase the risk of developing serious medical conditions such as high blood pressure, heart disease, and stroke. Since cardiovascular disease is the number one cause of illness and death in people with diabetes, it is especially important to limit your sodium intake. The majority of people's sodium intake comes from processed foods and restaurant meals—not the salt shaker.

People with diabetes should limit their sodium consumption to 2,300 milligrams (mg) a day. Lowering your sodium intake even more, to 1,500 mg a day, may benefit blood pressure in certain circumstances. The American Heart Association recommends 1,500 mg a day for African Americans; people diagnosed with hypertension, diabetes, or chronic kidney disease; and people over 51 years of age.

Recommendations to decrease sodium intake:
- Buy fresh or frozen (no sauce added) vegetables.
- Eat fresh poultry, fish, pork, and lean meat, rather than canned or processed meats.
- Buy low-sodium, lower sodium, reduced-sodium, or no-salt-added versions of packaged products.
- Limit your use of sauces, mixes, and "instant products," including flavored rice and ready-made pasta.
- Read the Nutrition Facts labels on food packages for milligrams of sodium, and compare products.
- Review the sodium content of foods online before eating at chain restaurants.
- Limit using the salt shaker. (In the next chapter we give you alternative ways to season your food!)

CHAPTER 4:

Tips and Tricks for Diabetic Recipes

- Do not eat out too much.
- Ensure to plan your meals before you go to the grocery store and keep in mind what you need while shopping.
- Always check out the entire nutrition label before purchasing a product. Check the sodium, saturated fat, total carbohydrates, sugar, and protein content of products before purchasing them. If a product contains one of these items you should purchase something else.
- Do not buy products that are highly processed or refined. These often contain high amounts of sugar or other preservatives such as high fructose corn syrup or artificial colors.
- Replace white rice with brown rice.
- Use herbs and spices or lemon juice to flavor foods instead of adding sugar.
- Bring your healthy snacks to work or school.
- When shopping for fruits and vegetables, choose the ones that are firm and have bright colors. Avoid vegetables such as carrots and potatoes which have skin that has become soft or wrinkly.
- Choose low fat for dairy products such as milk, yogurt, or cheese instead of regular milk and cheese.
- When preparing a meal, try to use a variety of vegetables in every meal.
- Make sure that the food that you eat does not contain too much sodium.
- If you do not have access to sugar substitutes, use fresh fruit as your sweetener instead. Do not add sugar directly to drinks or foods because it can cause calories to be absorbed more quickly by your body.
- Do not buy products that contain too much sugar or fat. Make sure that you read the labels and use the product in moderation. If you do not want to buy some high sugar or fat product, make your own version of it at home.
- Choose foods with high fiber content, such as whole grains.
- Buy lean meat and fish instead of fatty cuts.
- Make sure to add leafy greens at least once a day.
- Try to choose fresh fruits and vegetables over frozen products.
- Avoid eating too much peanut butter as well as making smoothies with this ingredient.
- Try to find healthy snacks that can help you feel full such as fruits, nuts, or low-fat yogurt.
- It is very important to eat three meals a day and no more. It is also best if those meals are spread throughout the day.
- 3 meals a day might be sufficient but eating 5–6 small meals a day will better improve your metabolism and keep your energy levels up throughout the day.
- Make sure not to drink diet soda or other sugar-free drinks that contain artificial sweeteners.
- It is best to drink low or no-fat milk. It is essential to avoid choosing full-fat milk as it can cause you to gain more weight and be unhealthy.
- Avoid eating too much fruit as it might clog the arteries and block the little blood vessels that help in clearing out cholesterol from your body.

- Do not make yourself sick by eating too much of any one food item. Avoid eating too much fat, sugar, or carbohydrates if you are trying to lose weight.
- Avoid eating foods that are high in salt and sodium. Also, try to not add salt to your food while cooking.
- If you are someone who has a sweet tooth then try to reduce your sugar intake or avoid sugar as much as possible.
- Make sure that cooked foods do not have more than 400 calories per serving.
- While shopping for healthy items, read the labels on them and try to get the ones that are low in fat and calories with no added sugars or other unhealthy ingredients.

CHAPTER 5:

CookingTricks, Tips, and Timesavers

Different Types of Cooking for Diabetic Recipes

An actual diabetes diagnosis can be both frightening and confusing. Along with the physical effects, there's the mental battle of what it will mean to your lifestyle. Feeling like you'll never enjoy food or drink again can be very heartbreaking.

There are many ways to help you enjoy your favorite foods even if you're diabetic. Following a diabetes diet is one way to help manage your diabetes, but it's not the only way. You can still enjoy the occasional treat without feeling guilty or without damaging your health.

Tips on Cooking With Diabetes

Once you've been diagnosed with diabetes, you may start to experience a lot of changes in your life. This can be painful and stressful. You're no longer able to indulge in your favorite foods. But it doesn't have to be like this! There are ways for you to still enjoy the culinary delights you once enjoyed. Here are some tips on how to cook while diabetic-friendly:

Sugar Substitutions

One thing that should never be skipped is sugar substitutes. Some people tend to think that they are as bad as sugar, but thankfully, they aren't. There are plenty of different kinds available for you to try. You can purchase them at your local grocery store or online depending on what your needs are like. The following four substitutes are fairly common and can be found in most supermarkets:

- **Sucralose:** This is one of the most popular sugar alternatives available today. It's 600 times sweeter than table sugar and doesn't add calories.
- **Sugar alcohols:** While these may cause some gastrointestinal discomfort, they do provide the same sweetening power as regular sugar. The most common is xylitol, and it's safe for dogs too!
- **Stevia:** 300 times sweeter than sugar and doesn't contain any calories. It's great for diabetics because it doesn't affect your blood sugar levels.
- **Aspartame:** This is the most common one used in many products, and it's 200 times sweeter than table sugar. You shouldn't have much trouble finding this in the supermarket either.

Sugar substitutes can be a lifesaver for diabetic recipes since they won't contribute any calories to your next meal, and they'll help lower blood glucose levels even more. Just remember that even though sugar substitutes seem like a perfect solution, they still count as extra calories in the long run.

Mixing Your Foods

Another way that you can increase the amount of flavor in your food is by mixing it. Mixing meats and sauces into vegetables is one of the easiest ways to do this. It makes your veggies taste a lot better and not so boring anymore.

You can also mix your sides (such as rice and beans) into the main dish if you want.

There are a few different steps to follow when mixing your foods. First, mix all of your vegetables in a large bowl. Then add the meat or sauce to the bowl and stir it around so that it's mixed evenly with all of the vegetables. Next, make sure that all of your ingredients are blended well.

Drying Fruits and Vegetables
If you have a dehydrator that's been sitting around for a while, now might be the time to start using it. Dehydrators can help you preserve the nutritional value of your fruits and vegetables. This means that consuming them won't cause any added sugar in your blood. There are several different kinds of dehydrators, and they vary in price and effectiveness.

Try dehydrating apples, strawberries, pears, apricots, prunes, or other fruit that you like. You can also dry out vegetables such as broccoli, carrots, mushrooms, and tomatoes. There are various recipes online that mention how you can make pancakes with these dehydrated ingredients.

Once you've used the dried fruits or vegetables, you can use them in your other dishes or throw them in the trash. You'll have to watch how much sugar goes into your food, so it's best to do this in small amounts at first.

Recipes to Use in Cooking While Diabetic-Friendly
The following recipes are some great ways to use ingredients normally used in sweet dishes. Since these ingredients won't add any extra sugar to your body, you can enjoy them without worry.

- **Pancakes:** If you're having trouble giving up your morning pancakes, try this diabetic-friendly pancake recipe:
  Boil 2 cups of rice in a saucepan. Add 1 cup of applesauce and some cinnamon to the mix. Use low-calorie pancake batter from a box. Pour the mixture into a cake pan and bake it in the oven at 325 degrees Fahrenheit for five minutes. Serve with syrup.
- **Baked apples:** Most muffin and cake recipes can be turned into baked apples instead. All you have to do is take out the flour that's included in the recipe and add some cinnamon to it instead. Then bake it as normal in an oven or microwave and turn it into an apple-pie filling when done.

Mixing high-fiber cereal with water or tea is another great way to relieve your craving for something sweet. Just look up diabetic-friendly recipes if you need inspiration.

Try Making Healthy Versions of Your Favorite Foods
You might feel like giving up on the foods that you love because they're not healthy for you anymore. But why stop eating them altogether? Instead, try adding fruit to make healthier versions of your favorite foods. Just remember that every slice of fruit counts as an extra snack in the long run.

If you want to add meat to your meals, use lean cuts and lots of vegetables. This will help you feel full for longer. And don't forget to stay away from processed foods, fatty meats, and refined sugars. The more processed the food is, the fewer nutrients it has in it, so stick with natural whole foods when possible.

If you can't give up on your favorite dessert because it tastes way too good, try baking healthier versions yourself. You can try making some healthier versions of your favorite cookies, pies, and cake recipes. You just have to remember that every slice of fruit you consume counts as an extra snack in the long run.

By keeping your fiber intake up, you will see that you can eat sweet treats without having any added sugars in your blood. Try out some of these recipes and see if they help with your craving for sweets. If you still find it extremely hard to stay away from sugar, consult a doctor about your condition.

CHAPTER 6:

Breakfast

The following are useful and easy breakfast recipes that can help in your battle against diabetes. No matter if you're just starting on your diabetes journey or are already all-too-familiar with Type 2 medical conditions, there's always room for improvement. That's where these recipes come in, a perfect way to stay healthy and active while learning the ins and outs of the condition.

1. Whole-Grain Breakfast Cookies

Preparation time: 20 minutes
Cooking time: 10 minutes
Servings: 18
Ingredients:
- 2 cups rolled oats
- ½ cup whole-wheat flour
- ¼ cup ground flaxseed
- 1 tsp baking powder
- 1 cup unsweetened applesauce
- 2 large eggs - 2 tbsp vegetable oil
- 2 tsp vanilla extract
- 1 tsp ground cinnamon
- ½ cup dried cherries
- ¼ cup unsweetened shredded coconut
- 2 oz dark chocolate, chopped

Directions:
1. Preheat the oven to 350°F.
2. In a large bowl, combine the oats, flour, flaxseed, and baking powder. Stir well to mix. In a medium bowl, whisk the applesauce, eggs, vegetable oil, vanilla, and cinnamon. Pour the wet mixture into the dry mixture, and stir until just combined.
3. Fold in cherries, coconut, and chocolate. Drop tbsp-size balls of dough onto a baking sheet. Bake for 10–12 minutes, until browned and cooked through.
4. Let cool for about 3 minutes, remove from the baking sheet, and cool completely before serving Store in an airtight container for up to 1 week.

Nutrition:
- Calories: 136 Total fat: 7 g
- Saturated fat: 3 g Protein: 4 g
- Carbs: 14 g Sugar: 4 g
- Fiber: 3 g Cholesterol: 21 mg
- Sodium: 11 mg

2. Blueberry Breakfast Cake

Preparation time: 15 minutes
Cooking time: 45 minutes
Servings: 12
Ingredients:
For the topping:
- ¼ cup finely chopped walnuts
- ½ tsp ground cinnamon
- 2 tbsp butter, chopped into small pieces
- 2 tbsp sugar

For the cake:
- Nonstick cooking spray
- 1 cup whole-wheat pastry flour
- 1 cup oat flour - ¼ cup sugar
- 2 tsp baking powder
- 1 large egg, beaten - ½ cup skim milk
- 2 tbsp butter, melted - 1 tsp grated lemon peel
- 2 cups fresh or frozen blueberries

Directions:
To make the topping:
1. In a small bowl, stir together the walnuts, cinnamon, butter, and sugar. Set aside.

To make the cake:
1. Preheat the oven to 350°F. Spray a 9-inch square pan with cooking spray. Set aside.

2. In a large bowl, stir together the pastry flour, oat flour, sugar, and baking powder.
3. Add the egg, milk, butter, and lemon peel, and stir until there are no dry spots. Stir in the blueberries, and gently mix until incorporated. Press the batter into the prepared pan, using a spoon to flatten it into the dish. Sprinkle the topping over the cake. Bake for 40–45 minutes or until a toothpick inserted into the cake comes out clean and serve.

Nutrition:
- Calories: 177 Total fat: 7 g
- Saturated fat: 3 g Protein: 4 g Carbs: 26 g
- Sugar: 9 g Fiber: 3 g Cholesterol: 26 mg
- Sodium: 39 mg

3. Whole-Grain Pancakes

Preparation time: 10 minutes
Cooking time: 15 minutes
Servings: 4–6
Ingredients:
- 2 cups whole-wheat pastry flour
- 4 tsp baking powder
- 2 tsp ground cinnamon
- ½ tsp salt
- 2 cups skim milk, plus more as needed
- 2 large eggs
- 1 tbsp honey
- Nonstick cooking spray
- Maple syrup, for serving
- Fresh fruit, for serving

Directions:
1. In a large bowl, stir together the flour, baking powder, cinnamon, and salt.
2. Add the milk, eggs, and honey, and stir well to combine. If needed, add more milk, 1 tbsp at a time, until there are no dry spots and you have a pourable batter.
3. Heat a large skillet over medium-high heat, and spray it with cooking spray.
4. Using a ¼-cup measuring cup, scoop 2–3 pancakes into the skillet at a time. Cook for a couple of minutes, until bubbles form on the surface of the pancakes, flip, and cook for 1–2 minutes more, until golden brown and cooked through. Repeat with the remaining batter.
5. Serve topped with maple syrup or fresh fruit.

Nutrition:
- Calories: 392 Total fat: 4 g
- Saturated fat: 1 g Protein: 15 g
- Carbs: 71 g Sugar: 11 g
- Fiber: 9 g Cholesterol: 95 mg
- Sodium: 396 mg

4. Buckwheat Grouts Breakfast Bowl

Preparation time: 5 minutes, plus overnight to soak
Cooking time: 10–12 minutes
Servings: 4
Ingredients:
- 3 cups skim milk
- 1 cup buckwheat grouts
- ¼ cup chia seeds
- 2 tsp vanilla extract
- ½ tsp ground cinnamon
- Pinch salt - 1 cup water
- ½ cup unsalted pistachios
- 2 cups sliced fresh strawberries
- ¼ cup cacao nibs (optional)

Directions:
1. In a large bowl, stir together the milk, groats, chia seeds, vanilla, cinnamon, and salt. Cover and refrigerate overnight.
2. The next morning, transfer the soaked mixture to a medium pot and add the water. Bring to a boil over medium-high heat, reduce the heat to maintain a simmer, and cook for 10–12 minutes, until the buckwheat is tender and thickened.
3. Transfer to bowls and serve, topped with the pistachios, strawberries, and cacao nibs (if using).

Nutrition:
- Calories: 340 Total fat: 8 g
- Saturated fat: 1 g Protein: 15 g
- Carbs: 52 g Sugar: 14 g
- Fiber: 10 g Cholesterol: 4 mg
- Sodium: 140 mg

5. Peach Muesli Bake

Preparation time: 10 minutes
Cooking time: 40 minutes
Servings: 8
Ingredients:
- Nonstick cooking spray
- 2 cups skim milk
- 1 ½ cup rolled oats
- ½ cup chopped walnuts
- 1 large egg
- 2 tbsp maple syrup
- 1 tsp ground cinnamon
- 1 tsp baking powder
- ½ tsp salt
- 2–3 peaches, sliced

Directions:
1. Preheat the oven to 375°F. Spray a 9-inch square baking dish with cooking spray. Set aside.
2. In a large bowl, stir together the milk, oats, walnuts, egg, maple syrup, cinnamon, baking powder, and salt. Spread half the mixture in the prepared baking dish.
3. Place half the peaches in a single layer across the oat mixture.
4. Spread the remaining oat mixture over the top. Add the remaining peaches in a thin layer over the oats. Bake for 35–40 minutes, uncovered until thickened and browned.
5. Cut into 8 squares and serve warm.

Nutrition:
- Calories: 138 Total fat: 3 g
- Saturated fat: 1 g Protein: 6 g
- Carbs: 22 g Sugar: 10 g
- Fiber: 3 g Cholesterol: 24 mg
- Sodium: 191 mg

6. Steel-Cut Oatmeal Bowl With Fruit and Nuts

Preparation time: 5 minutes
Cooking time: 20 minutes
Servings: 4
Ingredients:
- 1 cup steel-cut oats
- 2 cups almond milk
- ¾ cup water
- 1 tsp ground cinnamon
- ¼ tsp salt
- 2 cups chopped fresh fruit, such as blueberries, strawberries, raspberries, or peaches
- ½ cup chopped walnuts
- ¼ cup chia seeds

Directions:
1. In a medium saucepan over medium-high heat, combine the oats, almond milk, water, cinnamon, and salt.
2. Bring to a boil, reduce the heat to low, and simmer for 15–20 minutes, until the oats are softened and thickened.
3. Top each bowl with ½ cup of fresh fruit, 2 tbsp walnuts, and 1 tbsp chia seeds before serving

Nutrition:
- Calories: 288
- Total fat: 11 g
- Saturated fat: 1 g
- Protein: 10 g
- Carbs: 38 g
- Sugar: 7 g
- Fiber: 10 g
- Cholesterol: 0 mg
- Sodium: 329 mg

7. Whole-Grain Dutch Baby Pancake

Preparation time: 5 minutes
Cooking time: 25 minutes
Servings: 4
Ingredients:
- 2 tbsp coconut oil
- ½ cup whole-wheat flour
- ¼ cup skim milk
- 3 large eggs
- 1 tsp vanilla extract
- ½ tsp baking powder
- ¼ tsp salt
- ¼ tsp ground cinnamon
- Powdered sugar, for dusting

Directions:
1. Preheat the oven to 400°F.
2. Put the coconut oil in a medium oven-safe skillet, and place the skillet in the oven to melt the oil while it preheats.
3. In a blender, combine the flour, milk, eggs, vanilla, baking powder, salt, and cinnamon. Process until smooth.
4. Carefully remove the skillet from the oven and tilt it to spread the oil around evenly.
5. Pour the batter into the skillet and return it to the oven for 23–25 minutes, until the pancake puffs and lightly browns.
6. Remove, dust lightly with powdered sugar, cut into 4 wedges, and serve.

Nutrition:
- Calories: 195
- Total fat: 11 g
- Saturated fat: 7 g
- Protein: 8 g
- Carbs: 16 g
- Sugar: 1 g
- Fiber: 2 g
- Cholesterol: 140 mg
- Sodium: 209 mg

8. Mushroom, Zucchini, and Onion Frittata

Preparation time: 10 minutes
Cooking time: 20 minutes
Servings: 4
Ingredients:
- 1 tbsp extra-virgin olive oil
- ½ onion, chopped
- 1 medium zucchini, chopped
- 1 ½ cups sliced mushrooms
- 6 large eggs, beaten
- 2 tbsp skim milk
- Salt
- Freshly ground black pepper
- 1 oz Feta cheese, crumbled

Directions:
1. Preheat the oven to 400°F.
2. In a medium oven-safe skillet over medium-high heat, heat the olive oil.
3. Add the onion and sauté for 3–5 minutes, until translucent.
4. Add the zucchini and mushrooms, and cook for 3–5 more minutes, until the vegetables are tender.
5. Meanwhile, in a small bowl, whisk the eggs, milk, salt, and pepper. Pour the mixture into the skillet, stirring to combine, and transfer the skillet to the oven. Cook for 7–9 minutes, until set.
6. Sprinkle with the Feta cheese, and cook for 1–2 minutes more, until heated through.
7. Remove, cut into 4 wedges, and serve.

Nutrition:
- Calories: 178
- Total fat: 13 g
- Saturated fat: 4 g
- Protein: 12 g
- Carbs: 5 g
- Sugar: 3 g
- Fiber: 1 g
- Cholesterol: 285 mg
- Sodium: 234 mg

9. Spinach and Cheese Quiche

Preparation time: 10 minutes, plus 10 minutes to rest
Cooking time: 50 minutes
Servings: 4–6
Ingredients:
- Nonstick cooking spray
- 8 oz Yukon gold potatoes, shredded
- 1 tbsp extra-virgin olive oil, plus 2 tsp (divided)
- 1 tsp salt, divided
- Freshly ground black pepper
- 1 onion, finely chopped
- 1 (10 oz) bag of fresh spinach
- 4 large eggs
- ½ cup skim milk
- 1 oz Gruyere cheese, shredded

Directions:
1. Preheat the oven to 350°F. Spray a 9-inch pie dish with cooking spray. Set aside.

2. In a small bowl, toss the potatoes with 2 tsp olive oil, ½ tsp salt, and season with pepper.
3. Press the potatoes into the bottom and sides of the pie dish to form a thin, even layer.
4. Bake for 20 minutes, until golden brown. Remove from the oven and set aside to cool.
5. In a large skillet over medium-high heat, heat the remaining 1 tbsp olive oil.
6. Add the onion and sauté for 3–5 minutes, until softened.
7. By handfuls, add the spinach, stirring between each addition until it just starts to wilt before adding more. Cook for about 1 minute, until it cooks down.
8. In a medium bowl, whisk the eggs and milk. Add the gruyere, and season with the remaining ½ tsp salt and some pepper. Fold the eggs into the spinach. Pour the mixture into the pie dish and bake for 25 minutes, until the eggs are set.
9. Let rest for 10 minutes before serving

Nutrition:
- Calories: 445 Total fat: 14 g
- Saturated fat: 4 g Protein: 19 g
- Carbs: 68 g Sugar: 6 g
- Fiber: 7 g
- Cholesterol: 193 mg
- Sodium: 773 mg

10. Spicy Jalapeno Popper Deviled Eggs

Preparation time: 5 minutes
Cooking time: 5 minutes
Servings: 4
Ingredients:
- 4 large whole eggs, hardboiled
- 2 tbsp keto-friendly mayonnaise
- ¼ cup Cheddar cheese, grated
- 2 slices bacon, cooked and crumbled
- 1 jalapeno, sliced

Directions:
1. Cut eggs in half, remove the yolk, and put them in a bowl.
2. Lay egg whites on a platter.
3. Mix in the remaining ingredients and mash them with the egg yolks.
4. Transfer the yolk mixture back to the egg whites.
5. Serve and enjoy!

Nutrition:
- Calories: 176
- Fat: 14 g
- Carbs: 0.7 g
- Protein: 10 g

11. Lovely Porridge

Preparation time: 15 minutes
Cooking time: Nil
Servings: 2
Ingredients:
- 2 tbsp coconut flour
- 2 tbsp vanilla protein powder
- 3 tbsp golden flaxseed meal
- 1 ½ cups almond milk, unsweetened
- Powdered Erythritol

Directions:
1. Take a bowl and mix in flaxseed meal, protein powder, coconut flour and mix well.
2. Add mix to the saucepan (placed over medium heat).
3. Add almond milk and stir, let the mixture thicken.
4. Add your desired amount of sweetener and serve.
5. Enjoy!

Nutrition:
- Calories: 259
- Fat: 13 g
- Carbs: 5 g
- Protein: 16 g

12. Salty Macadamia Chocolate Smoothie

Preparation time: 5 minutes
Cooking time: Nil
Servings: 1
Ingredients:
- 2 tbsp macadamia nuts, salted

- ⅓ cup chocolate whey protein powder, low carb
- 1 cup almond milk, unsweetened

Directions:
1. Add the listed ingredients to your blender and blend until you have a smooth mixture.
2. Chill and enjoy it!

Nutrition:
- Calories: 165
- Fat: 2 g
- Carbs: 1 g
- Protein: 12 g

13. Basil and Tomato Baked Eggs

Preparation time: 10 minutes
Cooking time: 15 minutes
Servings: 4
Ingredients:
- 1 garlic clove, minced
- 1 cup canned tomatoes
- ¼ cup fresh basil leaves, roughly chopped
- ½ tsp chili powder
- 1 tbsp olive oil
- 4 whole eggs
- Salt and pepper to taste

Directions:
1. Preheat your oven to 375°F.
2. Take a small baking dish and grease it with olive oil.
3. Add garlic, basil, tomatoes, chili, and olive oil into a dish and stir.
4. Crack down eggs into a dish, keeping space between the two.
5. Sprinkle the whole dish with salt and pepper.
6. Place in oven and cook for 12 minutes until eggs are set and tomatoes are bubbling
7. Serve with basil on top.
8. Enjoy!

Nutrition:
- Calories: 235
- Fat: 16 g
- Carbs: 7 g
- Protein: 14 g

14. Cinnamon and Coconut Porridge

Preparation time: 5 minutes
Cooking time: 5 minutes
Servings: 4
Ingredients:
- 2 cups of water
- 1 cup 36% heavy cream
- ½ cup unsweetened dried coconut, shredded
- 2 tbsp flaxseed meal
- 1 tbsp butter
- 1 ½ tsp Stevia
- 1 tsp cinnamon
- Salt to taste
- Toppings as blueberries

Directions:
1. Add the listed ingredients to a small pot and mix well.
2. Transfer pot to stove and place it over medium-low heat.
3. Bring to mix to a slow boil.
4. Stir well and remove the heat.
5. Divide the mix into equal servings and let them sit for 10 minutes.
6. Top with your desired toppings and enjoy!

Nutrition:
- Calories: 171
- Fat: 16 g
- Carbs: 6 g
- Protein: 2 g

15. An Omelet of Swiss Chard

Preparation time: 5 minutes
Cooking time: 5 minutes
Servings: 4
Ingredients:
- 4 eggs, lightly beaten
- 4 cups Swiss chard, sliced
- 2 tbsp butter
- ½ tsp garlic salt
- Fresh pepper

Directions:
1. Take a non-stick frying pan and place it over medium-low heat.

2. Once the butter melts, add Swiss chard and stir cook for 2 minutes.
3. Pour egg into the pan and gently stir them into Swiss chard.
4. Season with garlic salt and pepper.
5. Cook for 2 minutes.
6. Serve and enjoy!

Nutrition:
- Calories: 260
- Fat: 21 g
- Carbs: 4 g
- Protein: 14 g

16. Cheesy Low-Carb Omelet

Preparation time: 5 minutes
Cooking time: 5 minutes
Servings: 5
Ingredients:
- 2 whole eggs
- 1 tbsp water
- 1 tbsp butter
- 3 thin slices of salami
- 5 fresh basil leaves
- 5 thin slices of fresh ripe tomatoes
- 2 oz fresh Mozzarella cheese
- Salt and pepper as needed

Directions:
1. Take a small bowl and whisk in eggs and water.
2. Take a non-stick sauté pan and place it over medium heat, add butter and let it melt.
3. Pour egg mixture and cook for 30 seconds.
4. Spread salami slices on half of the egg mix and top with cheese, tomatoes, and basil slices.
5. Season with salt and pepper according to your taste.
6. Cook for 2 minutes and fold the egg with the empty half.
7. Cover and cook on low for 1 minute.
8. Serve and enjoy!

Nutrition:
- Calories: 451
- Fat: 36 g
- Carbs: 3 g
- Protein: 33 g

17. Yogurt and Kale Smoothie

Preparation time: 10 minutes
Servings: 1
Ingredients:
- 1 cup whole milk yogurt
- 1 cup baby kale greens
- 1 pack of Stevia
- 1 tbsp MCT oil
- 1 tbsp sunflower seeds
- 1 cup of water

Directions:
1. Add listed ingredients to the blender.
2. Blend until you have a smooth and creamy texture.
3. Serve chilled and enjoy!

Nutrition:
- Calories: 329
- Fat: 26 g
- Carbs: 15 g
- Protein: 11 g

18. Bacon and Chicken Garlic Wrap

Preparation time: 15 minutes
Cooking time: 10 minutes
Servings: 4
Ingredients:
- 1 chicken fillet, cut into small cubes
- 8–9 thin slices of bacon, cut to fit cubes
- 6 garlic cloves, minced

Directions:
1. Preheat your oven to 400°F.
2. Line a baking tray with aluminum foil.
3. Add minced garlic to a bowl and rub each chicken piece with it.
4. Wrap bacon piece around each garlic chicken bite.
5. Secure with a toothpick.
6. Transfer bites to the baking sheet, keeping a little bit of space between them.
7. Bake for about 15–20 minutes until crispy.
8. Serve and enjoy!

Nutrition:
- Calories: 260 Fat: 19 g
- Carbs: 5 g Protein: 22 g

19. Grilled Chicken Platter

Preparation time: 5 minutes
Cooking time: 10 minutes
Servings: 6
Ingredients:
- 3 large chicken breast, sliced half lengthwise
- 10 oz spinach, frozen and drained
- 3 oz Mozzarella cheese, part-skim
- ½ cup of roasted red peppers, cut into long strips
- 1 tsp olive oil
- 2 garlic cloves, minced
- Salt and pepper as needed

Directions:
1. Preheat your oven to 400°F.
2. Slice 3 chicken breasts lengthwise.
3. Take a non-stick pan and grease it with cooking spray.
4. Bake for 2–3 minutes on each side.
5. Take another skillet and cook spinach and garlic in oil for 3 minutes.
6. Place chicken on an oven pan and top with spinach, roasted peppers, and Mozzarella.
7. Bake until the cheese melts.
8. Enjoy!

Nutrition:
- Calories: 195 Fat: 7 g
- Net carbs: 3 g Protein: 30 g

20. Parsley Chicken Breast

Preparation time: 10 minutes
Cooking time: 40 minutes
Servings: 4
Ingredients:
- 1 tbsp dry parsley
- 1 tbsp dry basil
- 4 chicken breast halves, boneless and skinless
- ½tsp salt
- ½tsp red pepper flakes, crushed
- 2 tomatoes, sliced

Directions:
1. Preheat your oven to 350°F.
2. Take a 9x13-inch baking dish and grease it up with cooking spray.
3. Sprinkle 1 tbsp parsley, 1 tsp basil, and spread the mixture over your baking dish.
4. Arrange the chicken breast halves over the dish and sprinkle garlic slices on top.
5. Take a small bowl and add 1 tsp parsley, 1 tsp basil, salt, basil, red pepper and mix well. Pour the mixture over the chicken breast.
6. Top with tomato slices and cover, bake for 25 minutes.
7. Remove the cover and bake for 15 minutes more.
8. Serve and enjoy!

Nutrition:
- Calories: 150
- Fat: 4 g
- Carbs: 4 g
- Protein: 25 g

21. Mustard Chicken

Preparation time: 10 minutes
Cooking time: 40 minutes
Servings: 4
Ingredients:
- 4 chicken breasts
- ½cup chicken broth
- 3–4tbsp mustard
- 3 tbsp olive oil
- 1 tsp paprika
- 1 tsp chili powder
- 1 tsp garlic powder

Directions:
1. Take a small bowl and mix mustard, olive oil, paprika, chicken broth, garlic powder, chicken broth, and chili.
2. Add chicken breast and marinate for 30 minutes.
3. Take a lined baking sheet and arrange the chicken.
4. Bake for 35 minutes at 375°F.
5. Serve and enjoy!

Nutrition:
- Calories: 531
- Fat: 23 g
- Carbs: 10 g
- Protein: 64 g

22. Balsamic Chicken

Preparation time: 10 minutes
Cooking time: 25 minutes
Servings: 6
Ingredients:
- 6 chicken breast halves, skinless and boneless
- 1 tsp garlic salt
- Ground black pepper
- 2 tbsp olive oil
- 1 onion, thinly sliced
- 14 ½ oz tomatoes, diced
- ½ cup balsamic vinegar
- 1 tsp dried basil - 1 tsp dried oregano
- 1 tsp dried rosemary
- ½ tsp dried thyme

Directions:
1. Season both sides of your chicken breasts thoroughly with pepper and garlic salt.
2. Take a skillet and place it over medium heat.
3. Add some oil and cook your seasoned chicken for 3–4 minutes per side until the breasts are nicely browned.
4. Add some onion and cook for another 3–4 minutes until the onions are browned.
5. Pour the diced-up tomatoes and balsamic vinegar over your chicken and season with some rosemary, basil, thyme, and rosemary. Simmer the chicken for about 15 minutes until they are no longer pink.
6. Take an instant-read thermometer and check if the internal temperature gives a reading of 165°F. If yes, then you are good to go!

Nutrition:
- Calories: 196 Fat: 7 g
- Carbs: 7 g Protein: 23 g

23. Greek Chicken Breast

Preparation time: 10 minutes
Cooking time: 25 minutes
Servings: 4
Ingredients:
- 4 chicken breast halves, skinless and boneless
- 1 cup extra-virgin olive oil
- 1 lemon, juiced
- 2 tsp garlic, crushed
- 1 ½ tsp black pepper
- ⅓ tsp paprika

Directions:
1. Cut 3 slits in the chicken breast.
2. Take a small bowl and whisk in olive oil, salt, lemon juice, garlic, paprika, and pepper and whisk for 30 seconds.
3. Place chicken in a large bowl and pour marinade.
4. Rub the marinade all over using your hand.
5. Refrigerate overnight.
6. Pre-heat grill to medium heat and oil the grate.
7. Cook chicken on the grill until the center is no longer pink.
8. Serve and enjoy!

Nutrition:
- Calories: 644
- Fat: 57 g
- Carbs: 2 g
- Protein: 27 g

24. Chipotle Lettuce Chicken

Preparation time: 10 minutes
Cooking time: 25 minutes
Servings: 6
Ingredients:
- 1 lb chicken breast, cut into strips
- Splash of olive oil
- 1 red onion, finely sliced
- 14 oz tomatoes
- 1 tsp chipotle, chopped
- ½ tsp cumin
- Pinch of sugar
- Lettuce as needed
- Fresh coriander leaves
- Jalapeno chilies, sliced
- Fresh tomato slices for garnish
- Lime wedges

Directions:
1. Take a non-stick frying pan and place it over medium heat.

2. Add oil and heat it up.
3. Add chicken and cook until brown.
4. Keep the chicken on the side.
5. Add tomatoes, sugar, chipotle, and cumin to the same pan and simmer for 25 minutes until you have a nice sauce.
6. Add chicken into the sauce and cook for 5 minutes.
7. Transfer the mix to another place.
8. Use lettuce wraps to take a portion of the mixture and serve with a squeeze of lemon.
9. Enjoy!

Nutrition:
- Calories: 332
- Fat: 15 g
- Carbs: 13 g
- Protein: 34 g

25. Stylish Chicken-Bacon Wrap

Preparation time: 5 minutes
Cooking time: 50 minutes
Servings: 3
Ingredients:
- 8 oz lean chicken breast
- 6 bacon slices
- 3 oz shredded cheese
- 4 slices ham

Directions:
1. Cut chicken breast into bite-sized portions.
2. Transfer shredded cheese onto ham slices.
3. Roll up chicken breast and ham slices in bacon slices.
4. Take a skillet and place it over medium heat.
5. Add olive oil and brown bacon for a while.
6. Remove rolls and transfer them to your oven.
7. Bake for 45 minutes at 325°F.
8. Serve and enjoy!

Nutrition:
- Calories: 275
- Fat: 11 g
- Carbs: 0.5 g
- Protein: 40 g

26. Healthy Cottage Cheese Pancakes

Preparation time: 10 minutes
Cooking time: 15
Servings: 1
Ingredients:
- ½ cup of Cottage cheese (low-fat)
- ⅓ cup egg whites (approx. 2 egg whites)
- ¼ cup of oats
- 1 tsp vanilla extract
- Olive oil cooking spray
- 1 tbsp Stevia (raw)
- Berries or sugar-free jam (optional)

Directions:
1. Begin by taking a food blender and adding the egg whites and Cottage cheese. Also add in the vanilla extract, a pinch of Stevia, and oats. Palpitate until the consistency is well smooth.
2. Get a non-stick pan and oil it nicely with the cooking spray. Position the pan on low heat.
3. After it has been heated, scoop out half of the batter and pour it into the pan. Cook for about 2½ minutes on each side.
4. Position the cooked pancakes on a serving plate and cover them with sugar-free jam or berries.

Nutrition:
- Calories: 205 Fat: 1.5 g
- Protein: 24.5 g
- Carbs: 19 g

27. Avocado Lemon Toast

Preparation time: 10 minutes
Cooking time: 13 minutes
Servings: 2
Ingredients:
- 2 slices of whole-grain bread
- 2 tbsp fresh cilantro (chopped)
- ¼ tsp lemon zest
- 1 pinch of fine sea salt
- ½ avocado
- 1 tsp fresh lemon juice
- 1 pinch of cayenne pepper
- ¼ tsp chia seeds

Directions:
1. Begin by getting a medium-sized mixing bowl and adding the avocado. Make use of a fork to crush it properly.
2. Then, add in the cilantro, lemon zest, lemon juice, sea salt, and cayenne pepper. Mix well until combined.
3. Toast the bread slices in a toaster until golden brown. It should take about 3 minutes.
4. Top the toasted bread slices with the avocado mixture and finalize by drizzling with chia seeds.

Nutrition:
- Calories: 72 Protein: 3.6 g
- Fat: 1.2 g Carbs: 11.6 g

28. Healthy Baked Eggs

Preparation time: 10 minutes
Cooking time: 1 hour
Servings: 6

Ingredients:
- 1 tbsp olive oil
- 2 garlic cloves
- 8 large eggs
- ½ tsp sea salt
- 3 cups shredded Mozzarella cheese (medium-fat)
- Olive oil spray
- 1 medium onion, chopped
- 8 oz spinach leaves
- 1 cup half-and-half
- 1 tsp black pepper
- ½ cup Feta cheese

Directions:
1. Begin by heating the oven to 375°F.
2. Get a glass baking dish and grease it with olive oil spray. Arrange aside.
3. Now take a non-stick pan and pour in the olive oil. Position the pan on allows heat and allows it heat.
4. Immediately you are done, toss in the garlic, spinach, and onion. Prepare for about 5 minutes. Arrange aside.
5. You can now get a large mixing bowl and add in the half, eggs, pepper, and salt. Whisk thoroughly to combine.
6. Put in the Feta cheese and chopped Mozzarella cheese (reserve ½cup of Mozzarella cheese for later).
7. Put the egg mixture and prepared spinach into the prepared glass baking dish. Blend well to combine. Drizzle the reserved cheese over the top.
8. Bake the egg mix for about 45 minutes.
9. Extract the baking dish from the oven and allow it to stand for 10 minutes.
10. Dice and serve!

Nutrition:
- Calories: 323 calories per serving
- Fat: 22.3 g
- Protein: 22.6 g
- Carbs: 7.9 g

29. Quick Low-Carb Oatmeal

Preparation time: 10 minutes
Cooking time: 15 minutes
Servings: 2

Ingredients:
- ½ cup almond flour
- 2 tbsp flax meal
- 1 tsp ground cinnamon
- 1 ½ cup unsweetened almond milk
- Salt as per taste
- 2 tbsp chia seeds
- 10–15 drops of liquid Stevia
- 1 tsp vanilla extract

Directions:
1. Begin by taking a large mixing bowl and adding the coconut flour, almond flour, ground cinnamon, flax seed powder, and chia seeds. Mix properly to combine.
2. Position a stockpot on low heat and add in the dry ingredients. Also add in the liquid Stevia, vanilla extract, and almond milk. Mix well to combine.
3. Prepare the flour and almond milk for about 4 minutes. Add salt if needed.
4. Move the oatmeal to a serving bowl and top with nuts, seeds, and pure and neat berries.

Nutrition:
- Protein: 11.7 g Fat. 24.3 g
- Carbs: 16.7 g

30. Tofu and Vegetable Scramble

Preparation time: 10 minutes
Cooking time: 15 minutes
Servings: 2
Ingredients:
- 16 oz firm tofu (drained)
- ½ tsp sea salt
- 1 tsp garlic powder
- ½ medium red onion
- 1 tsp cumin poder
- 1 tsp turmeric
- 1 tsp chili powder
- 1 medium green bell pepper
- 1 tsp garlic powder
- fresh coriander for garnishing
- ½ medium red onion
- 1 tsp cumin powder
- Lemon juice for topping

Directions:
1. Begin by preparing the ingredients. For this, you are to extract the seeds of the tomato and green bell pepper. Shred the onion, bell pepper, and tomato into small cubes.
2. Get a small mixing bowl and position the fairly hard tofu inside it. Make use of your hands to break the fairly hard tofu. Arrange aside.
3. Get a non-stick pan and add the onion, tomato, and bell pepper. Mix and cook for about 3 minutes.
4. Put the somewhat hard crumbled tofu into the pan and combine well.
5. Get a small bowl and put in the water, turmeric, garlic powder, cumin powder, and chili powder. Combine well and stream it over the tofu and vegetable mixture.
6. Allow the tofu and vegetable crumble to cook with seasoning for 5 minutes. Continuously stir so that the pan is not holding the ingredients.
7. Drizzle the tofu scramble with chili flakes and salt. Combine well.
8. Transfer the prepared scramble to a serving bowl and give it a proper spray of lemon juice.
9. Finalize by garnishing with pure and neat coriander. Serve while hot!

Nutrition:
- Calories: 238
- Carbs: 16.6 g
- Fat: 11 g

31. Breakfast Smoothie Bowl With Fresh Berries

Preparation time: 10 minutes
Cooking time: 5 minutes
Servings: 2
Ingredients:
- ½ cup unsweetened almond milk
- ½ tsp psyllium husk powder
- 2 oz chopped strawberries
- 1 tbsp coconut oil
- 3 cups crushed ice
- 5–10 drops of liquid Stevia
- ⅓ cup pea protein powder

Directions:
1. Begin by taking a blender and adding the mashed ice cubes. Allow them to rest for about 30 seconds.
2. Then put in the almond milk, shredded strawberries, pea protein powder, psyllium husk powder, coconut oil, and liquid Stevia. Blend well until it turns into a smooth and creamy puree.
3. Vacant the prepared smoothie into 2 glasses.
4. Cover with coconut flakes and pure and neat strawberries.

Nutrition:
- Calories: 166
- Fat: 9.2 g
- Carbs: 4.1 g
- Protein: 17.6 g

32. Chia and Coconut Pudding

Preparation time: 10 minutes
Cooking time: 5 minutes
Servings: 2
Ingredients:
- 7 oz light coconut milk
- 3–4 drops of liquid Stevia

- 1 kiwi
- ¼ cup chia seeds
- 1 clementine
- Shredded coconut (unsweetened)

Directions:
1. Begin by getting a mixing bowl and putting in the light coconut milk. Set in the liquid Stevia to sweeten the milk. Combine well.
2. Put the chia seeds into the milk and whisk until well combined. Arrange aside.
3. Scrape the clementine and carefully extract the skin from the wedges. Leave aside.
4. Also, scrape the kiwi and dice it into small pieces.
5. Get a glass vessel and gather the pudding For this, position the fruits at the bottom of the jar; then put a dollop of chia pudding Then spray the fruits and then put another layer of chia pudding
6. Finalize by garnishing with the rest of the fruits and chopped coconut.

Nutrition:
- Calories: 201 Protein: 5.4 g
- Fat: 10 g Carbs: 22.8 g

33. Tomato and Zucchini Sauté

Preparation time: 10 minutes
Cooking time: 43 minutes
Servings: 6
Ingredients:
- 1 tbsp vegetable oil
- 2 chopped tomatoes
- 1 chopped green bell pepper
- Freshly ground black pepper as per taste
- 1 sliced onion
- 2 lb zucchini (peeled and cut into 1-inch-thick slices)
- Salt as per taste
- ¼ cup uncooked white rice

Directions:
1. Begin by getting a non-stick pan and putting it over low heat. Stream in the oil and allow it to heat through.
2. Put in the onions and sauté for about 3 minutes.
3. Then pour in the zucchini and green peppers. Mix well and spice with black pepper and salt.
4. Reduce the heat and cover the pan with a lid. Allow the veggies to cook on low for 5 minutes.
5. While you're done, put in the water and rice. Place the lid back on and cook on low for 20 minutes.

Nutrition:
- Calories: 94 Fat: 2.8 g
- Protein: 3.2 g Carbs: 16.1 g

34. Steamed Kale With Mediterranean Dressing

Preparation time: 10 minutes
Cooking time: 25 minutes
Servings: 6
Ingredients:
- 12 cups chopped kale
- 1 tbsp olive oil
- 1 tsp soy sauce
- Freshly ground pepper as per taste
- 2 tbsp lemon juice
- 1 tbsp minced garlic
- Salt as per taste

Directions:
1. Get a gas steamer or an electric steamer and fill the bottom pan with water. If making use of a gas steamer, position it on high heat. Making use of an electric steamer, place it on the highest setting
2. Immediately the water comes to a boil, put in the shredded kale, and cover with a lid. Boil for about 8 minutes. The kale should be tender by now.
3. During the kale is boiling, take a big mixing bowl and put in the olive oil, lemon juice, soy sauce, garlic, pepper, and salt. Whisk well to mix.
4. Now toss in the steamed kale and carefully enclose it into the dressing Be assured the kale is well-coated.
5. Serve while it's hot!

Nutrition:
- Calories: 91 Fat: 3.5 g
- Protein: 4.6 g Carbs: 14.5 g

35. Healthy Carrot Muffins

Preparation time: 10 minutes
Cooking time: 40 minutes
Servings: 8
Ingredients:
Dry Ingredients:
- ¼ cup tapioca starch
- 1 tsp baking soda
- 1 tbsp cinnamon
- ¼ tsp cloves

Wet Ingredients:
- 1 tsp vanilla extract
- 1 ½ cups water
- 1 ½ cup carrots (shredded)
- 1 ¾ cup almond flour
- ½ cup granulated sweetener of choice
- 1 tsp baking powder
- 1 tsp nutmeg
- 1 tsp salt
- ⅓ cup coconut oil
- 4 tbsp flax meal
- 1 medium banana (mashed)

Directions:
1. Begin by heating the oven to 350°F.
2. Get a muffin tray and position paper cups in all the molds. Arrange aside.
3. Get a small glass bowl and put half a cup of water and the flax meal. Allow this rest for about 5 minutes. Your flax egg is prepared.
4. Get a large mixing bowl and put in the almond flour, tapioca starch, granulated sugar, baking soda, baking powder, cinnamon, nutmeg, cloves, and salt. Mix well to combine.
5. Conform a well in the middle of the flour mixture and stream in the coconut oil, vanilla extract, and flax egg Mix well to conform to a mushy dough.
6. Then, put in the chopped carrots and mashed banana. Mix until well-combined.
7. Make use of a spoon to scoop out an equal amount of mixture into 8 muffin cups.
8. Position the muffin tray in the oven and allow it to bake for about 40 minutes.
9. Extract the tray from the microwave and allow the muffins to stand for about 10 minutes.
10. Extract the muffin cups from the tray and allow them to chill until they reach room degree of hotness and coldness.
11. Serve and enjoy!

Nutrition:
- Calories: 189
- Fat: 13.9 g
- Protein: 3.8 g
- Carbs: 17.3 g

CHAPTER 7:

Meat

The following are useful, easy, and delicious meat recipes that can help in your battle against type 2 diabetes.

36. Fried Pork Chops

Preparation time: 15 minutes
Cooking time: 35 minutes
Servings: 2
Ingredients:
- 3 garlic cloves, ground - 2 tbsp olive oil
- 1 tbsp marinade - 4 thawed pork chops

Directions:
1. Mix the cloves of ground garlic, marinade, and oil. Then apply this mixture to the chops.
2. Put the chops in the air fryer at 360°C for 35 minutes.

Nutrition:
- Calories: 118 Fat: 3.41 g
- Carbs: 0 g Protein: 20.99 g
- Sugar: 0 g Cholesterol: 39 mg

37. Pork on a Blanket

Preparation time: 15 minutes
Cooking time: 10 minutes
Servings: 4
Ingredients:
- ½ puff pastry sheet, defrosted
- 16 thick smoked sausages
- 15 ml milk

Directions:
1. Preheat the air fryer to 200°C and set the timer to 5 minutes.
2. Cut the puff pastry into 64x38 mm strips.
3. Place a cocktail sausage at the end of the puff pastry and roll around the sausage, sealing the dough with some water.
4. Brush the top (with the seam facing down) of the sausages wrapped in milk and places them in the preheated air fryer.
5. Cook at 200°C until golden brown.

Nutrition:
- Calories: 381
- Fat: 5 g
- Carbs: 9.6 g
- Protein: 38 g
- Sugar: 1.8 g
- Cholesterol: 0 mg

38. Chicken Thighs

Preparation time: 15 minutes
Cooking time: 20 minutes
Servings: 2
Ingredients:
- 4 chicken thighs
- Salt to taste
- Pepper
- Mustard
- Paprika

Directions:
1. Before using the pot, it is convenient to turn it on for 5 minutes to heat it. Marinate the thighs with salt, pepper, mustard, and paprika.
2. Put your thighs in the air fryer for 10 minutes at 380°F.

3. After that time, turn the thighs and fry for 10 more minutes.
4. If necessary, you can use an additional 5 minutes depending on the size of the thighs so that they are well cooked.

Nutrition:
- Calories: 211
- Carbs: 6 g
- Fat: 11 g
- Protein: 19 g

39. Tasty Harissa Chicken

Preparation time: 15 minutes
Cooking time: 4 hours
Servings: 4
Ingredients:
- 1 lb chicken breasts, skinless and boneless
- ½ tsp ground cumin
- 1 cup harissa sauce
- ¼ tsp garlic powder
- ½ tsp kosher salt

Directions:
1. Flavor chicken with garlic powder, cumin, and salt.
2. Place chicken in the Slow Cooker.
3. Pour harissa sauce over the chicken.
4. Cover Slow Cooker on low for 4 hours.
5. Remove chicken from the Slow Cooker and shred using a fork.
6. Set shredded chicken on the Slow Cooker and stir well.

Nutrition:
- Calories: 235 Fat: 13 g
- Carbs: 1 g Protein: 2 g
- Sugar: 1 g
- Cholesterol: 130 mg

40. Pork Rind

Preparation time: 15 minutes
Cooking time: 1 hour
Servings: 4
Ingredients:
- 1kg pork rinds
- Salt
- ½ tsp black pepper coffee

Directions:
1. Preheat the air fryer. Set the time to 5 minutes and the temperature to 200°C.
2. Cut the bacon into cubes—1 finger wide.
3. Flavor with salt and a pinch of pepper.
4. Place in the basket of the air fryer. Set the time to 45 minutes and press the power button.
5. Shake the basket every 10 minutes so that the pork rinds stay golden brown equally.
6. Once they are ready, drain a little on the paper towel so they stay dry. Transfer to a plate and serve.

Nutrition:
- Calories: 282
- Fat: 23.41 g
- Carbs: 0 g
- Protein: 16.59
- Sugar: 0 g
- Cholesterol: 73 mg

41. Ginger Chili Broccoli

Preparation time: 15 minutes
Cooking time: 25 minutes
Servings: 4
Ingredients:
- 8 cups broccoli florets
- ½ cup olive oil
- Fresh juice of 2 limes
- 2 tbsp fresh ginger, grated
- 2 tsp chili pepper, chopped

Directions:
1. Add broccoli florets into the steamer and steam for 8 minutes.
2. Meanwhile, for dressing in a small bowl, combine lime juice, oil, ginger, and chili pepper.
3. Add steamed broccoli to a large bowl then pour dressing over broccoli. Toss well.

Nutrition:
- Calories: 239
- Fat: 20.8 g
- Carbs: 13.7 g
- Sugar: 3 g
- Protein: 4.5 g
- Cholesterol: 0 mg

42. Pork Tenderloin

Preparation time: 15 minutes
Cooking time: 45 minutes
Servings: 2–4
Ingredients:
- 1 lb pork
- 2 large eggs
- ¼ cup milk
- 2 cups seasoned breadcrumbs
- Salt and pepper to taste
- Nonstick cooking spray

Directions:
1. Slice the tenderloin into ½-inch slices.
2. Place the slices between two plastic sheets and tap them until each piece is ¼-inch thick.
3. In a large container, mix the eggs and milk.
4. In a separate container or dish, pour the breadcrumbs.
5. Introduce each piece of pork in the mixture of eggs and milk, letting the excess drain.
6. Then introduce the pork in the breadcrumbs, covering each side.
7. Place the covered pork on a wire rack for 30 minutes to make sure the cover adheres.
8. Preheat the air fryer to 400°F (204°C).
9. Spray the basket of the air fryer with non-stick cooking spray. Place the covered sirloin in the basket in a single layer.
10. Cook the sirloin for 10 minutes, then take it out, turn it over and sprinkle with more non-stick spray.
11. Cook for 5-minutes more or until both sides are crispy and golden brown.

Nutrition:
- Calories: 120
- Fat: 3.41 g
- Carbs: 0 g
- Protein: 20.99 g
- Sugar: 0 g
- Cholesterol: 65 mg

43. Chicken Soup

Preparation time: 15 minutes
Cooking time: 1 hour 20 minutes
Servings: 6
Ingredients:
- 4 lb chicken, cut into pieces
- 5 carrots, sliced thick
- 8 cups water
- 2 celery stalks, sliced 1-inch thick
- 2 large onions, sliced

Directions:
1. In a large pot add chicken, water, and salt. Bring to boil.
2. Add celery and onion to the pot and stir well.
3. Turn heat to medium-low and simmer.
4. Attach carrots and cover the pot with a lid and simmer for 40 minutes.
5. Detach the chicken from the pot and remove bones and cut the chicken into bite-size pieces.
6. Return chicken into the pot and stir well.

Nutrition:
- Calories: 89
- Fat: 6.33 g
- Carbs: 0 g
- Protein: 7.56 g
- Sugar: 0 g
- Cholesterol: 0 mg

44. Roasted Pork

Preparation time: 15 minutes
Cooking time: 30 minutes
Servings: 2–4
Ingredients:
- ½–2 kg pork meat (to roast)
- Salt
- Oil

Directions:
1. Join the cuts in an orderly manner.
2. Place the meat on the plate
3. Varnish with a little oil.
4. Place the roasts with the fat side down.
5. Cook in the air fryer at 180°C for 30 minutes.
6. Turn when you hear the beep.
7. Remove from the oven. Drain excess juice.
8. Let stand for 10 minutes on aluminum foil before serving

Nutrition:
- Calories: 820 Fat: 41 g
- Carbs: 0 g Protein: 20.99 g
- Sugar: 0 g Cholesterol: 120 mg

45. Marinated Loin Potatoes

Preparation time: 15 minutes
Cooking time: 1 hour 20 minutes
Servings: 2
Ingredients:
- 2 medium potatoes
- 4 fillets of marinated loin
- A little extra-virgin olive oil
- Salt

Directions:
1. Peel the potatoes and cut. Cut with match-sized mandolin, potatoes with a cane but very thin.
2. Wash and immerse in water for 30 minutes.
3. Drain and dry well.
4. Add a little oil and stir so that the oil permeates well in all the potatoes.
5. Go to the basket of the air fryer and distribute well.
6. Select 160°C, 10 minutes.
7. Take out the basket; shake so that the potatoes take off. Let the potato tender. If it is not, leave 5 more minutes.
8. Set the steaks on top of the potatoes.
9. Select 160°C, 10 minutes, and 180°F for 5 minutes again.

Nutrition:
- Calories: 136 Fat: 3.41 g Carbs: 0 g
- Protein: 20.99 g
- Sugar: 0 g

46. Homemade Flamingos

Preparation time: 15 minutes
Cooking time: 20 minutes
Servings: 4
Ingredients:
- 400 g very thin sliced pork fillets c/n
- 2 boiled and chopped eggs
- 100 g chopped Serrano ham
- 1 beaten egg
- Breadcrumbs

Directions:
1. Make a roll with the pork fillets. Introduce half-cooked egg and Serrano ham. So that the roll does not lose its shape, fasten with a string or chopsticks.
2. Pass the rolls through the beaten egg and then through the breadcrumbs until it forms a good layer.
3. Preheat the air fryer for a few minutes at 180°C.
4. Insert the rolls in the basket and set the timer for about 8 minutes at 180°C.

Nutrition:
- Calories: 482 Fat: 23.41 g
- Carbs: 0 g
- Protein: 16.59
- Sugar: 0 g
- Cholesterol: 173 mg

47. Meatloaf Reboot

Preparation time: 5 minutes
Cooking time: 9 minutes
Servings: 2
Ingredients:
- 4 slices of leftover meatloaf, cut about 1-inch thick.

Directions:
1. Preheat your air fryer to 350°F.
2. Spray each side of the meatloaf slices with cooking spray. Add the slices to the air fryer and cook for about 9–10 minutes.
3. Don't turn the slices halfway through the cooking cycle, because they may break apart. Instead, keep them on one side to cook to ensure they stay together

Nutrition:
- Calories: 201 Fat: 5 g
- Carbs: 9.6 g Protein: 38 g
- Sugar: 1.8 g
- Cholesterol: 10 mg

48. Tasty Chicken Tenders

Preparation time: 15 minutes
Cooking time: 25 minutes
Servings: 4
Ingredients:
- 1 ½lb chicken tenders
- 1 tbsp extra-virgin olive oil
- 1 tsp rotisserie chicken seasoning
- 2 tbsp BBQ sauce

Directions:
1. Add all ingredients except oil to a Ziplock bag.
2. Seal bag and place in the refrigerator for 2–3 hours.
3. Warm the oil in a large pan over medium heat.
4. Cook marinated chicken tenders in a pan until lightly brown and cooked.

Nutrition:
- Calories: 365 Fat: 16.1 g
- Carbohydrates: 2.8 g Sugar: 2 g
- Protein: 49.2 g Cholesterol: 151 mg

49. Creamy Mushroom Pork Chops

Preparation time: 10 minutes
Cooking time: 6 hours
Servings: 4
Ingredients:
- 4 pork chops
- 2 cups sliced mushrooms
- ½ cup chicken broth
- 2 tbsp tomato paste
- ½ tsp garlic powder
- Salt and pepper, to taste

Directions:
1. Place the pork inside your Slow Cooker.
2. In a bowl, combine the broth, tomato paste, and garlic powder and season with salt and pepper.
3. Top the pork with the mushrooms.
4. Pour the tomato mixture over.
5. Put the lid on and cook for 6 hours on low.
6. Serve and enjoy!

Nutrition:
- Calories: 215
- Total fats: 15 g
- Carbs: 4 g
- Protein: 22 g
- Fiber: 0.7 g

50. Pork and Sweet Potato Mash

Preparation time: 10 minutes
Cooking time: 4 hours
Servings: 4
Ingredients:
- 1 ¼ lb pork loin, cut into chunks
- 1 lb sweet potatoes, peeled and cut into cubes
- ½ tsp thyme
- ½ tsp salt
- ½ tsp paprika
- ½ tsp garlic powder
- 1 small onion, diced
- 1 cup beef broth

Directions:
1. Set the potatoes at the bottom of your Slow Cooker.
2. Set the meat on top.
3. Combine the broth with the rest of the ingredients.
4. Pour the mixture over the meat and potatoes.
5. Put the lid on and cook for 4 hours on high.
6. Open the lid and transfer the meat to a plate.

7. Transfer the potatoes to a bowl, along with the juices from the pot.
8. Mash until creamy and serve with pork chunks.
9. Serve and enjoy!

Nutrition:
- Calories: 340
- Total fats: 10 g
- Carbs: 23 g
- Protein: 36 g
- Fiber: 4 g

51. Lamb Roast

Preparation time: 10 minutes
Cooking time: 8 hours
Servings: 6
Ingredients:
- 2 ¼ lb leg of lamb
- 3 carrots, sliced
- 1 onion, chopped
- 2 garlic cloves, minced
- 2 rosemary sprigs
- ½ cup red wine
- 1 beef stock cube
- Salt and pepper, to taste

Directions:
1. Flavor the lamb generously with salt and pepper.
2. Add the lamb to your Slow Cooker.
3. Place the remaining ingredients in a bowl, crumble the stock cube inside, stir to combine, and pour over the lamb.
4. Add the rosemary sprigs inside and put the lid on.
5. Cook for 8 hours on low.
6. Open the lid and shred the lamb inside the pot. Stir to make sure it is equally moist.
7. Serve and enjoy!

Nutrition:
- Calories: 270
- Total fats: 7 g
- Carbs: 11 g
- Protein: 34 g
- Fiber: 2 g

52. Burgundy Lamb Shanks

Preparation time: 10 minutes
Cooking time: 8 hours
Servings: 4
Ingredients:
- 4 lamb shanks
- ½ onion, chopped
- 1 carrot, chopped
- 1 cup burgundy
- 2 garlic cloves, minced
- 1 tbsp parsley flakes
- 1 tsp thyme
- 1 tsp beef bouillon granules
- ¼ tsp oregano
- Salt and pepper, to taste

Directions:
1. Flavor the lamb generously with salt and pepper and place inside your Slow Cooker.
2. Arrange the carrots, onion, and garlic on top.
3. Combine the rest of the ingredients in a bowl, and pour over the lambs.
4. Place the lid of your Slow Cooker on, and cook for 8 hours on low.
5. Serve and enjoy!

Nutrition:
- Calories: 450
- Total fats: 25 g
- Carbs: 6 g
- Protein: 42 g
- Fiber: 1 g

53. Fruity Pork Roast

Preparation time: 10 minutes
Cooking time: 5 hours
Servings: 6
Ingredients:
- 2 ½ lb pork roast
- 7 oz dried fruit
- 2 tsp garlic pepper
- ½ cup water
- 1 tbsp chopped chipotle
- 2 tsp cornstarch
- 1 tbsp water

Directions:
1. Cut the meat into chunks and sprinkle it with garlic pepper.
2. Place inside the Slow Cooker.
3. Add the water, chipotle, and fruit inside.
4. Stir gently and place the lid on.
5. Cook for 5 hours on high.
6. Whisk in the cornstarch and cook for 30 more minutes on high.
7. Let sit before slicing or shredding.
8. Serve and enjoy!

Nutrition:
- Calories: 338
- Total fats: 12 g
- Carbs: 35 g
- Protein: 34 g
- Fiber: 2.5 g

54. Pork Carnitas

Preparation time: 10 minutes
Cooking time: 5 hours
Servings: 6
Ingredients:
- 12 corn tortillas
- 2 lb boneless pork shoulder
- 28 oz canned chicken broth
- 3 bay leaves
- 1 tsp oregano
- 4 garlic cloves, minced
- 1 tbsp black peppercorn
- 2 tsp cumin seeds
- Salt and pepper, to taste
- ⅓ cup sour cream
- ⅓ cup salsa

Directions:
1. Flavor the pork with some salt and pepper.
2. Place it inside the Slow Cooker.
3. Cut a small cheesecloth piece and add the peppercorns, cumin seeds, oregano, bay leaves, and garlic at the center. Bring up the corners together and tie with kitchen string to make a pouch.
4. Add the spice bag to the Slow Cooker.
5. Add the broth and place the lid on.
6. Cook for 5 hours on high.
7. Open the lid, discard the spice bag, and shred the pork inside the cooker.
8. Serve in tortillas along with some sour cream and salsa.
9. Enjoy!

Nutrition:
- Calories: 320
- Total fats: 10 g
- Carbs: 24 g
- Protein: 32 g
- Fiber: 4 g

55. Spiced Lamb Shoulder With Carrots

Preparation time: 10 minutes
Cooking time: 4 hours
Servings: 6
Ingredients:
- 2 lb lamb shoulder
- ½ lb carrots, sliced
- ½ onion, chopped
- ¼ cup fresh mint
- ½ tsp minced ginger
- ½ tsp turmeric
- ¼ tsp cinnamon
- ¼ tsp nutmeg
- ¼ tsp coriander
- ½ tsp garlic powder
- ½ tsp paprika
- ½ cup beef broth
- Salt and pepper, to taste

Directions:
1. Pour the broth into your Slow Cooker.
2. Merge all of the spices in a small bowl.

3. Rub this mixture all over the lamb.
4. Place the lamb inside your Slow Cooker, along with the carrots and onions.
5. Top with the chopped mint.
6. Set the lid on and cook for 4 hours on high.
7. Let sit for 10 minutes before slicing or shredding
8. Serve and enjoy!

Nutrition:
- Calories: 267
- Total fats: 15 g
- Carbs: 6 g
- Protein: 28 g
- Fiber: 1.4 g

56. Pineapple Pork Tacos

Preparation time: 15 minutes
Cooking time: 6 hours
Servings: 6
Ingredients:
- 2 lb pork loin roast, fat trimmed
- ½ cup lime juice
- ⅓ cup apple juice
- 2 tsp paprika
- 2 tbsp vinegar
- 1 tbsp chili powder
- ¾ tsp salt
- ¼ tsp black pepper
- 2 cups diced pineapple
- ¼ cup diced red onion
- 2 cups shredded cabbage
- 1 cup diced cucumber
- 12 corn tortillas

Directions:
1. Combine the spices (set aside ¼ tsp salt) in a small bowl and rub all over the meat.
2. Set in the Slow Cooker and pour the apple juice around (not over).
3. Put the lid on and cook on low for 6 hours.
4. In the meantime, combine the remaining salt, lime juice, pineapple, cabbage, cucumber, and onion. Place in a fridge until ready to serve.
5. Open the lid and shred the pork.
6. Attach the vinegar to the meat and stir to coat well.
7. Serve the meat in tortillas, topped with the lime pineapple mixture.
8. Serve and enjoy!

Nutrition:
- Calories: 306
- Total fats: 5 g
- Carbs: 31 g
- Protein: 35
- Fiber: 4 g

57. Lamb Tagine

Preparation time: 10 minutes
Cooking time: 7 hours
Servings: 4–6
Ingredients:
- 1 lb lamb, leaner cut
- 2 carrots, sliced
- 1 can of chickpeas, drained
- 1 can of diced tomatoes, undrained
- 1 onion, diced
- 1 tbsp olive oil
- 7 oz dried apricots
- 1 cup chicken stock
- 1 tbsp minced ginger
- 1 tsp paprika
- 2 tsp cumin
- ¼ tsp cinnamon
- Salt and pepper, to taste

Directions:
1. Warm the olive oil in a pan.
2. Add the lamb and cook until it becomes brown on all sides.
3. Add the onions and carrots and cook for a couple of minutes.
4. Whisk in the garlic and cook just until fragrant.

5. Stir in the remaining ingredients and transfer to your Slow Cooker.
6. Cover the pot and cook for 7 hours on low.
7. Serve and enjoy!

Nutrition:
- Calories: 470
- Total fats: 9 g
- Carbs: 49 g
- Protein: 23 g
- Fiber: 10 g

58. Barbecue Pulled Pork

Preparation time: 10 minutes
Cooking time: 8 hours
Servings: 6
Ingredients:
- 2 lb boneless pork loin
- 1 tbsp paprika
- 8 oz sugar-free barbecue sauce
- ½ onion, diced
- 2 garlic cloves, minced
- ½ cup water
- 1 tsp salt
- ½ tsp black pepper

Directions:
1. Set the water into the Slow Cooker and add everything but the meat.
2. Stir well to combine.
3. Now, gently place the meat in, and put the lid on.
4. Cook on low for 8 hours.
5. Grab two forks, open the lid, and shred within the pot.
6. Serve as desired and enjoy!

Nutrition:
- Calories: 240 Total fats: 11 g
- Carbs: 2 g Protein: 25 g
- Fiber: 0.5 g

59. Zoodles Carbonara

Preparation time: 10 minutes
Cooking time: 25 minutes
Servings: 4
Ingredients:
- 6 slices of bacon, cut into pieces
- 1 red onion, finely chopped
- 3 zucchini, cut into noodles
- 1 cup peas
- ½ tsp sea salt
- 3 garlic cloves, minced
- 3 large eggs, beaten
- 1 tbsp heavy cream
- Pinch red pepper flakes
- ½ cup grated Parmesan cheese

Directions:
1. Cook the bacon until browned, about 5 minutes.
2. Attach the onion to the bacon fat in the pan and cook, stirring, until soft, 3–5 minutes. Add the zucchini, peas, and salt. Cook, stirring, until the zucchini softens, about 3 minutes. Attach the garlic and cook, stirring constantly, for 5 minutes.
3. In a small bowl, whisk together the eggs, cream, and red pepper flakes. Add to the vegetables.
4. Remove the pan from the stovetop and stir for 3 minutes, allowing the heat of the pan to cook the eggs without setting them.
5. Set the bacon in the pan and stir to mix.
6. Serve topped with Parmesan cheese, if desired.

Nutrition:
- Calories: 326 Total fat: 24 g
- Saturated fat: 8 g
- Sodium: 555 mg Carbs: 15 g
- Fiber: 4 g
- Protein: 14 g

60. Pork and Apple Skillet

Preparation time: 10 minutes
Cooking time: 20 minutes
Servings: 4
Ingredients:
- 1 lb ground pork
- 1 red onion, thinly sliced
- 2 apples, peeled, cored, and thinly sliced
- 2 cups shredded cabbage
- 1 tsp dried thyme
- 2 garlic cloves, minced
- ¼ cup apple cider vinegar
- 1 tbsp Dijon mustard

- ½ tsp sea salt
- ⅛ tsp freshly ground black pepper

Directions:
1. In a large skillet, cook the ground pork, crumbling it with a spoon, until browned.
2. Add the onion, apples, cabbage, and thyme to the fat in the pan. Cook the vegetables until soft, about 5 minutes.
3. Attach the garlic and cook, stirring constantly, for 5 minutes.
4. Set the pork in the pan.
5. In a small bowl, pour together the vinegar, mustard, salt, and pepper. Add to the pan. Bring to a simmer. Cook, stirring, until the sauce thickens, about 2 minutes.

Nutrition:
- Calories: 364 Total fat: 24 g
- Saturated fat: 9 g
- Sodium: 260 mg Carbs: 19 g
- Fiber: 4 g Protein: 20 g

61. Vegetable Beef Soup

Preparation time: 10 minutes
Cooking time: 15 minutes
Servings: 4
Ingredients:
- 1 lb ground beef
- 1 onion, chopped
- 2 celery stalks, chopped
- 1 carrot, chopped
- 1 tsp dried rosemary
- 6 cups low-sodium beef or chicken broth
- ½ tsp sea salt
- ⅛ tsp freshly ground black pepper
- 2 cups peas

Directions:
1. Cook the ground beef, crumbling with the side of a spoon, until browned, about 5 minutes.
2. Add the onion, celery, carrot, and rosemary. Cook, stirring occasionally until the vegetables start to soften, about 5 minutes.
3. Add the broth, salt, pepper, and peas. Bring to a simmer. Reduce the heat and simmer, stirring, until warmed through, about 5 minutes more.

Nutrition:
- Calories: 355
- Total fat: 17 g
- Saturated fat: 7 g
- Sodium: 362 mg
- Carbs: 18 g
- Fiber: 5 g
- Protein: 34 g

62. Open-Faced Pub-Style Bison Burgers

Preparation time: 10 minutes
Cooking time: 15 minutes
Servings: 4
Ingredients:
- 2 tbsp extra-virgin olive oil
- 1 onion, thinly sliced
- 1 lb ground bison
- 1 tsp sea salt, divided
- 1 cup blue cheese crumbles
- 4 slices of sourdough bread
- 1 garlic clove, halved
- Pub sauce

Directions:
1. In a large skillet over medium-high heat, heat the olive oil until it shimmers. Add the onion. Cook for about 5 minutes.
2. Set the onion aside, wipe out the skillet with a paper towel and return it to the stove at medium-high heat. Season the bison with the salt and form it into 4 patties. Brown the patties in the hot skillet until they reach an internal temperature of 140°F, about 5 minutes per side.
3. Sprinkle the blue cheese over the tops of the burgers and remove the skillet from

the heat. Cover the skillet and allow the cheese to melt.
4. Meanwhile, toast the bread and then rub the garlic halves over the pieces of toast to flavor them.
5. To assemble, put a piece of toast on a plate. Top with onion slices, place a burger patty on top, and then spoon the sauce over the patty.

Nutrition:
- Calories: 390
- Total fat: 23 g
- Saturated fat: 4 g
- Sodium: 793 mg
- Carbs: 22 g
- Fiber: 1 g
- Protein: 27 g

63. Broccoli Beef Stir-Fry

Preparation time: 15 minutes
Cooking time: 15 minutes
Servings: 4
Ingredients:
- 2 tbsp extra-virgin olive oil
- 1 lb sirloin steak, cut into ¼-inch-thick strips
- 2 cups broccoli florets
- 1 garlic clove, minced
- 1 tsp peeled and grated fresh ginger
- 2 tbsp reduced-sodium soy sauce
- ¼ cup beef broth
- ½ tsp Chinese hot mustard
- Pinch red pepper flakes

Directions:
1. In a large skillet over medium-high heat, heat the olive oil until it shimmers. Add the beef. Cook, stirring, until it browns, 3–5 minutes. With a slotted spoon, detach the beef from the oil and set it aside on a plate.
2. Add the broccoli to the oil. Cook, stirring until it is crisp-tender, about 4 minutes.
3. Add the garlic and ginger and cook, stirring constantly, for 30 seconds.
4. Set the beef to the pan, along with any juices that have collected.
5. In a small bowl, whisk together the soy sauce, broth, mustard, and red pepper flakes.
6. Attach the soy sauce mixture to the skillet and cook, stirring, until everything warms through, about 3 minutes.

Nutrition:
- Calories: 227 Total fat: 11 g
- Saturated fat: 2 g
- Sodium: 375 mg
- Carbs: 5 g Fiber: 1 g
- Protein: 27 g

64. Beef and Pepper Fajita Bowls

Preparation time: 10 minutes
Cooking time: 15 minutes
Servings: 4
Ingredients:
- 4 tbsp extra-virgin olive oil, divided
- 1 head cauliflower, riced
- 1 lb sirloin steak, cut into ¼-inch-thick strips
- 1 red bell pepper, seeded and sliced
- 1 onion, thinly sliced
- 2 garlic cloves, minced
- Juice of 2 limes
- 1 tsp chili powder

Directions:
1. In a large skillet over medium-high heat, warm 2 tbsp olive oil until it shimmers. Add the cauliflower. Cook until it softens, about 3 minutes. Set aside.
2. Clean out the skillet with a paper towel. Attach the remaining 2 tbsp oil to the skillet, and heat it on medium-high until it shimmers. Add the steak and cook, stirring occasionally, until it browns, about 3 minutes. Use a slotted spoon to remove the steak from the oil in the pan and set it aside.
3. Attach the bell pepper and onion to the pan. Cook, until they start to brown, about 5 minutes.
4. Attach the garlic and cook, stirring constantly, for 30 seconds.
5. Set the beef along with any juices that have collected and the cauliflower to the

pan. Add the lime juice and chili powder. Cook, stirring until everything is warmed through, 2–3 minutes.

Nutrition:
- Calories: 310 Total fat: 18 g
- Saturated fat: 3 g Sodium: 93 mg
- Carbs: 13 g Fiber: 3 g Protein: 27 g

65. Lamb Kofta Meatballs With Cucumber Quick-Pickled Salad

Preparation time: 10 minutes
Cooking time: 15 minutes
Servings: 4
Ingredients:
- ¼ cup red wine vinegar
- Pinch red pepper flakes
- 1 tsp sea salt, divided
- 2 cucumbers, peeled and chopped
- ½ red onion, finely chopped
- 1 lb ground lamb
- 2 tsp ground coriander
- 1 tsp ground cumin
- 3 garlic cloves, minced
- 1 tbsp fresh mint, chopped

Directions:
1. Preheat the oven to 375°F. Set a rimmed baking sheet with parchment paper.
2. In a medium bowl, merge the vinegar, red pepper flakes, and ½ tsp salt. Attach the cucumbers and onion and toss to combine. Set aside.
3. In a large bowl, mix the lamb, coriander, cumin, garlic, mint, and remaining ½ tsp salt. Form the mixture into 1-inch meatballs and place them on the prepared baking sheet.
4. Bake until the lamb reaches 140°F internally, about 15 minutes.
5. Serve with the salad on the side.

Nutrition:
- Calories: 345 Total fat: 27 g
- Saturated fat: 12 g
- Sodium: 362 mg
- Carbs: 7 g
- Fiber: 1 g
- Protein: 20 g

66. Turkey Scaloppini

Preparation time: 10 minutes
Cooking time: 20 minutes
Servings: 4
Ingredients:
- ½ cup whole-wheat flour
- ½ tsp sea salt
- ¼ tsp freshly ground black pepper
- 3 tbsp extra-virgin olive oil
- 12 oz turkey breast, cut into ½-inch-thick cutlets and pounded flat (see headnote)
- 1 garlic clove, minced
- ½ cup dry white wine
- 2 tbsp chopped fresh rosemary
- 1 cup low-sodium chicken broth
- 2 tbsp salted butter, very cold, cut into small pieces

Directions:
1. Preheat the oven to 200°F. Line a baking sheet with parchment paper.
2. In a medium bowl, whip together the flour, salt, and pepper.
3. In a large skillet over medium-high heat, warm the olive oil until it shimmers.
4. Working in batches with one or two pieces of turkey at a time (depending on how much room you have in the pan), dredge the turkey cutlets in the flour and pat off any excess. Cook in the hot oil until the turkey is cooked through, about 3 minutes per side. Add more oil if needed.
5. Place the cooked cutlets on the lined baking sheet and keep them warm in the oven while you cook the remaining turkey and make the pan sauce.
6. Once all the turkey is cooked and warming in the oven, add the garlic to the pan and cook, stirring constantly, for 30 seconds. Add the wine and use the side of a spoon to scrape any browned bits off the bottom of the pan. Simmer, stirring, for 1 minute. Add the rosemary and chicken broth. Simmer, stirring, until it thickens, 1–2 minutes more.
7. Whisk in the cold butter, one piece at a time, until incorporated. Return the turkey cutlets to the sauce and turn once

to coat. Serve with any remaining sauce spooned over the top.

Nutrition:
- Calories: 344 Total fat: 20 g
- Saturated fat: 7 g Sodium: 266 mg
- Carbs: 15 g Fiber: 2 g Protein: 24 g

67. Ground Turkey Taco Skillet

Preparation time: 10 minutes
Cooking time: 20 minutes
Servings: 4
Ingredients:
- 3 tbsp extra-virgin olive oil
- 1 lb ground turkey
- 1 onion, chopped
- 1 green bell pepper, seeded and chopped
- ½ tsp sea salt
- 1 small head cauliflower, grated
- 1 cup corn kernels
- ½ cup prepared salsa
- 1 cup shredded pepper Jack cheese

Directions:
1. In a large non-stick skillet over medium-high heat, heat the olive oil until it shimmers.
2. Add the turkey. Cook, crumbling with a spoon, until browned, about 5 minutes.
3. Add the onion, bell pepper, and salt. Cook until the vegetables soften, for about 4–5 minutes.
4. Add the cauliflower, corn, and salsa. Cook, stirring, until the cauliflower rice softens, for about 3 minutes more.
5. Sprinkle with the cheese. Reduce heat to low, cover, and allow the cheese to melt, for about 2–3 minutes.

Nutrition:
- Calories: 448
- Total fat: 30 g
- Saturated fat: 10 g
- Sodium: 649 mg
- Carbs: 18 g
- Fiber: 4 g
- Protein: 30 g

68. Turkey Meatloaf Meatballs

Preparation time: 10 minutes
Cooking time: 20 minutes
Servings: 4
Ingredients:
- ¼ cup tomato paste
- 1 tbsp honey
- 1 tbsp Worcestershire sauce
- ½ cup milk
- ½ cup whole-wheat bread crumbs
- 1 lb ground turkey
- 1 onion, grated
- 1 tbsp Dijon mustard
- 1 tsp dried thyme
- ½ tsp sea salt

Directions:
1. Preheat the oven to 375°F. Set a rimmed baking sheet with parchment paper.
2. In a small saucepan on medium-low heat, whisk together the tomato paste, honey, and Worcestershire sauce. Bring to a simmer and then remove from the heat.
3. In a large bowl, combine the milk and bread crumbs. Let rest for 5 minutes.
4. Add the ground turkey, onion, mustard, thyme, and salt. Using your hands, mix well without overmixing
5. Form into 1-inch meatballs and set on the prepared baking sheet. Brush the tops with the tomato paste mixture.
6. Bake until the meatballs reach 165°F internally, about 15 minutes.

Nutrition:
- Calories: 285 Total fat: 11 g
- Saturated fat: 3 g Sodium: 465 mg
- Carbs: 22 g Fiber: 2 g Protein: 24

69. Citrus Pork Tenderloin

Preparation time: 10 minutes
Cooking time: 30 minutes
Servings: 4
Ingredients:
- ¼ cup freshly squeezed orange juice
- 2 tsp orange zest
- 1 tsp low-sodium soy sauce
- 1 tsp honey
- 1 tsp grated fresh ginger
- 2 tsp minced garlic
- 1 ½ lb (680 g) pork tenderloin roast, fat trimmed
- 1 tbsp extra-virgin olive oil

Directions:
1. Combine the orange juice and zest, soy sauce, honey, ginger, and garlic in a large bowl. Stir to mix well. Dunk the pork in the bowl and press to coat well.
2. Wrap the bowl in plastic and refrigerate to marinate for at least 2 hours.
3. Preheat the oven to 400°F (205°C).
4. Detach the bowl from the refrigerator and discard the marinade.
5. Heat the olive oil in an oven-safe skillet over medium-high heat until shimmering
6. Add the pork and sear for 5 minutes. Flip the pork halfway.
7. Arrange the skillet in the preheated oven and roast the pork for 25 minutes or until well browned. Flip the pork halfway.
8. Transfer the pork to a plate. Allow cooling before serving.

Nutrition:
- Calories: 228 Fat: 9.0 g
- Protein: 34.0 g Carbs: 4.0 g
- Fiber: 0 g Sugar: 3.0 g Sodium: 486 mg

70. Beef and Sweet Potato Stew

Preparation time: 20 minutes
Cooking time: 1 hour 10 minutes
Servings: 6
Ingredients:
- 2 lb (907 g) top sirloin steak, diced
- 1 ½ lb (680 g) sweet potato, peeled and cut into ½-inch cubes
- ½ lb (227 g) Cremini mushrooms, quartered
- 2 stalks of celery, diced
- 1 red onion, diced
- 1 carrot, peeled and diced
- 2 tbsp fresh parsley, chopped
- 4 sprigs of fresh thyme
- 4 cups low-sodium beef broth
- ½ cup dry red wine
- ¼ cup flour
- 3 garlic cloves, diced
- 2 tbsp tomato paste
- 2 tbsp olive oil
- 2 bay leaves
- Salt and ground black pepper, to taste

Directions:
1. Heat oil in a large stockpot over medium heat. Season steak with salt and pepper and add to pot. Cook, until brown on all sides. Remove from pot and set aside.
2. Add onion, carrot, and celery. Cook, until tender.
3. Add garlic and mushrooms and cook another 3–4 minutes. Whisk in flour and tomato paste and cook until lightly browned, for about 1 minute.
4. Add the broth, thyme, bay leaves, and steak.
5. Add sweet potato and cook 20 minutes or until potatoes are tender and the stew has thickened. Discard bay leaves and thyme sprigs. Stir in parsley and serve.

Nutrition:
- Calories: 420 Fat: 15.0 g
- Protein: 51.0 g Carbs: 14.1 g
- Fiber: 2.0 g
- Sugar: 4.1 g
- Sodium: 175 mg

71. Pork Diane

Preparation time: 10 minutes
Cooking time: 20 minutes
Servings: 4
Ingredients:
- 2 tsp Worcestershire sauce
- 1 tbsp freshly squeezed lemon juice

- ¼ cup low-sodium chicken broth
- 2 tsp Dijon mustard
- 4 (5 oz/142 g) boneless pork top loin chops, about 1-inch thick
- Sea salt and freshly ground black pepper, to taste - 1 tsp extra-virgin olive oil
- 2 tsp chopped fresh chives
- 1 tsp lemon zest

Directions:
1. Combine the Worcestershire sauce, lemon juice, broth, and Dijon mustard in a bowl. Stir to mix well.
2. On a clean work surface, massage the pork chops with salt and ground black pepper.
3. Warm the olive oil.
4. Add the pork chops and sear for 16 minutes or until well browned. Flip the pork halfway through the cooking time. Transfer to a plate and set aside.
5. Pour the sauce mixture into the skillet and cook for 2 minutes or until warmed through and slightly thickened. Mix in the chives and lemon zest.
6. Baste the pork with the sauce mixture and serve immediately.

Nutrition:
- Calories: 200 Fat: 8.0 g
- Protein: 30.0 g Carbs: 1.0 g
- Fiber: 0 g Sugar: 1.0 g Sodium: 394 mg

72. Pork Souvlakia With Tzatziki Sauce

Preparation time: 20 minutes
Cooking time: 12 minutes
Servings: 4
Ingredients:
- ¼ cup lemon juice
- 1 tbsp dried oregano
- ¼ tsp salt
- ¼ tsp ground black pepper
- 1 lb (454 g) pork tenderloin, cut into 1-inch cubes
- 1 tbsp olive oil

For the Tzatziki sauce:
- ½ cup plain Greek yogurt
- 1 large cucumber, peeled, deseeded, and grated
- 1 tbsp fresh lemon juice
- 4 garlic cloves, minced or grated
- ¼ tsp ground black pepper

Special equipment:
- 8 bamboo skewers, soaked in water

Directions:
1. Combine the lemon juice, oregano, salt, and ground black pepper in a large bowl. Stir to mix well.
2. Dunk the pork cubes in the bowl of mixture, and then toss to coat well. Wrap the bowl in plastic and refrigerate to marinate for 10 minutes or overnight.
3. Preheat the oven to 450°F (235°C) or broil. Grease a baking sheet with olive oil.
4. Remove the bowl from the refrigerator. Run the bamboo skewers through the pork cubes. Set the skewers on the baking sheet, and then brush with marinade.
5. Broil the skewers in the preheated oven for 12 minutes or until well browned. Flip skewers at least 3 times during the broiling.
6. Meanwhile, combine the ingredients for the Tzatziki sauce in a small bowl.
7. Remove the skewers from the oven and baste with the Tzatziki sauce and serve immediately.

Nutrition:
- Calories: 260
- Fat: 7.0 g
- Protein: 28.0 g
- Carbs: 21.0 g
- Fiber: 3.0 g
- Sugar: 3.0 g
- Sodium: 360 mg

73. Beef, Tomato, and Pepper Tortillas

Preparation time: 15 minutes
Cooking time: 0 minutes
Servings: 6
Ingredients:
- 6 whole wheat flour tortillas (10-inch)
- 6 large romaine lettuce leaves
- 12 oz (340 g) cooked deli roast beef, thinly sliced
- 1 cup diced red bell peppers
- 1 cup diced tomatoes
- 1 tbsp red wine vinegar
- 1 tsp cumin
- ¼ tsp freshly ground black pepper
- 1 tbsp olive oil

Directions:
1. Unfold the tortillas on a clean work surface, and then top each tortilla with a lettuce leaf. Divide the roast beef over the leaf.
2. Combine the remaining ingredients in a bowl. Stir to mix well. Pour the mixture over the beef.
3. Fold the tortillas over the fillings, and then roll them up. Serve immediately.

Nutrition:
- Calories: 295
- Fat: 6.0 g
- Protein: 19.0 g
- Carbs: 43.0 g
- Fiber: 6.0 g
- Sugar: 3.0 g
- Sodium: 600 mg

74. Classic Stroganoff

Preparation time: 15 minutes
Cooking time: 20 minutes
Servings: 5
Ingredients:
- 5 oz (142 g) cooked egg noodles
- 2 tsp olive oil
- 1 lb (454 g) beef tenderloin tips, boneless, sliced into 2-inch strips
- 1 ½ cups white button mushrooms, sliced
- ½ cup onion, minced
- 1 tbsp all-purpose flour
- ½ cup dry white wine
- 1 (14.5 oz/411 g) can of fat-free, low-sodium beef broth
- 1 tsp Dijon mustard
- ½ cup fat-free sour cream
- ¼ tsp salt
- ¼ tsp black pepper

Directions:
1. Put the cooked egg noodles on a large plate.
2. Warmth the olive oil.
3. Add the beef and sauté for 3 minutes or until lightly browned. Detach the beef from the skillet and set it on the plate with noodles.
4. Add the mushrooms and onion to the skillet and sauté for 5 minutes or until tender and the onion browns.
5. Add the flour and cook for a minute. Add the white wine and cook for 2 more minutes.
6. Add the beef broth and Dijon mustard. Bring to a boil. Keep stirring Reduce the heat to low and simmer for another 5 minutes.
7. Attach the beef back to the skillet and simmer for an additional 3 minutes. Add the remaining ingredients and simmer for 1 minute.
8. Pour them over the egg noodles and beef, and serve immediately.

Nutrition:
- Calories: 275 Fat: 7.0 g
- Protein: 23.0 g Carbs: 29.0 g
- Fiber: 4.0 g Sugar: 3.0 g
- Sodium: 250 mg

75. Ritzy Beef Stew

Preparation time: 20 minutes
Cooking time: 2 hours
Servings: 6
Ingredients:
- 2 tbsp all-purpose flour
- 1 tbsp Italian seasoning
- 2 lb (907 g) top round, cut into ¾-inch cubes

- 2 tbsp olive oil
- 4 cups low-sodium chicken broth, divided
- 1 ½lb (680 g) Cremini mushrooms, rinsed, stems removed, and quartered
- 1 large onion, coarsely chopped
- 3 garlic cloves, minced
- 3 medium carrots, peeled and cut into ½-inch pieces
- 1 cup frozen peas
- 1 tbsp fresh thyme, minced
- 1 tbsp red wine vinegar
- ½tsp freshly ground black pepper

Directions:
1. Combine the flour and Italian seasoning in a large bowl. Dredge the beef cubes in the bowl to coat well.
2. Heat the olive oil in a pot over medium heat until shimmering.
3. Add the beef to the single layer in the pot and cook for 2–4 minutes or until golden brown on all sides. Flip the beef cubes frequently.
4. Detach the beef from the pot and set it aside, then add ¼ cup of chicken broth to the pot.
5. Add the mushrooms and sauté for 4 minutes or until soft. Remove the mushrooms from the pot and set them aside.
6. Set ¼ cup of chicken broth in the pot. Add the onions and garlic to the pot and sauté for 4 minutes or until translucent.
7. Put the beef back into the pot and pour in the remaining broth. Bring to a boil.
8. Reduce the heat to low and cover. Simmer for 45 minutes. Stir periodically.
9. Add the carrots, mushroom, peas, and thyme to the pot and simmer for 45 more minutes or until the vegetables are soft.
10. Open the lid, drizzle with red wine vinegar, and season with black pepper. Stir and serve in a large bowl.

Nutrition:
- Calories: 250 Fat: 7.0 g
- Protein: 25.0 g Carbs: 24.0 g
- Fiber: 3.0 g Sugar: 5.0 g
- Sodium: 290 mg

76. Slow Cooked Beef and Vegetables Roast

Preparation time: 15 minutes
Cooking time: 4 hours
Servings: 4
Ingredients:
- 2 medium celery stalks, halved lengthwise and cut into 3-inch pieces
- 4 medium carrots, scrubbed, halved lengthwise, and cut into 3-inch pieces
- 1 medium onion, cut in eighths
- 1¼lb (567 g) lean chuck roast, boneless, trimmed of fat 2 tsp Worcestershire sauce
- 1 tbsp balsamic vinegar - 2 tbsp water
- 1 tbsp onion soup mix - 1 tbsp olive oil
- ½tsp ground black pepper

Directions:
1. Grease a Slow Cooker with olive oil.
2. Set the celery, carrots, and onion in the Slow Cooker, then add the beef.
3. Top them with Worcestershire sauce, balsamic vinegar, and water, and then sprinkle with onion soup mix and black pepper. Cover and cook on high for 4 hours. Allow to cool for 20 minutes, and then serve them on a large plate.

Nutrition:
- Calories: 250 Fat: 6.0 g
- Protein: 33.0 g Carbs: 15.0 g
- Fiber: 3.0 g Sugar: 6.0 g Sodium: 510 mg

77. Easy Lime Lamb Cutlets

Preparation time: 4 hours 20 minutes
Cooking time: 8 minutes
Servings: 4
Ingredients:
- ¼ cup freshly squeezed lime juice

- 2 tbsp lime zest
- 2 tbsp chopped fresh parsley
- Sea salt and freshly ground black pepper, to taste
- 1 tbsp extra-virgin olive oil
- 12 lamb cutlets (about 1 ½lb/680 g in total)

Directions:
1. Combine the lime juice and zest, parsley, salt, black pepper, and olive oil in a large bowl. Stir to mix well.
2. Dunk the lamb cutlets in the bowl of the lime mixture, and then toss to coat well. Wrap the bowl in plastic and refrigerate to marinate for at least 4 hours.
3. Preheat the oven to 450°F (235°C) or broil. Line a baking sheet with aluminum foil.
4. Remove the bowl from the refrigerator and let sit for 10 minutes, and then discard the marinade. Arrange the lamb cutlets on the baking sheet.
5. Broil the lamb in the preheated oven for 8 minutes or until it reaches your desired doneness. Flip the cutlets with tongs to make sure they are cooked evenly.
6. Serve immediately.

Nutrition:
- Calories: 297
- Fat: 18.8 g
- Protein: 31.0 g
- Carbs: 1.0 g
- Fiber: 0 g
- Sugar: 0 g
- Sodium: 100 mg

78. Sumptuous Lamb and Pomegranate Salad

Preparation time: 8 hours 35 minutes
Cooking time: 30 minutes
Servings: 8
Ingredients:

- 1 ½cups pomegranate juice
- 4 tbsp olive oil, divided
- 1 tbsp ground cinnamon
- 1 tsp cumin
- 1 tbsp ground ginger
- 3 garlic cloves, chopped
- Salt and freshly ground black pepper, to taste
- 1 (4 lb/1.8 kg) lamb leg, deboned, butterflied, and fat trimmed
- 2 tbsp pomegranate balsamic vinegar
- 2 tsp Dijon mustard
- ½cup pomegranate seeds
- 5 cups baby kale
- 4 cups fresh green beans, blanched
- ¼ cup toasted walnut halves
- 2 fennel bulbs, thinly sliced
- 2 tbsp Gorgonzola cheese

Directions:
1. Mix the pomegranate juice, 1 tbsp olive oil, cinnamon, cumin, ginger, garlic, salt, and black pepper in a large bowl. Stir to mix well.
2. Dunk the lamb leg in the mixture and press to coat well. Wrap the bowl in plastic and refrigerate to marinate for at least 8 hours.
3. Remove the bowl from the refrigerator and let sit for 20 minutes. Pat the lamb dry with paper towels.
4. Preheat the grill to high heat.
5. Brush the grill grates with 1 tbsp olive oil, then arrange the lamb on the grill grates.
6. Grill for 30 minutes.
7. Remove the lamb from the grill and wrap it with aluminum foil. Let stand for 15 minutes.
8. Meanwhile, combine the vinegar, mustard, salt, black pepper, and remaining olive oil in a separate large bowl. Stir to mix well.
9. Add the remaining ingredients and lamb leg to the bowl and toss to combine well. Serve immediately.

Nutrition:
- Calories: 380 Fat: 21.0 g
- Protein: 32.0 g
- Carbs: 16.0 g
- Fiber: 5.0 g
- Sugar: 6.0 g
- Sodium: 240 mg

79. Pork Fillet on Lentils

Preparation time: 10 minutes
Cooking time: 25 minutes
Servings: 2
Ingredients:
- 200 g pork tenderloin
- 80 g red lentils
- 2 onions
- 4 tsp oil
- Curry
- 4 spring onions
- 1 apple

Directions:
1. Wash the pork tenderloin, pat dry, and cut into small medallions. Peel and dice the onions. Wash the leek and cut it into small rings. Peel the apple, remove the core and cut it into wedges.
2. Fry the onions, leeks, and apple wedges in a pan with hot oil. Add the curry and the lentils. Punch with 100 ml of water. Put on the lid and simmer for 12 minutes. Add salt and pepper.
3. Fry the medallions vigorously in a second pan with hot oil (3 minutes on each side). Add salt and pepper.
4. Serve the meat with lentil vegetables.

Nutrition:
- Calories: 275 Fat: 7.0 g
- Protein: 23.0 g
- Carbs: 29.0 g
- Fiber: 4.0 g
- Sugar: 3.0 g
- Sodium: 250 mg

80. Turkey Rolls

Preparation time: 8 hours 35 minutes
Cooking time: 40 minutes
Servings: 2
Ingredients:
- 2 turkey schnitzel (100 g each)
- 400 g leek
- 60 g long-grain rice
- 2 slices of salmon ham
- 50 g Gouda (1 slice)
- 250 ml vegetable stock

Directions:
1. Wash the leek and cut off the ends. Put 4 leaves aside and blanch for 4 minutes. Cut the remaining leek into rings.
2. Prepare the vegetable stock.
3. Wash the turkey schnitzel, pat dry, and then place on the leek leaves. Halve the cheese slices and place a slice of cheese and a salmon ham on top of the turkey. Roll up the turkey escalope, pinch it with a wooden skewer and fry it in a pan with hot oil. Pour the curry over the skewers. Deglaze with the broth. Put on the lid and let simmer for ¼ hour.
4. Soak rice in salted boiling water for 20 minutes. Steam the leek in a pan with hot oil. Serve the rice with the leek and turkey rolls.

Nutrition:
- Calories: 200
- Fat: 8.0 g
- Protein: 30.0 g
- Carbs: 1.0 g
- Fiber: 0 g
- Sugar: 1.0 g
- Sodium: 394 mg

81. Turkey Escalope Pan

Preparation time: 8 hours 35 minutes
Cooking time: 30 minutes
Servings: 2
Ingredients:
- 320 g potatoes
- 100 g carrots
- 300 g pointed cabbage
- 2 turkey schnitzel
- 2 slices of Emmental
- 4 tbsp oil
- 150 ml vegetable broth

Directions:
1. Peel the potatoes and cut them into small cubes.
2. Peel the carrots. Wash the cabbage and shake it dry. Cut both into small pieces
3. Prepare the vegetable stock.
4. Peel the onion and cut it into small cubes.

5. Wash turkey schnitzel, dab it and fry in a pan with hot oil for 5–10 minutes. Turn in half the time. Remove turkey from heat and keep warm.
6. Sauté the onions in a pan with hot. Add the potatoes and carrots and fry briefly. Deglaze with the vegetable stock. Put a lid on the pot and cook everything for ¼ hour. After about 5 minutes, add the cabbage. Mix well. Season with salt and pepper and then serve.

Nutrition:
- Calories: 250
- Fat: 7.0 g
- Protein: 25.0 g
- Carbs: 24.0 g
- Fiber: 3.0 g
- Sugar: 5.0 g
- Sodium: 290 mg

82. Schnitzel With Chinese Cabbage

Preparation time: 8 hours 35 minutes
Cooking time: 25 minutes
Servings: 2
Ingredients:
- 150 g pork schnitzel
- 2 red peppers
- 400 g Chinese cabbage
- 100 g mushrooms
- 2 tbsp sesame oil
- Sambal Olenek
- Asia fund
- 1 paprika (noble sweet)

Directions:
1. Wash the peppers; remove the stalk, core, and threads. Cut the bell pepper into small pieces.
2. Wash Chinese cabbage, shake dry, remove the stalk, and cut the cabbage into small pieces
3. . Wash, clean, and slice the mushrooms.
4. Wash the schnitzel, dab it with a kitchen towel, cut it into small strips, and then fry in a pan with the sesame oil.
5. Add paprika and mushrooms.
6. Season with 1 tsp Sambal oiled and paprika powder.
7. Stir everything well and fry for about 3–5 minutes over medium heat.
8. Deglaze with the Asia fund. Add the Chinese cabbage.
9. Simmer briefly, season to taste, and serve on a plate.

Nutrition:
- Calories: 228
- Fat: 9.0 g
- Protein: 34.0 g
- Carbs: 4.0 g
- Fiber: 0 g
- Sugar: 3.0 g
- Sodium: 486 mg

83. Lemon Chicken With Basil

Preparation time: 15 minutes
Cooking time: 1 hour
Servings: 4
Ingredients:
- 1kg chopped chicken
- 1–2 lemons
- Basil, salt, and ground pepper
- Extra virgin olive oil

Directions:
1. Put the chicken in a bowl with a jet of extra-virgin olive oil.
2. Put salt, pepper, and basil.
3. Bind well and let stand for at least 30 minutes stirring occasionally.
4. Put the pieces of chicken in the air fryer basket and take the air fryer.
5. Select 30 minutes.
6. Occasionally remove.
7. Take out and put another batch.
8. Do the same operation.

Nutrition:
- Calories: 126
- Fat: 6 g
- Carbohydrates: 0 g
- Protein: 18 g
- Sugar: 0 g

84. Mississippi Style Pot Roast

Preparation time: 15 minutes
Cooking time: 8 hours
Servings: 8
Ingredients:
- 3 lb chuck roast
- 6–8 pepperoncini
- 1 envelope au jus gravy mix
- 1 envelope ranch dressing mix

Directions:
1. Place roast in a Crock-Pot. Sprinkle both envelopes of mixes over top.
2. Place the peppers around the roast.
3. Cover and cook.
4. Set roast to a large bowl and shred using 2 forks. Attach it back to the Crock-Pot and bring remove the pepperoncini, chop, and stir back into the roast.
5. Serve.

Nutrition:
- Calories: 379
- Total carbs: 3 g
- Protein: 56 g
- Fat: 14 g
- Sugar: 1 g
- Fiber: 0 g

85. Pesto Chicken

Preparation time: 15 minutes
Cooking time: 35 minutes
Servings: 6
Ingredients:
- 1 ¾ lb chicken breasts, skinless, boneless, and slice
- ½ cup Mozzarella cheese, shredded
- ¼ cup pesto

Directions:
1. Add chicken and pesto to a mixing bowl and mix until well coated.
2. Place in refrigerator for 2–3 hours.
3. Grill chicken over medium heat until completely cooked.
4. Sprinkle cheese over chicken and serve.

Nutrition:
- Fat: 303 g Carbs: 13 g
- Protein: 1 g Sugar: 1 g Cholesterol: 122 mg

86. Chicken and Tofu

Preparation time: 1 hour 15 minutes
Cooking time: 25 minutes
Servings: 6
Ingredients:
- 2 tbsp olive oil, divided
- 2 tbsp orange juice
- 1 tbsp Worcestershire sauce
- 1 tbsp low-sodium soy sauce
- 1 tsp ground turmeric
- 1 tsp dry mustard
- 8 oz chicken breast, cooked and sliced into cubes
- 8 oz extra-firm tofu, drained and sliced into cubed
- 2 carrots, sliced into thin strips
- 1 cup mushroom, sliced
- 2 cups fresh bean sprouts
- 3 green onions, sliced
- 1 red sweet pepper, sliced into strips

Directions:
1. In a bowl, mix half of the oil with the orange juice, Worcestershire sauce, soy sauce, turmeric, and mustard.
2. Coat all sides of chicken and tofu with the sauce. Marinate for 1 hour.
3. In a pan over medium heat, add 1 tbsp oil.
4. Add carrot and cook for 2 minutes.
5. Add mushroom and cook for another 2 minutes.
6. Add bean sprouts, green onion, and sweet pepper. Cook for 2–3 minutes.
7. Stir in the chicken and heat through.

Nutrition:
- Calories: 285 Total fat: 9 g
- Saturated fat: 1 g Cholesterol: 32 mg
- Sodium: 331 mg Total carbs: 30 g
- Dietary fiber: 4 g Total sugars: 4 g
- Protein: 20 g Potassium: 559 mg

87. Chicken and Peanut Stir-Fry

Preparation time: 15 minutes
Cooking time: 15 minutes
Servings: 4
Ingredients:
- 3 tbsp lime juice

- ½ tsp lime zest
- 4 garlic cloves, minced
- 2 tsp chili bean sauce
- 1 tbsp fish sauce
- 1 tbsp water
- 2 tbsp peanut butter
- 3 tsp oil, divided
- 1 lb chicken breast, sliced into strips
- 1 red sweet pepper, sliced into strips
- 3 green onions, sliced thinly
- 2 cups broccoli, shredded
- 2 tbsp peanuts, chopped

Directions:
1. In a bowl, merge the lime juice, lime zest, garlic, chili bean sauce, fish sauce, water, and peanut butter.
2. Mix well.
3. In a pan over medium-high heat, attach 2 tsp oil. Cook the chicken until golden on both sides.
4. Pour in the remaining oil.
5. Add the pepper and green onions.
6. Add the chicken, broccoli, and sauce.
7. Cook for 2 minutes.
8. Top with peanuts before serving

Nutrition:
- Calories: 368 Total fat: 11 g
- Saturated fat: 2 g Cholesterol: 66 mg
- Sodium: 556 mg Total carbs: 34 g
- Dietary fiber: 3 g Total sugars: 4 g
- Protein: 32 g Potassium: 482 mg

88. Honey Mustard Chicken

Preparation time: 15 minutes
Cooking time: 12 minutes
Servings: 4
Ingredients:
- 2 tbsp honey mustard
- 2 tsp olive oil
- Salt to taste
- 1 lb chicken tenders
- 1 lb baby carrots, steamed
- Chopped parsley

Directions:
1. Preheat your oven to 450°F.
2. Mix honey mustard, olive oil, and salt.
3. Coat the chicken tenders with the mixture.
4. Place the chicken on a single layer on the baking pan.
5. Bake for 10–12 minutes.
6. Serve with steamed carrots and garnish with parsley.

Nutrition:
- Calories: 366 Total fat: 8 g
- Saturated fat: 2 g Cholesterol: 63 mg
- Sodium: 543 mg Total carbs: 46 g
- Dietary fiber: 8 g Total sugars: 13 g
- Protein: 33 g
- Potassium: 377 mg

89. Lemon Garlic Turkey

Preparation time: 1 hour 10 minutes
Cooking time: 5 minutes
Servings: 4
Ingredients:
- 4 turkey breasts fillet
- 2 garlic cloves, minced
- 1 tbsp olive oil
- 3 tbsp lemon juice
- 1 oz Parmesan cheese, shredded
- Pepper to taste
- 1 tbsp fresh sage, snipped
- 1 tsp lemon zest

Directions:
1. Pound the turkey breast until flat.
2. In a bowl, merge the olive oil, garlic, and lemon juice. Add the turkey to the bowl.
3. Marinate for 1 hour.
4. Broil for 5 minutes until the turkey is fully cooked. Sprinkle cheese on top at the last minute of cookingIn a bowl, mix the pepper, sage, and lemon zest.
5. Whisk this mixture on top of the turkey before serving

Nutrition:
- Calories: 188 Total fat: 7 g
- Saturated fat: 2 g Cholesterol: 71 mg
- Sodium: 173 mg Total carbs: 2 g
- Dietary fiber: 0 g
- Total sugars: 0 g
- Protein: 29 g
- Potassium: 264 mg

90. Chicken and Spinach

Preparation time: 15 minutes
Cooking time: 13 minutes
Servings: 4
Ingredients:
- 2 tbsp olive oil
- 1 lb chicken breast fillet, sliced into small pieces
- Salt and pepper to taste
- 4 garlic cloves, minced
- 1 tbsp lemon juice
- ½ cup dry white wine
- 1 tsp lemon zest
- 10 cups fresh spinach, chopped
- 4 tbsp Parmesan cheese, grated

Directions:
1. Pour oil into a pan.
2. Season the chicken with salt and pepper.
3. Cook in the pan for 7 minutes until golden on both sides.
4. Attach the garlic and cook for 1 minute.
5. Stir in the lemon juice and wine.
6. Sprinkle lemon zest on top.
7. Simmer for 5 minutes.
8. Add the spinach and cook until wilted.
9. Serve with Parmesan cheese.

Nutrition:
- Calories: 334
- Total fat: 12 g
- Saturated fat: 3 g
- Cholesterol: 67 mg
- Sodium: 499 mg
- Total carbs: 25 g
- Protein: 29 g
- Potassium: 685 mg

91. Greek Chicken Lettuce Wraps

Preparation time: 1 hour 15 minutes
Cooking time: 8 minutes
Servings: 4
Ingredients:
- 2 tbsp freshly squeezed lemon juice
- 1 tsp lemon zest
- 5 tsp olive oil, divided
- 3 tsp garlic, minced and divided
- 1 tsp dried oregano
- ¼ tsp red pepper, crushed
- 1 lb chicken tenders
- 1 cucumber, sliced in half and grated
- Salt and pepper to taste
- ¾ cup non-fat Greek yogurt
- 2 tsp fresh mint, chopped
- 2 tsp fresh dill, chopped
- 4 lettuce leaves
- ½ cup red onion, sliced
- 1 cup tomatoes, chopped

Directions:
1. In a bowl, merge the lemon juice, lemon zest, half oil, half garlic, and red pepper.
2. Coat the chicken with the marinade.
3. Marinate it for 1 hour.
4. Toss grated cucumber in salt.
5. Squeeze to release liquid.
6. Add the yogurt, dill, salt, pepper, remaining garlic, and remaining oil.
7. Grill the chicken per side.
8. Shred the chicken and put it on top of the lettuce leaves.
9. Top with the yogurt mixture, onion, and tomatoes.
10. Wrap the lettuce leaves and secure them with a toothpick.

Nutrition:
- Calories: 353 Total fat: 9 g
- Saturated fat: 1 g
- Cholesterol: 58 mg
- Sodium: 559 mg
- Total carbs: 33 g
- Dietary fiber: 6 g
- Total sugars: 6 g
- Protein: 37 g
- Potassium: 459 mg

92. Lemon Chicken With Kale

Preparation time: 10 minutes
Cooking time: 19 minutes
Servings: 4
Ingredients:
- 1 tbsp olive oil
- 1 lb chicken thighs, trimmed
- Salt and pepper to taste
- ½ cup low-sodium chicken stock
- 1 lemon, sliced
- 1 tbsp fresh tarragon, chopped
- 4 garlic cloves, minced
- 6 cups baby kale

Directions:
1. Set olive oil in a pan over medium heat.
2. Season the chicken with salt and pepper.
3. Cook until golden brown on both sides.
4. Pour in the stock.
5. Add the lemon, tarragon, and garlic.
6. Simmer for 15 minutes.
7. Add the kale and cook for 4 minutes.

Nutrition:
- Calories: 374 Total fat: 19 g
- Saturated fat: 4 g Cholesterol: 76 mg
- Sodium: 378 mg Total carbs: 26 g
- Dietary fiber: 3 g Total sugars: 2 g
- Protein: 25 g Potassium: 677 mg

93. Pumpkin, Bean, and Chicken Enchiladas

Preparation time: 35 minutes
Cooking time: 25 minutes
Servings: 4
Ingredients:
- 2 tsp olive oil - ½ cup chopped onion
- 1 jalapeno, seeded and chopped
- 1 (15 oz) can of pumpkin
- 1 ½ cup water, more if needed
- 1 tsp chili powder - ½ tsp salt
- ½ tsp ground cumin
- 1 cup canned no-salt-added red kidney beans, rinsed and drained
- 1 ½ cup shredded cooked chicken breast
- ½ cup shredded part-skim Mozzarella cheese
- 8 (6-inch) whole-wheat tortillas, softened
- Salsa and lime wedges

Directions:
1. Lightly coat a 2-qt. rectangular baking dish with cooking spray and preheat the oven to 400°F. In a saucepan, warm oil over medium heat. Add jalapeno and onion and stir-fry until onion is tender, for about 5 minutes. Stir in cumin, salt, chili powder, 1 ½ cups water, and pumpkin, and heat through. Add more water if needed.
2. Set beans in a bowl and mash slightly with a fork. Stir in ¼ cup of the cheese, the chicken, and half of the pumpkin mixture.
3. Scoop ⅓ cup bean mixture onto each tortilla. Roll up tortillas. Place in the baking dish (seam sides down). Pour the remaining pumpkin mixture over the enchiladas. Bake, covered, for 15 minutes. Sprinkle with the remaining ¼ cup cheese. Bake, uncovered until heated through, for about 10 minutes more.
4. Serve with salsa and lime wedges.

Nutrition:
- Calories: 357 Fat: 8 g
- Carbs: 44 g Protein: 28 g

94. Mu Shu Chicken

Preparation time: 20 minutes
Cooking time: 6 hours
Servings: 6
Ingredients:
- ½ cup hoisin sauce
- 2 tbsp water

- 4 tsp toasted sesame oil
- 1 tbsp cornstarch
- 1 tbsp reduced-sodium soy sauce
- 3 garlic cloves, minced
- 1 (16 oz) package of shredded cabbage with carrots (coleslaw mix)
- 1 cup coarsely shredded carrots
- 12 oz skinless, boneless chicken thighs
- 6 (8-inch) whole wheat flour tortillas
- Green onions

Directions:
1. Merge the first six ingredients in a bowl (through garlic).
2. In a Slow Cooker, combine shredded carrots and coleslaw mix.
3. Cut chicken into 1/8-inch slices and cut each slice in half lengthwise. Place chicken on top of the cabbage mix. Drizzle with 1/4 cup of the hoisin mixture.
4. Heat tortillas according to package directions. Fill tortillas with chicken mixture.
5. Top with green onions and serve.

Nutrition:
- Calories: 269 Fat: 8 g
- Carbs: 34 g Protein: 16 g

95. Stove-Top Chicken, Macaroni, and Cheese

Preparation time: 10 minutes
Cooking time: 30 minutes
Servings: 5
Ingredients:
- 1 ½ cup dried multigrain or elbow macaroni
- 12 oz skinless, boneless chicken breast halves, cut into 1-inch pieces
- ¼ cup chopped onion
- 1 (6 ½ oz) package of light semisoft cheese with garlic and fine herbs
- 1 ⅔ cup fat-free milk
- 1 tbsp all-purpose flour
- ¾ cup shredded reduced-fat Cheddar cheese
- 2 cups fresh baby spinach
- 1 cup cherry tomatoes, quartered

Directions:
1. Cook macaroni according to package directions. Drain.
2. Meanwhile, coat a skillet with cooking spray. Heat skillet over medium-high heat.
3. Add onion and chicken until chicken is no longer pink, about 4–6 minutes. Stirring frequently. Remove from heat and stir in semisoft cheese until melted.
4. In a bowl, whisk together flour and milk until smooth. Gradually stir the milk mixture into the chicken mixture. Cook and stir until bubbly and thickened. Lower heat and gradually attach Cheddar cheese. Stirring until melted.
5. Attach cooked macaroni, cook and stir for 1–2 minutes or until heated through.
6. Stir in spinach. Top with cherry tomatoes and serve.

Nutrition:
- Calories: 369 Fat: 12 g
- Carbs: 33 g Protein: 33 g

96. Chicken Sausage Omelets With Spinach

Preparation time: 20 minutes
Cooking time: 10 minutes
Servings: 2
Ingredients:
- 2 cups fresh spinach
- ½ (from a 7oz) package of frozen fully cooked chicken and maple breakfast sausage links, thawed and chopped
- 3 eggs, lightly beaten
- 2 tbsp water
- ¼ cup shredded part-skim Mozzarella cheese
- 2 green onions, green tops only, thinly sliced
- ½ cup grape tomatoes, quartered
- ¼ cup fresh basil leaves, thinly sliced

Directions:
1. Coat a skillet with non-stick cooking spray. Heat over medium heat.

2. Add sausage and spinach. Cook until sausage is heated. Remove from the skillet.
3. In a bowl, whip together the water and eggs. Attach egg mixture to skillet and cook until egg is set and shiny.
4. Spoon spinach and sausage mixture over half of the omelet. Sprinkle with cheese and green onions. Set the opposite side of the omelet over the sausage mixture.
5. Cook for 1 minute or until filling is heated and cheese is melted.
6. Transfer to a plate and cut in half. Transfer half of the omelet to a second plate.
7. Top with tomatoes and basil and serve.

Nutrition:
- Calories: 252
- Fat: 16 g
- Carbs: 5 g
- Protein: 21 g

97. Chicken-Broccoli Salad With Buttermilk Dressing

Preparation time: 20 minutes
Cooking time: 0 minutes
Servings: 4
Ingredients:
- 3 cups packaged shredded broccoli slaw mix
- 2 cups coarsely chopped cooked chicken breast
- ½ cup dried cherries
- ⅓ cup sliced celery
- ¼ cup chopped red onion
- ⅓ cup buttermilk
- ⅓ cup light mayonnaise
- 1 tbsp honey
- 1 tbsp cider vinegar
- 1 tsp dry mustard
- ½ tsp salt
- ⅛ tsp black pepper
- 4 cups fresh baby spinach

Directions:
1. Merge the first five ingredients in a bowl (through onion). In a small bowl, whisk together the next seven ingredients (through pepper). Pour buttermilk mixture over broccoli mixture. Toss to gently mix.
2. Cover and chill for 2–24 hours.
3. Add baby spinach and serve.

Nutrition:
- Calories: 278
- Fat: 7 g
- Carbs: 29 g
- Protein: 26 g

98. Country-Style Wedge Salad with Turkey

Preparation time: 10 minutes
Cooking time: 0 minutes
Servings: 4
Ingredients:
- 1 head bibb or butterhead lettuce, quartered
- 1 recipe for Buttermilk-Avocado dressing
- 2 cups shredded cooked turkey breast
- 1 cup halved grape
- 2 hard-cooked eggs, chopped
- 4 slices of low-sodium, less-fat bacon, crisp-cooked, and crumbled
- ¼ cup finely chopped red onion
- Cracked black pepper

Directions:
1. Arrange one lettuce quarter on each plate. Drizzle half of the dressing over wedges. Top with turkey, eggs, and tomatoes. Drizzle with the remaining dressing Sprinkle with onion, bacon, and pepper.
2. To make the buttermilk-avocado dressing: in a blender, combine ¾ cup buttermilk, ½ avocado, 1 tbsp parsley, ¼ tsp each salt, onion powder, dry mustard, black pepper, and 1 garlic clove, minced. Cover and blend until smooth.

Nutrition:
- Calories: 228
- Fat: 9 g
- Carbs: 8 g
- Protein: 29 g

99. Turkey Kabob Pitas

Preparation time: 25 minutes
Cooking time: 15 minutes
Servings: 4
Ingredients:
- 1 tsp whole cumin seed, lightly crushed
- 1 cup shredded cucumber
- ⅓ cup seeded and chopped Roma tomato
- ¼ cup slivered red onion
- ¼ cup shredded radishes
- ¼ cup snipped fresh cilantro
- ¼ tsp black pepper
- 1 lb turkey breast, cut into thin strips
- 1 recipe curry blend
- ¼ cup plain fat-free Greek yogurt
- 4 (6-inch) whole-wheat pita bread rounds

Directions:
1. Soak wooden skewers in water for 30 minutes. Toast the cumin seeds for 1 minute and transfer them to a bowl. Add the next six ingredients to the bowl (through pepper). Mix.
2. In another bowl, combine curry blend and turkey. Stir to coat. Thread turkey onto skewers. Grill kabobs, uncovered until turkey is no longer pink. Turning kabobs occasionally. Remove turkey from skewers. Spread Greek yogurt on pita bread. Spoon cucumber mixture over yogurt. Top with grilled turkey. Serve.

To make the curry blend:
1. In a bowl, combine 2 tsp olive oil, 1 tsp curry powder, ½tsp, each ground turmeric, ground cumin, ground coriander, ¼tsp ground ginger, and⅛tsp salt and cayenne pepper.

Nutrition:
- Calories: 343 Fat: 6 g
- Carbs: 40 g Protein: 35 g

100. Chicken Broth—Easy Slow-Cooker Method

Preparation time: 35 minutes
Cooking time: 25 minutes
Servings: 4
Ingredients:
- 1 small onion, chopped
- 2 carrots, peeled and chopped
- 2 celery stalks and leaves, chopped
- 1 bay leaf - 4 sprigs parsley
- 6 black peppercorns
- ¼ cup dry white wine
- 2 lb chicken pieces, skin removed
- 4½ cup water

Directions:
1. Attach all the ingredients except water to a Slow Cooker. The chicken pieces and vegetables should be loosely layered and fill no more than ¾ of the Slow Cooker.
2. Add enough water to just cover the ingredients. Cover the Slow Cooker. Set Slow Cooker to high until the mixture almost reaches a boil, and then reduce heat to low. Allow simmering overnight or up to 16 hours, checking occasionally and adding more water, if necessary. Remove chicken pieces and drain on paper towels to absorb any fat. Allow cooling; remove meat from bones. Strain vegetables from broth and discard.
3. Set broth in a covered container and refrigerate for several hours or overnight, allowing the fat to congeal on top. Remove hardened fat and discard.
4. To separate broth into small amounts for use when you steam vegetables or potatoes, fill up an ice cube tray with stock. Let freeze, then remove cubes from tray and store in a labeled freezer bag Common ice cube trays allow for ⅛ cup or 2 tbsp liquid per section.

Reduced broth:
Reducing broth is the act of boiling it to decrease the amount of water so you're left with a richer broth. Boiling non-fat, canned chicken broth won't reduce it as a homemade broth would. The broth from this recipe will be richer than what most recipes call for, so unless you need reduced broth, thin it with water as needed. Assuming you remove the fat from the broth, it will be a free exchange.

Nutrition:
- Calories: 374 Saturated fat: 4 g
- Cholesterol: 76 mg Sodium: 378 mg
- Total carbs: 26 g Dietary fiber: 3 g
- Protein: 25 g Potassium: 677 mg

101. Oven-Fried Chicken Thighs

Preparation time: 35 minutes
Cooking time: 25 minutes
Servings: 4
Ingredients:
- 4 chicken thighs, skin removed
- 1 tbsp unbleached, white all-purpose flour
- 1 large egg white
- ½ tsp sea salt
- ½ tsp olive oil (optional; see Comparison Analysis for using olive oil)
- 1 tbsp rice flour
- 1 tbsp cornmeal

Directions:
1. Preheat the oven to 350°F. Set a baking sheet with non-stick cooking spray.
2. Rinse and dry chicken thighs. Put white flour on a plate.
3. In a small, shallow bowl, whip the egg white with the sea salt. Add olive oil if using and mix well.
4. Put rice flour and cornmeal on another plate and mix.
5. Roll each chicken thigh in the white flour, then dip it into the egg mixture, and then roll it in the rice flour mixture.
6. Place thighs on a rack so they aren't touching Bake for 35–45 minutes until meat juices run clear.

Nutrition:
- Calories: 78.53
- Protein: 9.46 g
- Carbs: 4.65 g
- Fat: 2.27 g
- Cholesterol: 34.03 mg
- Sodium: 331.03 mg
- Fiber: 0.06 g

102. Another Healthy "Fried" Chicken

Preparation time: 35 minutes
Cooking time: 25 minutes
Servings: 4
Ingredients:
- 10 oz raw boneless, skinless chicken breasts (fat trimmed off)
- ½ cup non-fat plain yogurt
- ½ cup bread crumbs
- 1 tsp garlic powder
- 1 tsp paprika
- ¼ tsp dried thyme

Directions:
1. Preheat the oven to 350°F. Set a baking pan with non-stick cooking spray.
2. Cut the chicken breast into 4 equal pieces. Marinate chicken pieces in the yogurt for several minutes.
3. On a plate, mix the bread crumbs, garlic, paprika, and thyme.
4. Dredge the chicken in the crumb mixture. Arrange on the prepared pan and bake for 20 minutes. To give the chicken a deep golden color, place the pan under the broiler for at least 5 minutes. Watch closely to ensure the chicken "crust" doesn't burn.

Nutrition:
- Calories: 369
- Fat: 12 g
- Carbs: 33 g
- Protein: 33 g

103. Buttermilk Ranch Chicken Salad

Preparation time: 35 minutes
Cooking time: 25 minutes
Servings: 4
Ingredients:
- 1 cup chopped cooked chicken breast
- ½ cup sliced cucumber
- ½ cup chopped celery
- ½ cup sliced carrots
- 1 tbsp real mayonnaise
- 3 tbsp non-fat plain yogurt
- ½ cup non-fat Cottage cheese
- ½ tsp cider vinegar
- 1 tsp brown sugar
- 1 tsp Dijon mustard
- ½ cup buttermilk
- 2 tbsp dried parsley
- 1 garlic clove, minced
- 2 tbsp grated Parmesan cheese

- ¼ tsp sea salt (optional)
- ¼ tsp freshly ground pepper (optional)
- 4 cup salad greens - ½ cup red onion slices
- Fresh parsley for garnish (optional)

Directions:
1. In a large bowl merge the chicken, cucumber, celery, and carrots.
2. In a blender or food processor, merge the mayonnaise, yogurt, Cottage cheese, vinegar, brown sugar, mustard, buttermilk, parsley, garlic, cheese, salt, and pepper and process until smooth. Pour over the chicken mixture in the bowl. Chill for at least 2 hours.
3. To serve, arrange 1 cup of salad greens on each of 4 serving plates. Set each salad with an equal amount of chicken salad. Garnish with red onion slices and fresh parsley, if desired.

Nutrition:
- Calories: 269 Fat: 8 g
- Carbs: 34 gProtein: 16 g

104. Pineapple-Orange Grilled Chicken Breasts

Preparation time: 35 minutes
Cooking time: 25 minutes
Servings: 4
Ingredients:
- 6 oz pineapple juice
- 4 oz orange juice
- ¼ cup cider vinegar
- 1 tbsp fresh tarragon, chopped
- ½ tbsp fresh rosemary
- 1 lb boneless chicken breast

Directions:
1. About 3–4 hours before you are ready to grill, make the marinade: In a large shallow dish, combine the pineapple juice, orange juice, vinegar, tarragon, and rosemary.
2. Add the raw chicken breasts to the marinade. Cover and refrigerate for 3–4 hours. Turn pieces of chicken over during the marinade process to cover with it.
3. Heat the grill to medium-high.
4. Place the chicken on the grill. Grill each side, until the chicken is cooked through.

Nutrition:
- Calories: 334
- Total fat: 12 g
- Saturated fat: 3 g
- Cholesterol: 67 mg
- Sodium: 499 mg

105. Herbed Chicken and Brown Rice

Preparation time: 35 minutes
Cooking time: 25 minutes
Servings: 4
Ingredients:
- 1 tbsp canola oil
- 4 (4oz) boneless chicken breast pieces, skin removed
- ¾ tsp garlic powder
- ¾ tsp dried rosemary
- 1 (10½ oz) can of low-fat, reduced-sodium chicken broth
- ⅓ cup water
- 2 cups uncooked instant brown rice

Directions:
1. Warmth oil. Add the chicken and sprinkle it with half the garlic powder and half the crushed rosemary. Cover and cook through. Remove chicken from skillet and set aside.
2. Add broth and water to the skillet. Stir to deglaze the pan and bring to a boil. Whisk in rice and remaining garlic powder and rosemary.
3. Set with the chicken and cover. Cook on low heat for 5 minutes.

4. Detach from heat and let stand, covered, for 5 minutes.

Nutrition:
- Calories: 78.53
- Protein: 9.46 g
- Carbs: 4.65 g
- Fat: 2.27 g
- Cholesterol: 34.03 mg
- Sodium: 331.03 mg
- Fiber: 0.06 g

106. Walnut Chicken

Preparation time: 35 minutes
Cooking time: 25 minutes
Servings: 4
Ingredients:
- ¾lb (12 oz) raw boneless, skinless chicken breast
- 1 tsp sherry
- 1 egg white
- 2 tsp peanut oil
- 2 drops of toasted sesame oil (optional)
- ⅓cup ground walnuts

Directions:
1. Preheat the oven to 350°F.
2. Cut the chicken into bite-sized pieces. Sprinkle the pieces with sherry and set them aside.
3. In a small bowl, whip the egg white and oils until frothy.
4. Fold chicken pieces into the egg mixture, and then roll the pieces individually in chopped walnuts.
5. Set the chicken pieces on a baking sheet treated with non-stick cooking spray. Bake for 10–15 minutes, or until walnuts are lightly browned and chicken juices run clear. (Walnuts make the fat ratio of this dish high, so serve it with steamed vegetables and rice to bring the ratios into balance.)

Nutrition:
- Calories: 252
- Fat: 16 g
- Carbs: 5 g
- Protein: 21 g

107. Easy Chicken Paprika

Preparation time: 15 minutes
Cooking time: 30 minutes
Servings: 4
Ingredients:
- 1 cup of Cream of Chicken Soup
- ½cup skim milk
- 2 tsp sweet paprika
- ⅛tsp ground red pepper (optional)
- ¼lb(4 oz) chopped cooked boneless, skinless chicken
- 1 ½cups sliced steamed mushrooms
- ½cup diced steamed onion
- ½cup non-fat plain yogurt
- 4 cups cooked medium-sized egg noodles

Directions:
1. In a saucepan, combine the soup, skim milk, paprika, and pepper (if using), and whisk until well mixed. Bring to a boil over medium heat, stirring occasionally.
2. Reduce heat to low and stir in chicken, mushrooms, and onion. Cook until chicken and vegetables are heated through, about 10 minutes. Stir in yogurt.
3. To serve, put 1 cup of warm, cooked noodles on each of the four plates. Set each portion with an equal amount of chicken mixture. Garnish by sprinkling with additional paprika, if desired.

Nutrition:
- Calories: 353
- Total fat: 9 g
- Saturated fat: 1 g
- Cholesterol: 58 mg
- Sodium: 559 mg
- Total carbs: 33 g

108. Chicken and Broccoli Casserole

Preparation time: 15 minutes
Cooking time: 30 minutes
Servings: 4
Ingredients:
- 2 cups broccoli
- ½lb(8 oz) cooked chopped chicken
- ½cup skim milk

- ⅛ cup (2 tbsp) real mayonnaise
- ¼ tsp curry powder
- 1 recipe Condensed Cream of Chicken Soup
- 1 tbsp lemon juice
- ½ cup (2 oz) grated Cheddar cheese
- ½ cup bread crumbs
- 1 tsp melted butter
- 1 tsp olive oil

Directions:
1. Preheat the oven to 350°F. Treat an 11x7-inch casserole dish with non-stick spray.
2. Steam broccoli until tender, then drain.
3. Spread out chicken on the bottom of the dish. Cover with steamed broccoli.
4. In a medium bowl, combine the milk, mayonnaise, curry powder, soup, and lemon juice. Pour mixture over broccoli.
5. In a small bowl, merge the cheese, bread crumbs, butter, and oil. Sprinkle over the top of the casserole. Bake for 30 minutes.

Nutrition:
- Calories: 269
- Fat: 8 g
- Carbs: 34 g
- Protein: 16 g

109. Chicken and Green Bean Stovetop Casserole

Preparation time: 15 minutes
Cooking time: 30 minutes
Servings: 4
Ingredients:
- 1 recipe for Condensed Cream of Chicken Soup
- ¼ cup skim milk
- 2 tsp Worcestershire sauce
- 1 tsp real mayonnaise
- ½ tsp onion powder
- ¼ tsp garlic powder
- ¼ tsp ground black pepper
- 1 (4 oz) can of sliced water chestnuts, drained
- 2½ cups frozen green beans, thawed
- 1 cup sliced mushrooms, steamed
- ½ lb (8 oz) cooked chopped chicken
- 1⅓ cup cooked brown long-grain rice

Directions:
1. In a saucepan, combine the soup, milk, Worcestershire, mayonnaise, onion powder, garlic powder, and pepper, and bring to a boil.
2. Reduce heat; add the water chestnuts, green beans, mushrooms, and chicken. Serve over rice.

Nutrition:
- Calories: 234
- Total fat: 2 g
- Saturated fat: 1 g
- Cholesterol: 100 mg
- Sodium: 308 mg
- Total carbs: 10 g

110. Chicken and Asparagus in White Wine Sauce

Preparation time: 35 minutes
Cooking time: 25 minutes
Servings: 4
Ingredients:
- 4 boneless, skinless chicken breast halves
- ½ tbsp butter
- 1 tbsp olive oil
- 1 tsp garlic, finely chopped
- ½ cup onion, finely chopped
- 10 oz asparagus spears, cut diagonally into 2-inch pieces
- ½ lb mushrooms
- ¼ cup dry white wine
- ¼ cup water
- 1 tbsp chopped parsley
- Salt and pepper, to taste

Directions:
1. Pound the chicken pieces to ¼-inch thickness.
2. Melt butter and olive oil in a large skillet over medium heat. Add chopped garlic and onions and sauté for 1–2 minutes.
3. Add chicken and cook for 5 minutes, or until the chicken is brown on both sides. Remove chicken and set aside.
4. Add the asparagus and mushrooms to a skillet. Cook for 2–3 minutes.
5. Return the chicken to the skillet; add white wine and water. Bring to a quick boil. Boil to reduce the liquid.
6. Set heat. Cover and simmer for 3 minutes, or until the chicken and vegetables are tender. Attach chopped parsley, salt, and pepper to taste, and serve.

Nutrition:
- Calories: 252
- Fat: 16 g
- Carbs: 5 g
- Protein: 21 g

111. Chicken Kalamata

Preparation time: 15 minutes
Cooking time: 25 minutes
Servings: 4
Ingredients:
- 2 tbsp olive oil
- 1 cup chopped onion
- 1 tsp minced garlic
- 1 ½ cup chopped green peppers
- 1 lb boneless, skinless chicken cut into 4 pieces
- 2 cups diced tomatoes
- 1 tsp oregano
- ½ cup pitted, chopped Kalamata olives

Directions:
1. Heat the olive oil over medium heat in a large skillet. Add the onions, garlic, and peppers. Sauté for about 5 minutes until the onions are translucent.
2. Add the chicken pieces. Cook until lightly brown.
3. Add the tomatoes and oregano. Reduce heat and simmer for 20 minutes.
4. Add the olives and simmer for an additional 10 minutes before serving.

Nutrition:
- Calories: 124 Carbs: 17.4 g
- Fat: 4.4 g Protein: 4.7 g
- Fiber: 4 g

112. Chicken Breasts in Balsamic Vinegar Sauce

Preparation time: 15 minutes
Cooking time: 25 minutes
Servings: 4
Ingredients:
- 1 lb boneless chicken
- 4 pieces pinch salt
- ¼ tsp pepper
- 1 tbsp butter
- 1 tbsp olive oil
- ¼ cup red onion, chopped
- 2 tsp finely chopped garlic
- 3 tbsp balsamic vinegar
- 1 ½ cup low-sodium chicken broth
- 1 tsp oregano

Directions:
1. Sprinkle the chicken with salt and pepper.
2. Dissolve butter and olive oil in a large skillet over medium heat. Add the chicken and cook until browned, about 5 minutes on each side.
3. Reduce heat and cook for 12 minutes. Transfer to a platter, cover, and keep warm.
4. Add the red onions and garlic to the skillet. Sauté over medium heat for 3 minutes, scraping up the browned bits.
5. Add the balsamic vinegar and bring to a boil. Boil for 3 minutes, or until reduced to a glaze, stirring constantly.
6. Add the chicken broth. Boil. Detach sauce from heat and add the chopped oregano. Spoon sauce over chicken and serve immediately.

Nutrition:
- Calories: 357 Fat: 8 g
- Carbs: 44 g
- Protein: 28 g

113. Easy Herbed Chicken

Preparation time: 10 minutes
Cooking time: 5 hours
Servings: 6
Ingredients:
- 1 tbsp olive oil
- ½ tsp thyme
- 1 tsp basil
- ¼ tsp oregano
- 1 tsp paprika
- ½ tsp salt
- ¼ tsp pepper
- ¼ tsp garlic powder
- ¼ cup chicken broth
- 16 oz chicken, boneless and skinless

Directions:
1. Combine the oil with the herbs and spices.
2. Rub all over the chicken.
3. Place the chicken inside your Slow Cooker.
4. Pour the chicken broth around (not over) your chicken.
5. Place the lid on and cook for 5 hours on low.
6. Serve and enjoy!

Nutrition:
- Calories: 210
- Total fats: 8 g
- Carbs: 14 g
- Protein: 22 g
- Fiber: 1 g

114. Tomato and Pepper Steak

Preparation time: 10 minutes
Cooking time: 6 hours
Servings: 6
Ingredients:
- 1 ½ beef round steak, cut into chunks
- ¼ cup reduced-sodium soy sauce
- 1 onion, chopped
- 1 large green pepper, chopped
- 4 tomatoes, chopped
- Salt and pepper, to taste

Directions:
1. Place the meat in a non-stick skillet and brown over medium heat for a couple of minutes. Skip this step if you enjoy your beef under-cooked.
2. Place the steak in your Slow Cooker.
3. Combine the rest of the ingredients in a bowl.
4. Pour the mixture over the steak.
5. Place the lid on and cook for 6 hours on low.
6. Serve and enjoy!

Nutrition:
- Calories: 230 Total fats: 8 g Carbs: 111 g
- Protein: 28 g Fiber: 2 g

115. Mexican Meatloaf

Preparation time: 15 minutes
Cooking time: 5 hours
Servings: 8
Ingredients:
- 12 saltines, crushed
- 2 lb lean ground beef
- 2 tbsp Worcestershire sauce
- 6 tbsp sugar-free ketchup
- 1 onion, chopped
- 2 tsp minced garlic
- 1 tsp paprika
- Salt and pepper, to taste

Directions:
1. Chop some strips of aluminum foil and place them inside, criss-crossed, so you can lift up the meatloaf when done.
2. Place all of the ingredients in a large bowl.
3. Mix well until incorporated, then shape with your hands into a meatloaf.
4. Place inside the Slow Cooker.
5. Put the lid on and cook for 5 hours on low. The meatloaf should no longer be pink—you can check with a meat thermometer; it is done when it reaches 160°F.
6. Lift up the meatloaf using the foil strips.
7. Let sit for 15 minutes before slicing
8. Serve and enjoy!

Nutrition:
- Calories: 225 Total fats: 10 g
- Carbs: 10 g
- Protein: 23 g
- Fiber: 1 g

116. Provencal Chuck

Preparation time: 10 minutes
Cooking time: 7 hours
Servings: 8
Ingredients:
- 2 lb beef chuck
- 2 cups sliced carrots
- 1 large onion, chopped
- ½ cup beef broth
- 1 cup dry red wine
- 3 tsp minced garlic
- 1 tbsp tomato paste
- 14 oz canned diced tomatoes
- 1 tsp thyme
- ½ tsp paprika
- Salt and pepper, to taste

Directions:
1. Cut the chuck into chunks—brown in a skillet if you want to, though this is optional.
2. Place the meat in your Slow Cooker.
3. Add the rest of the ingredients there.
4. Stir to combine well.
5. Place the lid on and cook on low.
6. Serve over pasta, rice, or mashed potatoes.
7. Enjoy!

Nutrition:
- Calories: 240 Total fats: 12 g
- Carbs: 8 g Protein: 23 g
- Fiber: 2 g

117. Shredded Chili Beef

Preparation time: 10 minutes
Cooking time: 5 hours
Servings: 6
Ingredients:
- 3 lb chuck roast, boneless
- 2 sweet onions, sliced
- 1 tbsp paprika
- 2 tbsp swerve
- 1 green chili, diced
- 28 canned diced tomatoes, undrained
- 1 tsp chili powder
- 1 tsp garlic powder
- ½ tsp black pepper
- 1 tsp salt

Directions:
1. Combine the paprika, swerve, salt, pepper, and chili pepper, in a small bowl.
2. Rub the mixture into the meat.
3. Place the chuck inside the Slow Cooker.
4. Top with sliced onions and diced chili.
5. Pour the diced tomatoes over.
6. Set the lid on and cook for 8 hours on low.
7. Open the lid and shred inside the cooker.
8. Serve and enjoy!

Nutrition:
- Calories: 278 Total fats: 15 g
- Carbs: 14 g Protein: 22 g Fiber: 2.5 g

118. Asian Beef and Broccoli

Preparation time: 10 minutes
Cooking time: 5 hours 30 minutes
Servings: 6
Ingredients:
- 2 lb boneless beef
- 3 garlic cloves, minced
- 1 cup beef broth
- 3 tbsp swerve
- ¼ cup water
- 12 oz frozen broccoli florets
- ½ cup sodium-reduced soy sauce
- 4 tbsp cornstarch
- 1 tbsp sesame oil
- Salt and pepper, to taste

Directions:
1. Place the oil, garlic, broth, and soy sauce, in the Slow Cooker. Stir to combine.
2. Cut the beef into chunks and add to the Slow Cooker.
3. Set the lid on and cook for 5 hours on low.
4. In a small bowl, whisk together the water and cornstarch.
5. Open the lid and pour over the beef.
6. Add the broccoli, stir to combine everything, and put the lid back on.
7. Cook on high for 30 minutes.
8. Serve and enjoy!

Nutrition:
- Calories: 260 Total fats: 9 g
- Carbs: 16 g
- Protein: 27 g
- Fiber: 3 g

119. Beef Bourguignon

Preparation time: 10 minutes
Cooking time: 8 hours
Servings: 12
Ingredients:
- 3 lb beef - 8 bacon strips
- 1 ¾ cup dry red wine
- 2 cups sliced onion
- 1 tsp thyme
- 1 bay leaf
- 1 tsp salt
- ½ tsp pepper
- 2 garlic cloves, minced
- 1 lb mushrooms, sliced

Directions:
1. Set the bacon in a pan over medium heat and cook until crisp. Transfer to a plate.
2. Attach the beef to the pan and brown just a little bit.
3. Add onion and cook for a minute.
4. Transfer everything to your Slow Cooker.
5. Add the rest of the ingredients and stir well to combine.
6. Place the lid on. Cook for 8 hours on low.
7. Serve topped with crisp bacon.
8. Enjoy!

Nutrition:
- Calories: 290 Total fats: 16 g
- Carbs: 8 g Protein: 25 g Fiber: 1 g

120. Chili Flank Steak

Preparation time: 10 minutes
Cooking time: 5 hours
Servings: 6
Ingredients:
- 1 onion, sliced
- 1 ½ lb flank steak, cut in half
- 4 oz canned green chilis
- ⅓ cup beef broth
- 2 tbsp vinegar
- 1 tsp chili powder
- 1 tsp garlic powder
- ½ tsp paprika
- Salt and pepper, to taste

Directions:
1. Combine the beef broth, chilies, and seasonings.
2. Place the steak inside your Slow Cooker.
3. Arrange the onion slices on top.
4. Pour the chili mixture over.
5. Place the lid on and cook for 5 hours on low.
6. Let sit for 10 minutes so the juices can set before slicing
7. Serve and enjoy!

Nutrition:
- Calories: 219
- Total fats: 11 g
- Carbs: 4 g
- Protein: 20 g
- Fiber: 1 g

121. Beef and Peas

Preparation time: 10 minutes
Cooking time: 5 hours
Servings: 6
Ingredients:
- 4 cups frozen peas
- 1 lb beef, cut into chunks
- 2 tsp paprika
- 1 cup beef broth
- ½ can of diced tomatoes
- 1 onion, diced
- 1 tsp garlic powder
- Salt and pepper, to taste

Directions:
1. Place everything except the peas in your Slow Cooker.
2. Stir to combine well.
3. Put the lid on and cook on low.
4. Add the peas, stir to incorporate well, and put the lid back on.
5. Cook for another hour on low.

6. Serve and enjoy!

Nutrition:
- Calories: 309
- Total fats: 15.2 g
- Carbs: 15.8 g
- Protein: 27 g
- Fiber: 4.5 g

122. Classic Steak

Preparation time: 10 minutes
Cooking time: 5 hours
Servings: 4
Ingredients:
- 4 steaks (4 oz)
- ½ tsp thyme
- 1 tbsp olive oil
- ½ tsp paprika
- ½ tsp garlic powder
- ½ cup beef broth
- Salt and pepper, to taste

Directions:
1. In a small bowl, merge the oil, thyme, paprika, and garlic powder. Add some salt and pepper, to taste.
2. Brush this mixture over the steaks.
3. Place the steak inside the Slow Cooker.
4. Pour the beef broth around the steaks (not over).
5. Place the lid and cook for 5 hours on low.
6. Serve and enjoy!

Nutrition:
- Calories: 210 Total fats: 12 g
- Carbs: 1 g Protein: 20 g Fiber: 0 g

123. Satay Beef

Preparation time: 10 minutes
Cooking time: 5 hours
Servings: 6
Ingredients:
- 1 onion, chopped
- 1 lb rump steak, cut into cubes
- 1 red bell pepper, chopped
- 1 tbsp sodium-reduced soy sauce
- 1 tsp garlic powder
- 1 tsp Swerve
- ½ cup coconut milk
- ½ cup beef broth
- 1 tsp ground ginger
- 1 tsp chili flakes
- Salt and pepper, to taste

Directions:
1. Place the beef in a non-stick skillet and brown for a couple of minutes over medium heat.
2. Bring to your Slow Cooker and attach the rest of the ingredients there.
3. Stir well to combine and place the lid on.
4. Cook for 8 hours on low.
5. Serve and enjoy!

Nutrition:
- Calories: 240 Total fats: 28 g
- Carbs: 9 g Protein: 35 g Fiber: 2 g

124. Roasted Chicken Breasts

Preparation time: 15 minutes
Cooking time: 30 minutes
Servings: 4
Ingredients:
- Non-stick cooking spray
- 4 oz chicken breasts (skinless, boneless)
- 1 tbsp salt (optional)
- ½ tbsp black pepper - 1 tbsp olive oil
- ¼ cup lemon juice
- 2 tbsp garlic (minced)
- 1 ½ tbsp paprika

Directions:
1. Heat oven to 350°F. Spray a baking sheet with cooking oil.
2. Bring the chicken breasts to the baking sheet.
3. In a small bowl, mix salt, pepper, olive oil, lemon juice, and garlic and whisk.
4. You can use a brush or pour lemon juice mixture over all pieces of chicken breast.
5. Cover each chicken breast uniformly with paprika. Bake in the oven for 35 minutes at 165°F. Leave the chicken breasts covered with foil for 10–15 minutes. Then slice and serve.

Nutrition:
- Calories: 240 Total fats: 12 g
- Carbs: 8 g Protein: 23 g
- Fiber: 2 g

125. Sticky Chicken

Preparation time: 15 minutes
Cooking time: 30 minutes
Servings: 6
Ingredients:
- 6 chicken drumsticks
- 6 chicken thighs
- 3 tbsp light soy sauce
- 2 tbsp agave nectar
- Lemon juice
- 6 garlic cloves, finely chopped
- 1 tbsp ginger, finely chopped
- 3 tbsp ground allspice
- 1 finely chopped green chili

Directions:
1. Put the soy sauce, agave nectar, lemon juice, garlic, ginger, allspice, and chili into a large bowl
2. Mix well all the ingredients.
3. Cut the chicken.
4. Fill with marinade.
5. Leave in the fridge overnight.
6. Heat the oven to 200°C.
7. Put the chicken in a roasting tin. Sprinkle leftover marinade.
8. Roast the chicken in the oven for forty minutes.
9. Take out the chicken when it gets sticky and golden.
10. You can serve it with homemade coleslaw.

Nutrition:
- Calories: 225 Total fats: 10 g
- Carbs: 10 g Protein: 23 g Fiber: 1 g

126. Stuffed Greek-Style Chicken Breasts

Preparation time: 15 minutes
Cooking time: 30 minutes
Servings: 4
Ingredients:
- 45 oz boneless, skinless chicken breast cut into halves
- 4 water-packed canned artichoke hearts, minced
- ¼ cup onion, minced
- 1 tbsp crushed dried oregano, preferably Greek - Salt (optional)
- Freshly ground pepper
- 1 tsp olive oil
- 1 cup fat-free unsalted canned chicken broth
- ¼ cup plus half tbsp fresh lemon juice
- 4 slices of lemon
- 2 tbsp cornstarch
- Chopped parsley for garnish

Directions:
1. Remove any obvious chicken fat, rinse it and pat it dry. Season the chicken with salt and pepper.
2. Place the halves with the flat side of a meat mallet between 2 pieces of plastic wrap and pound until the chicken is very thin and flat.
3. Mix the heart of the artichoke, ginger, and oregano.
4. To form a log, put equal amounts of the artichoke mixture into the middle of each pounded chicken breast. Just roll up with a toothpick or skewer, secure.
5. Heat the oil over low heat in a non-stick pan. On both ends, add chicken and brown equally. Do not feel bad if some of the stuffing drops out. The sauce would be flavored.
6. Pour on the lemon juice and broth.
7. Cover chicken with lemon slices, cover, and boil (about 15–20 minutes) until chicken is cooked through.
8. Shift chicken, discarding toothpicks/skewers, to a tray. Keep warm (it can work well by wrapping it in foil and placing it in the oven).
9. Merge cornstarch with the remaining 1 ½tsplemon juice using a fork. Apply to the skillet and whisk until slightly thickened, over high fire. Spoon the chicken with lemon sauce. Garnish with boiled parsley and lemon slices.

Nutrition:
- Calories: 260 Total fats: 9 g
- Carbs: 16 g Protein: 27 g Fiber: 3 g

CHAPTER 8:

Seafood

The following are useful, easy, and delicious seafood recipes that can help in your battle against type 2 diabetes.

127. Cheesy Salmon Fillets

Preparation time: 15 minutes
Cooking time: 20 minutes
Servings: 2–3
Ingredients:
For the salmon fillets:
- 2 pieces (4 oz each) of salmon fillets, choose even cuts
- ½ cup sour cream, reduced-fat
- ¼ cup Cottage cheese, reduced-fat
- ¼ cup Parmigiano-Reggiano cheese, freshly grated

For the garnish:
- Spanish paprika
- ½ piece of 1 lemon, cut into wedges

Directions:
1. Preheat the air fryer to 330°F.
2. To make the salmon fillets, mix sour cream,
3. Cottage cheese, and Parmigiano-Reggiano cheese in a bowl.
4. Layer salmon fillets in the Air fryer basket. Fry for 20 minutes or until cheese turns golden brown.
5. To assemble, place a salmon fillet and sprinkle paprika.
6. Garnish with lemon wedges and squeeze lemon juice on top. Serve.

Nutrition:
- Calories: 274
- Carbs: 1 g
- Fat: 19 g
- Protein: 24 g
- Fiber: 0.5 g

128. Salmon With Asparagus

Preparation time: 5 minutes
Cooking time: 10 minutes
Servings: 3
Ingredients:
- 1 lb salmon, sliced into fillets
- 1 tbsp olive oil -Salt and pepper, as needed
- 1 bunch of asparagus, trimmed
- 2 garlic cloves, minced
- Zest and juice of ½ lemon
- 1 tbsp butter, salted

Directions:
1. Spoon the butter and olive oil into a large pan and heat it over medium-high heat.
2. Once it becomes hot, place the salmon and season it with salt and pepper.
3. Cook for 4 minutes per side and then cook the other side. Stir in the garlic and lemon zest to it. Cook for further 2 minutes or until slightly browned. Off the heat and squeeze the lemon juice over it. Serve it hot.

Nutrition:
- Calories: 409 Carbs: 2.7 g
- Protein: 32.8 g Fat: 28.8 g
- Sodium: 497 mg

129. Shrimp in Garlic Butter

Preparation time: 5 minutes
Cooking time: 20 minutes
Servings: 4
Ingredients:
- 1 lb shrimp, peeled and deveined
- ¼ tsp red pepper flakes
- 6 tbsp butter, divided
- ½ cup chicken stock
- Salt and pepper, as needed
- 2 tbsp parsley, minced
- 5 garlic cloves, minced
- 2 tbsp lemon juice

Directions:
1. Heat a large bottomed skillet over medium-high heat.
2. Spoon in 2tbspthe butter and melt it. Add the shrimp.
3. Season it with salt and pepper. Sear for 4 minutes or until shrimp gets cooked.
4. Transfer the shrimp to a plate and stir in the garlic.
5. Sauté for 30 seconds or until aromatic.
6. Pour the chicken stock and whisk it well. Allow it to simmer for 5–10 minutes or until it has reduced to half.
7. Spoon the remaining butter, red pepper, and lemon juice into the sauce. Mix.
8. Continue cooking for another 2 minutes.
9. Take off the pan from the heat and add the cooked shrimp to it.
10. Garnish with parsley and transfer to the serving bowl.
11. Enjoy.

Nutrition:
- Calories: 307 Carbs: 3 g
- Protein: 27 g Fat: 20 g
- Sodium: 522 mg

130. Baked Salmon With Garlic Parmesan Topping

Preparation time: 5 minutes
Cooking time: 20 minutes
Servings: 4
Ingredients:
- 1 lb wild-caught salmon filets
- 2 tbsp margarine

From the store cupboard:
- ¼ cup reduced-fat Parmesan cheese, grated
- ¼ cup light mayonnaise
- 2–3 garlic cloves, diced
- 2 tbsp parsley
- Salt and pepper

Directions:
1. Heat the oven to 350°F and line a baking pan with parchment paper.
2. Place salmon on pan and season with salt and pepper.
3. In a medium skillet, over medium heat, melt butter. Add garlic and cook, stirring 1 minute.
4. Reduce heat to low and add remaining ingredients. Stir until everything is melted and combined.
5. Spread evenly over salmon and bake for 15 minutes for thawed fish or 20 for frozen. Salmon is done when it flakes easily with a fork. Serve.

Nutrition:
- Calories: 408 Total carbs: 4 g
- Protein: 41 g
- Fat: 24 g
- Sugar: 1 g
- Fiber: 0 g

131. Baked Seafood Casserole

Preparation time: 20 minutes
Cooking time: 30 minutes
Servings: 6
Ingredients:
- 12 oz shrimp, peeled and deveined
- 12 oz cod, cut into 1-inch squares
- 2 medium leeks, white part only, cut into matchstick pieces
- 2 stalks of celery, diced
- 1 cup half-n-half
- 4 tbsp margarine

From the store cupboard:
- 1 cup dry white wine
- 1 cup water
- ½ cup reduced-fat Parmesan cheese, grated
- ¼ cup super fine almond flour
- 2 small bay leaves whole
- 2 ½ tsp Old Bay seasoning
- ½ tsp xanthan gum
- ¼ tsp sea salt

Directions:
1. Heat oven to 400°F.
2. Poach the seafood: In a large, heavy pot, combine wine, water, bay leaves, and ½ tsp Old Bay. Bring just to boiling over med-high heat. Reduce heat to low and simmer for 3 minutes.
3. Add shrimp and cook until they start to turn pink. Transfer to a bowl. Repeat for cod.
4. Turn the heat back to med-high heat and continue simmering poaching liquid until it is reduced to about 1 cup. Remove from heat, strain, and save for later.
5. In a separate large saucepan melt 2 tbsp margarine over med-high heat. Add leeks and celery and season with salt. Cook, stirring occasionally until vegetables are soft.
6. In an 8-inch square baking dish, layer vegetables, and seafood.
7. In the same saucepan used for the vegetables, melt 1 tbsp margarine. Stir in xanthan gum and stir to coat. After xanthan is coated gradually stir in the reserved poaching liquid. Bring to a simmer scraping up the browned bits on the bottom of the pan.
8. When the sauce starts to thicken, stir in half-n-half. Bring back to a simmer and cook, stirring frequently, until the sauce has the same texture as gravy. Taste and adjust seasoning as desired. Pour over seafood in the baking dish.
9. In a food processor or blender, combine the almond flour, Parmesan, 2 tsp Old Bay, and 1 tbsp margarine. Process until thoroughly combined. Sprinkle over casserole and bake 20 minutes or until topping is brown and crisp. Serve.

Nutrition:
- Calories: 344
- Total carbs: 9 g
- Protein: 30 g
- Fat: 17 g
- Sugar: 2 g
- Fiber: 1 g

132. BBQ Oysters With Bacon

Preparation time: 20 minutes
Cooking time: 10 minutes
Servings: 2
Ingredients:
- 1 dozen fresh oysters, shucked and left on the half shell
- 3 slices thick-cut bacon, cut into thin strips
- Juice of ½ lemon

From the store cupboard:
- ⅓ cup sugar-free ketchup
- ¼ cup Worcestershire sauce
- 1 tsp horseradish
- Dash of hot sauce
- Lime wedges for garnish
- Rock salt

Directions:
1. Heat oven to broil. Line a shallow baking dish with rock salt. Place the oysters snugly into the salt.
2. In a large bowl, combine the remaining ingredients and mix well.

3. Add a dash of Worcestershire to each oyster then top with bacon mixture. Cook 10 minutes, or until bacon is crisp. Serve with lime wedges.

Nutrition:
- Calories: 234 Total carbs: 10 g
- Protein: 13 g
- Fat: 13 g
- Sugar: 9 g
- Fiber: 0 g

133. Blackened Shrimp

Preparation time: 5 minutes
Cooking time: 5 minutes
Servings: 4
Ingredients:
- 1 ½ lb shrimp, peel and devein
- 4 lime wedges
- 4 tbsp cilantro, chopped

From the store cupboard:
- 4 garlic cloves, diced
- 1 tbsp chili powder
- 1 tbsp paprika
- 1 tbsp olive oil
- 2 tsp Splenda brown sugar
- 1 tsp cumin
- 1 tsp oregano
- 1 tsp garlic powder
- 1 tsp salt
- ½ tsp pepper

Directions:
1. In a small bowl combine seasonings and Splenda brown sugar.
2. Heat oil in a skillet over med-high heat. Add shrimp, in a single layer, and cook for 1–2 minutes per side.
3. Add seasonings, and cook, stirring, for 30 seconds. Serve garnished with cilantro and a lime wedge.

Nutrition:
- Calories: 252
- Total carbs: 7 g
- Protein: 39 g
- Fat: 7 g
- Sugar: 2 g
- Fiber: 1 g

134. Cajun Catfish

Cooking time: 15 minutes
Preparation time: 5 minutes
Servings: 4
Ingredients:
- 4 (8 oz) catfish fillets

From the store cupboard:
- 2 tbsp olive oil
- 2 tsp garlic salt
- 2 tsp thyme
- 2 tsp paprika
- ½ tsp cayenne pepper
- ½ tsp red hot sauce
- ¼ tsp black pepper
- Nonstick cooking spray

Directions:
1. Heat oven to 450°F. Spray a 9x13-inch baking dish with cooking spray.
2. In a small bowl whisk together everything but catfish. Brush both sides of fillets, using all the spice mix.
3. Bake 10–13 minutes or until fish flakes easily with a fork. Serve.

Nutrition:
- Calories: 366
- Total carbs: 0 g
- Protein: 35 g
- Fat: 24 g
- Sugar: 0 g
- Fiber: 0 g

135. Cajun Flounder and Tomatoes

Preparation time: 10 minutes
Cooking time: 15 minutes
Servings: 4
Ingredients:
- 4 flounder fillets
- 2 ½ cups tomatoes, diced
- ¾ cup onion, diced
- ¾ cup green bell pepper, diced

From the store cupboard:
- 2 garlic cloves, diced fine
- 1 tbsp Cajun seasoning
- 1 tsp olive oil

Directions:
1. Heat oil in a large skillet over med-high heat. Add onion and garlic and cook 2 minutes, or until soft. Add tomatoes, peppers, and spices, and cook for 2–3 minutes until tomatoes soften.
2. Lay fish over top. Cover, reduce heat to medium, and cook for 5–8 minutes, or until fish flakes easily with a fork. Transfer fish to serving plates and top with sauce.

Nutrition:
- Calories: 194 Total carbs: 8 g
- Net carbs: 6 g Protein: 32 g
- Fat: 3 g Sugar: 5 g Fiber: 2 g

136. Cajun Shrimp and Roasted Vegetables

Preparation time: 5 minutes
Cooking time: 15 minutes
Servings: 4
Ingredients:
- 1 lb large shrimp, peeled and deveined
- 2 zucchinis, sliced
- 2 yellow squash, sliced
- ½ bunch asparagus, cut into thirds
- 2 red bell pepper, cut into chunks

From the store cupboard:
- 2 tbsp olive oil
- 2 tbsp Cajun seasoning
- Salt and pepper, to taste

Directions:
1. Heat oven to 400°F.
2. Combine shrimp and vegetables in a large bowl. Add oil and seasoning and toss to coat.
3. Spread evenly on a large baking sheet and bake for 15–20 minutes, or until vegetables are tender. Serve.

Nutrition:
- Calories: 251 Total carbs: 13 g
- Net carbs: 9 g
- Protein: 30 g
- Fat: 9 g
- Sugar: 6 g
- Fiber: 4 g

137. Cilantro Lime Grilled Shrimp

Preparation time: 5 minutes
Cooking time: 5 minutes
Servings: 6
Ingredients:
- 1 ½ lb large shrimp raw, peeled, deveined with tails on
- Juice and zest of 1 lime
- 2 tbsp fresh cilantro chopped

From the store cupboard:
- ¼ cup olive oil
- 2 garlic cloves, diced fine
- 1 tsp smoked paprika
- ¼ tsp cumin
- ½ tsp salt
- ¼ tsp cayenne pepper

Directions:
1. Place the shrimp in a large Ziplock bag
2. Mix remaining ingredients in a small bowl and pour over shrimp. Let marinate for 20–30 minutes.
3. Heat up the grill. Skewer the shrimp and cook for 2–3 minutes, per side, just until they turn pink. Be careful not to overcook them. Serve garnished with cilantro.

Nutrition:
- Calories: 317
- Total carbs: 4 g
- Protein: 39 g
- Fat: 15 g
- Sugar: 0 g
- Fiber: 0 g

138. Coconut Shrimp

Preparation time: 15 minutes
Cooking time: 20 minutes
Servings: 6
Ingredients:
- 2 lb jumbo shrimp, peel, devein and pat dry
- 2 eggs

From the store cupboard:
- ¾ cup unsweetened coconut
- ¾ cup coconut flour
- ½ cup sunflower oil
- 1 tbsp Creole seasoning

- 2 tsp Splenda
- 1 tsp salt
- ½ tsp garlic powder
- Sriracha Dipping sauce

Directions:
1. Heat oil in a pot over med-high heat, you need about 3-inch of oil.
2. In a medium bowl, combine coconut, flour, Creole seasoning, salt, garlic powder, and Splenda.
3. In a small bowl beat the eggs.
4. Dip shrimp in the eggs and then the coconut mixture to coat. Cook, ⅓ of the shrimp at a time, for 2–3 minutes, or until golden brown. Transfer to a paper towel-lined plate.
5. Serve hot with Sriracha dipping sauce, or your favorite dipping sauce.

Nutrition:
- Calories: 316 Total carbs: 10 g
- Net carbs: 7 g Protein: 29 g
- Fat: 17 g Sugar: 6 g Fiber: 3 g

139. Crab Cakes

Preparation time: 10 minutes
Cooking time: 10 minutes
Servings: 8
Ingredients:
- 1 lb lump blue crabmeat
- 1 tbsp red bell pepper, diced fine
- 1 tbsp green bell pepper, diced fine
- 1 tbsp fresh parsley, chopped fine
- 2 eggs
- ¼ tsp fresh lemon juice

From the store cupboard:
- ¼ cup lite mayonnaise, plus 1 tbsp
- ¼ cup Dijon mustard
- 2 tbsp sunflower oil
- 1 tbsp baking powder
- 1 tbsp Worcestershire sauce
- 1 ½ tsp Old Bay

Directions:
1. In a small bowl, whisk together ¼ cup mayonnaise, Dijon mustard, Worcestershire, and lemon juice until combined. Cover and chill until ready to serve.
2. In a large bowl, mix crab, bell peppers, parsley, eggs, 1 tbsp mayonnaise, baking powder, and Old Bay seasoning until ingredients are combined.
3. Heat oil in a large skillet over med-high heat. Once the oil is hot, drop 2 tbsp crab mixture into a hot skillet. They will be loose but as the egg cooks, they will hold together.
4. Cook for 2 minutes or until firm, then flip and cook for other minutes. Transfer to a serving plate. Serve with mustard dipping sauce.

Nutrition:
- Calories: 96
- Total carbs: 3 g
- Protein: 12 g
- Fat: 4 g
- Sugar: 1 g
- Fiber: 0 g

140. Crab Frittata

Preparation time: 10 minutes
Cooking time: 50 minutes
Servings: 4
Ingredients:
- 4 eggs
- 2 cups lump crabmeat
- 1 cup half-n-half
- 1 cup green onions, diced

From the store cupboard:
- 1 cup reduced-fat Parmesan cheese, grated
- 1 tsp salt
- 1 tsp pepper
- 1 tsp smoked paprika
- 1 tsp Italian seasoning
- Nonstick cooking spray

Directions:
1. Heat oven to 350°F. Spray an 8-inch springform pan or pie plate with cooking spray.
2. In a large bowl, whisk together the eggs and half-n-half. Add seasonings and Parmesan cheese, and stir to mix.

3. Stir in the onions and crab meat. Pour into a prepared pan and bake 35–40 minutes, or eggs are set and the top is lightly browned.
4. Let cool for 10 minutes, then slice and serve warm or at room temperature.

Nutrition:
- Calories: 276
- Total carbs: 5 g
- Net carbs: 4 g
- Protein: 25 g
- Fat: 17 g
- Sugar: 1 g
- Fiber: 1 g

141. Crispy Baked Flounder With Green Beans

Preparation time: 10 minutes
Cooking time: 20 minutes
Servings: 4
Ingredients:
- 1 lb flounder
- 2 cups green beans
- 4 tbsp margarine
- 8 basil leaves

From the store cupboard:
- 1 ¾ oz pork rinds
- ½ cup reduced-fat Parmesan cheese
- 3 garlic cloves
- Salt and pepper to taste
- Nonstick cooking spray

Directions:
1. Heat oven to 350°F. Spray a baking dish with cooking spray.
2. Steam green beans until they are almost tender, about 15 minutes, less if you use frozen or canned beans. Lay green beans in the prepared dish.
3. Place the fish filets over the green beans and season with salt and pepper.
4. Place the garlic, basil, pork rinds, and Parmesan in a food processor and pulse until the mixture resembles crumbs. Sprinkle over fish. Cut margarine into small pieces and place on top.
5. Bake 15–20 minutes or until fish flakes easily with a fork. Serve.

Nutrition:
- Calories: 358
- Total carbs: 5 g
- Protein: 39 g
- Fat: 20 g
- Sugar: 1 g
- Fiber: 2 g

142. Crockpot Fish and Tomatoes

Preparation time: 10 minutes
Cooking time: 2 hours 30 minutes
Servings: 4
Ingredients:
- 1 lb cod
- 1 bell pepper, diced
- 1 small onion, diced

From the store cupboard:
- 1 (15 oz) can of tomatoes, diced
- ⅓ cup low-sodium vegetable broth
- 1 garlic clove, diced fine
- ½ tsp basil
- ½ tsp oregano
- ½ tsp salt
- ¼ tsp pepper

Directions:
1. Place the onion, bell pepper, tomatoes, and garlic in the crockpot. Stir to mix.
2. Place fish on top. Sprinkle with herbs and seasonings. Pour broth over top.
3. Cover and cook on high for 1–2 hours, or low for 2–4 hours.

Nutrition:
- Calories: 165 Total carbs: 11 g
- Net carbs: 8 g Protein: 28 g
- Fat: 1 g Sugar: 6 g Fiber: 3 g

143. Crunchy Lemon Shrimp

Preparation time: 5 minutes
Cooking time: 10 minutes
Servings: 4
Ingredients:
- 1 lb raw shrimp, peeled and deveined
- 2 tbsp Italian parsley, roughly chopped
- 2 tbsp lemon juice, divided

From the store cupboard:
- ⅔ cup panko bread crumbs
- 2½ tbsp olive oil, divided
- Salt and pepper, to taste

Directions:
1. Heat oven to 400°F.
2. Place the shrimp evenly in a baking dish and sprinkle with salt and pepper. Drizzle on 1 tbsp lemon juice and 1 tbsp olive oil. Set aside.
3. In a medium bowl, combine parsley, remaining lemon juice, bread crumbs, remaining olive oil, and ¼ tsp each of salt and pepper. Layer the panko mixture evenly on top of the shrimp.
4. Bake 8–10 minutes or until shrimp are cooked through and the panko is golden brown.

Nutrition:
- Calories: 283 Total carbs: 15 g
- Net carbs: 14 g Protein: 28 g
- Fat: 12 g Sugar: 1 g Fiber: 1 g

144. Dill Smoked Salmon Over Noodles

Preparation time: 10 minutes
Cooking time: 10 minutes
Servings: 4
Ingredients:
- 6 oz smoked salmon, chopped
- Juice from ½ a lemon
- ¼ cup half-n-half
- 3 tbsp margarine
- 2 tbsp fresh dill, diced

From the store cupboard:
- Homemade noodles
- ½ cup low-sodium chicken broth
- ½ cup dry white wine
- 1 tbsp olive oil
- 2 garlic cloves, diced fine
- Salt and pepper, to taste

Directions:
1. Heat oil and margarine in a large skillet over med-high heat. Add garlic and cook for 30 seconds.
2. Add broth, wine, and lemon juice. Cook until sauce is reduced by half, about 4 minutes.
3. Stir in the half-n-half and noodles and cook for 2 minutes, or until noodles are done.
4. Stir in the salmon and salt and pepper to taste. Serve garnished with fresh dill.

Nutrition:
- Calories: 273 Total carbs: 4 g
- Protein: 14 g Fat: 21 g
- Sugar: 0 g
- Fiber: 0 g

145. Fisherman's Pie

Preparation time: 15 minutes
Cooking time: 25 minutes
Servings: 4
Ingredients:
- 12 shrimp, peel and devein
- 8 oz cod, cut into 1-inch pieces
- 4 oz salmon, cut into 1-inch pieces
- 1 slice bacon
- 4 cups cheesy cauliflower puree
- ½ cup onion, diced
- ¼ cup heavy cream
- 2 tbsp butter
- 1 tbsp fresh parsley, diced

From the store cupboard:
- 1 cup low-sodium vegetable broth
- ½ cup dry white wine
- 1 garlic clove, diced fine
- ¼ tsp celery salt
- Salt and pepper, to taste
- Nonstick cooking spray

Directions:
1. Heat oven to 400°F. Spray a large casserole dish or 4 small ones with cooking spray.
2. Melt butter in a medium saucepan over medium heat. Add onion and cook until soft. Add the garlic and cook 1 minute more.
3. Pour in the wine and broth and cook for 5 minutes.

4. Stir in cream, bacon, and celery salt and simmer for 5 minutes, until bacon is cooked through and most of the fat has rendered off. Remove the slice of bacon, chop it up and add it back to the pot.
5. Add the seafood, parsley, salt, and pepper to taste and simmer for 2–3 minutes. Transfer mixture to the prepared casserole dish.
6. Place the cauliflower in a large Ziplock bag, or pastry bag, and snip off one corner. Pipe the cauliflower in small rosettes to cover the top. Bake 8–10 minutes, or until heated through and the top is lightly browned, you may need to broil it for 1–2 minutes to reach the browned color. Serve.

Nutrition:
- Calories: 338 Total carbs: 10 g
- Net carbs: 7 g Protein: 38 g
- Fat: 14 g Sugar: 3 g Fiber: 3 g

146. Garlic Shrimp With Sun-Dried Tomatoes

Preparation time: 10 minutes
Cooking time: 30 minutes
Servings: 4
Ingredients:
- ½ lb shrimp, peeled and deveined
- 4 oz sun-dried tomatoes
- 1 cup half-n-half

From the store cupboard:
- 1 cup reduced-fat Parmesan cheese
- 4 garlic cloves, diced fine
- 2 tbsp olive oil
- 1 tsp dried basil
- ¼ tsp salt
- ¼ tsp paprika
- ¼ tsp crushed red pepper
- ½ recipe homemade pasta, cook and drain

Directions:
1. Heat oil in a large skillet over medium heat. Add garlic and tomatoes and cook for 1 minute.
2. Add shrimp, sprinkle with salt and paprika, and cook for about 2 minutes.
3. Add half-n-half, basil, and crushed red pepper, and bring to boil. Reduce heat to simmer. Whisk the Parmesan cheese into the hot cream and stir to melt the cheese, on low heat.
4. Remove from heat. Add pasta and stir to coat. Serve.

Nutrition:
- Calories: 353 Total carbs: 23 g
- Net carbs: 20 g Protein: 37 g
- Fat: 22 g Sugar: 3 g Fiber: 3 g

147. Tuna Sweet Corn Casserole

Preparation time: 10 minutes
Cooking time: 35 minutes
Servings: 2
Ingredients:
- 3 small tins of tuna
- ½ lb sweet corn kernels
- 1lb chopped vegetables
- 1 cup low-sodium vegetable broth
- 2tbsp spicy seasoning

Directions:
1. Mix all the ingredients in your Instant Pot.
2. Cook on "Stew" for 35 minutes.
3. Release the pressure naturally.

Nutrition:
- Calories: 300
- Carbs: 6 g
- Sugar: 1 g
- Fat: 9 g
- GL: 2

148. Lemon Pepper Salmon

Preparation time: 10 minutes
Cooking time: 10 minutes
Servings: 4
Ingredients:
- 3 tbsp ghee or avocado oil
- 1 lb skin-on salmon filet
- 1 julienned red bell pepper
- 1 julienned green zucchini
- 1 julienned carrot
- ¾ cup water
- A few sprigs of parsley, tarragon, dill, basil, or a combination

- ½ sliced lemon
- ½ tsp black pepper
- ¼ tsp sea salt

Directions:
1. Add the water and the herbs to the bottom of the Instant Pot and put it in a wire steamer rack making sure the handles extend upwards.
2. Place the salmon filet onto the wire rack, with the skin side facing down.
3. Drizzle the salmon with ghee, season with black pepper and salt, and top with the lemon slices.
4. Close and seal the Instant Pot, making sure the vent is turned to "Sealing."
5. Select the "Steam" setting and cook for 3 minutes.
6. While the salmon cooks, julienne the vegetables and set them aside.
7. Once done, quickly release the pressure, and then press the "Keep Warm/Cancel" button.
8. Uncover and wear oven mitts, carefully remove the steamer rack with the salmon.
9. Remove the herbs and discard them.
10. Add the vegetables to the pot and put the lid back on.
11. Select the "Sauté" function and cook for 1–2 minutes.
12. Serve the vegetables with salmon and add the remaining fat to the pot.
13. Pour a little of the sauce over the fish and vegetables if desired.

Nutrition:
- Calories: 296 Carbs: 8 g
- Fat: 15 g Protein: 31 g
- Potassium (K): 1084 mg
- Sodium(Na): 284 mg

149. Green Salmon Florentine

Preparation time: 10 minutes
Cooking time: 30 minutes
Servings: 4
Ingredients:
- ½ sweet onion, finely chopped
- 1 tsp minced garlic
- 3 cups baby spinach
- 1 cup kale, tough stems removed, torn into 3-inch pieces
- 4 (5 oz/142 g) salmon fillets
- 1 tsp extra-virgin olive oil
- Salt and freshly ground black pepper

Directions:
1. Preheat the oven to 350°F (180°C).
2. Set a large skillet and attach the oil.
3. Sauté the onion and garlic until softened and translucent, about 3 minutes.
4. Add the spinach and kale and sauté until the greens wilt, about 5 minutes.
5. Detach the skillet from the heat and season the greens with salt and pepper.
6. Place the salmon fillets so they are nestled in the greens and partially covered by them.
7. Bake the salmon until it is opaque, about 20 minutes.
8. Serve immediately.

Nutrition:
- Calories: 282
- Fat: 15.9 g
- Protein: 28.9 g
- Carbs: 4.1 g
- Fiber: 1.1 g
- Sugar: 0.9 g
- Sodium: 92 mg

150. Seared Scallops With Orange Sauce

Preparation time: 10 minutes
Cooking time: 10 minutes
Servings: 4
Ingredients:
- 2 lb (907 g) sea scallops, patted dry
- 1 tbsp minced garlic
- ¼ cup freshly squeezed orange juice
- 1 tsp orange zest
- 2 tsp chopped fresh thyme, for garnish
- Sea salt and freshly ground black pepper
- 2 tbsp extra-virgin olive oil

Directions:
1. In a bowl, flavor the scallops with salt and pepper. Set aside.
2. Warm the olive oil until shimmering

3. Add the garlic and sauté for about 3 minutes, stirring occasionally, or until the garlic is softened.
4. Attach the scallops and cook each side for about 4 minutes or until the scallops are lightly browned and firm.
5. Remove the scallops from the heat to a plate and cover with foil to keep warm. Set aside.
6. Pour the orange juice and zest into the skillet and stir, scraping up any cooked bits.
7. Drizzle the scallops with the orange sauce and sprinkle the thyme on top for garnish before serving

Nutrition:
- Calories: 268
- Fat: 8.2 g
- Protein: 38.2 g
- Carbs: 8.3 g
- Fiber: 0 g
- Sugar: 1.1 g
- Sodium: 360 mg

151. Cod Fillet With Quinoa and Asparagus

Preparation time: 5 minutes
Cooking time: 15 minutes
Servings: 4
Ingredients:
- ½ cup uncooked quinoa
- 4 (4 oz/113 g) cod fillets
- ½ tsp garlic powder, divided
- 24 asparagus spears, cut the bottom 1 ½-inch off
- 1 cup half-and-half
- ¼ tsp salt
- ¼ tsp freshly ground black pepper
- 1 tbsp avocado oil

Directions:
1. Put the quinoa in a pot of salted water. Bring to a boil. Set the heat to low and simmer for 15 minutes or until the quinoa is soft and has a white "tail." Cover and turn off the heat. Let sit for 5 minutes.
2. On a clean work surface, rub the cod fillets with ¼ tsp garlic powder, salt, and pepper.
3. Heat the avocado oil in a non-stick skillet over medium-low heat.
4. Add the cod fillets and asparagus to the skillet and cook for 8 minutes or until they are tender. Flip the cod and shake the skillet halfway through the cooking time.
5. Pour the half-and-half into the skillet, and sprinkle with the remaining garlic powder. Set up the heat to high and simmer for 2 minutes until creamy.
6. Divide the quinoa, cod fillets, and asparagus into four bowls and serve warm.

Nutrition:
- Calories: 258 Fat: 7.9 g
- Protein: 25.2 g Carbs: 22.7 g
- Fiber: 5.2 g
- Sugar: 3.8 g
- Sodium: 410 mg

152. Red Cabbage and Mushroom Pot Stickers

Preparation time: 12 minutes
Cooking time: 11–18 minutes
Servings: 12
Ingredients:
- 1 cup shredded red cabbage
- ¼ cup chopped button mushrooms
- ¼ cup grated carrot
- 2 tbsp minced onion
- 2 garlic cloves, minced
- 2 tsp grated fresh ginger
- 12 gloze/potsticker wrappers
- 2 ½ tsp olive oil, divided

Directions:
1. In a baking pan, combine the red cabbage, mushrooms, carrot, onion, garlic, and ginger. Add 1 tbsp water. Set in the air fryer and bake at 370°F (188°C) for 3–6 minutes, until the vegetables are crisp-tender. Drain and set aside.
2. Working one at a time, place the potsticker wrappers on a work surface. Top each wrapper with a scant 1 tbsp of the filling. Fold half of the wrapper over the other half to form a half-circle. Dab

one edge with water and press both edges together.
3. To the baking pan, add 1¼ tsp olive oil. Put half of the potstickers, seam-side up, in the pan. Air fry for 5 minutes or until the bottoms are light golden brown. Add 1 tbsp water and return the pan to the Air Fryer.
4. Air fry for 4–6 minutes more, or until hot. Repeat with the remaining potstickers, the remaining 1¼ tsp oil, and 1 tbsp water. Serve immediately.

Nutrition:
- Calories: 88 Fat: 3 g
- Protein: 2 g
- Carbs: 14 g
- Fiber: 1 g
- Sugar: 1 g
- Sodium: 58 mg

153. Grilled Shrimp Skewers

Preparation time: 10 minutes
Cooking time: 12 minutes
Servings: 4
Ingredients:
- 1 lb (454 g) shrimp, shelled and deveined
- ½ cup plain Greek yogurt
- ½ tbsp chili paste
- ½ tbsp lime juice
- Chopped green onions, for garnish

Special equipment:
- Wooden skewers, soaked in water

Directions:
1. Set the shrimp onto skewers, piercing once near the tail and once near the head. You can place about 5 shrimps on each skewer.
2. Preheat the grill to medium.
3. Set the shrimp skewers on the grill and cook for about 6 minutes, flipping the shrimp halfway through, or until the shrimp are totally pink and opaque.
4. Meanwhile, make the yogurt and chili sauce: In a small bowl, stir together the yogurt, chili paste, and lime juice.
5. Transfer the shrimp skewers to a large plate. Scatter the green onions on top for garnish and serve with the yogurt and chili sauce on the side.

Nutrition:
- Calories: 122 Fat: 0.8 g
- Protein: 26.1 g Carbs: 2.9 g
- Fiber: 0.5 g Sugar: 1.3 g
- Sodium: 175 mg

154. Tuna Salad

Preparation time: 15 minutes
Cooking time: 20 minutes
Servings: 2
Ingredients:
- 2 (5 oz) cans of water-packed tuna, drained
- 2 tbsp fat-free plain Greek yogurt
- Salt and ground black pepper, as required
- 2 medium carrots, peeled and shredded
- 2 apples, cored and chopped
- 2 cups fresh spinach, torn

Directions:
1. In a large bowl, add the tuna, yogurt, salt, and black pepper and gently, stir to combine.
2. Add the carrots and apples and stir to combine.
3. Serve immediately.

Nutrition:
- Calories: 306 Total fat: 1.8 g
- Saturated fat: 0 g
- Cholesterol: 63 mg
- Total carbs: 38 g
- Sugar: 26 g
- Fiber: 7.6 g
- Sodium: 324 mg
- Potassium: 602 mg
- Protein: 35.8 g

155. Herring and Veggies Soup

Preparation time: 15 minutes
Cooking time: 25 minutes
Servings: 5
Ingredients:
- 2 tbsp olive oil
- 1 shallot, chopped
- 2 small garlic cloves, minced
- 1 jalapeño pepper, chopped
- 1 head cabbage, chopped
- 1 small red bell pepper
- 1 small yellow bell pepper
- 5 cups low-sodium chicken broth
- 2 (4 oz) boneless herring fillets, cubed
- ¼ cup fresh cilantro, minced
- 2 tbsp fresh lemon juice
- Ground black pepper, as required
- 2 scallions, chopped

Directions:
1. In a large soup pan, warm the oil over medium heat and sauté shallot and garlic for 2–3 minutes.
2. Add the cabbage and bell peppers and sauté for about 3–4 minutes.
3. Attach the broth and bring it to a boil over high heat.
4. Now, reduce the heat to medium-low and simmer for about 10 minutes.
5. Add the herring cubes and cook for about 5–6 minutes.
6. Stir in the cilantro, lemon juice, salt, and black pepper and cook for about 1–2 minutes.
7. Serve hot with the topping of scallion.

Nutrition:
- Calories: 215
- Total fat: 11.2 g
- Saturated fat: 2.1 g
- Cholesterol: 35 mg
- Total carbs: 14.7 g
- Sugar: 7 g
- Fiber: 4.5 g
- Sodium: 152 mg
- Potassium: 574 mg
- Protein: 15.1 g

156. Salmon Soup

Preparation time: 15 minutes
Cooking time: 20 minutes
Servings: 4
Ingredients:
- 1 tbsp olive oil
- 1 yellow onion, chopped
- 1 garlic clove, minced
- 4 cups low-sodium chicken broth
- 1 lb boneless salmon, cubed
- 2 tbsp fresh cilantro, chopped
- Ground black pepper, as required
- 1 tbsp fresh lime juice

Directions:
1. In a large pan warm the oil over medium heat and sauté the onion for about 5 minutes.
2. Add the garlic and sauté for about 1 minute. Stir in the broth and bring to a boil over high heat.
3. Now, set the heat and simmer for about 10 minutes. Add the salmon and soy sauce and cook for about 3–4 minutes.
4. Stir in black pepper, lime juice, and cilantro, and serve hot.

Nutrition:
- Calories: 208 Total fat: 10.5 g
- Saturated fat: 1.5 g Cholesterol: 50 mg
- Total carbs: 3.9 g
- Sugar: 1.2 g Fiber: 0.6 g
- Sodium: 121 mg Potassium: 331 mg
- Protein: 24.4 g

157. Salmon and Shrimp Stew

Preparation time: 20 minutes
Cooking time: 21 minutes
Servings: 6
Ingredients:

- 2 tbsp olive oil - ½cup onion, chopped finely - 2 garlic cloves, minced
- 1 Serrano pepper, chopped
- 1 tsp smoked paprika
- 4 cups fresh tomatoes, chopped
- 4 cups low-sodium chicken broth
- 1 lb salmon fillets, cubed
- 1 lb shrimp, peeled and deveined
- 2 tbsp fresh lime juice - ¼ cup fresh basil, chopped - ¼ cup fresh parsley, chopped
- Ground black pepper, as required
- 2 scallions, chopped

Directions:

1. In a large soup pan, melt coconut oil over medium-high heat and sauté the onion for about 5–6 minutes. Add the garlic, Serrano pepper, and smoked paprika and sauté for about 1 minute. Add the tomatoes and broth and bring to a gentle simmer over medium heat. Simmer for about 5 minutes.
2. Add the salmon and simmer for about 3–4 minutes. Stir in the remaining seafood and cook for about 4–5 minutes.
3. Stir in the lemon juice, basil, parsley, sea salt, and black pepper, and remove from heat.
4. Serve hot with the garnishing of scallion.

Nutrition:

- Calories: 271 Total fat: 11 g
- Saturated fat: 1.8 g Cholesterol: 193 mg
- Total carbs: 8.6 g Sugar: 3.8 g
- Fiber: 2.1 g Sodium: 273 mg
- Potassium: 763 mg Protein: 34.7 g

158. Salmon Curry

Preparation time: 15 minutes
Cooking time: 30 minutes
Servings: 6
Ingredients:

- 6 (4 oz) salmon fillets
- 1 tsp ground turmeric, divided
- Salt, as required
- 3 tbsp olive oil, divided
- 1 yellow onion, chopped finely
- 1 tsp garlic paste
- 1 tsp fresh ginger paste
- 3–4 green chilies, halved
- 1 tsp red chili powder
- ½tsp ground cumin
- ½tsp ground cinnamon
- ¾ cup fat-free plain Greek yogurt, whipped
- ¾ cup filtered water
- 3 tbsp fresh cilantro, chopped

Directions:

1. Season each salmon fillet with ½tsp turmeric and salt.
2. In a large skillet, melt 1 tbsp of butter over medium heat and cook the salmon fillets for about 2 minutes per side.
3. Transfer the salmon onto a plate.
4. In the same skillet, dissolve the remaining butter over medium heat and sauté the onion for about 4–5 minutes.
5. Add the garlic paste, ginger paste, green chilies, remaining turmeric and spices. Sauté for about 1 minute.
6. Now, reduce the heat to medium-low.
7. Slowly, add the yogurt and water, stirring continuously until smooth.
8. Cover the skillet and simmer for about 10–15 minutes or until the desired doneness of the sauce.
9. Carefully, add the salmon fillets and simmer for about 5 minutes.
10. Serve hot with the garnishing of cilantro.

Nutrition:

- Calories: 242 Total fat: 14.3 g
- Saturated fat: 2 g
- Cholesterol: 51 mg
- Total carbs: 4.1 g
- Sugar: 2 g
- Fiber: 0.8 g
- Sodium: 98 mg
- Potassium: 493 mg
- Protein: 25.4 g

159. Salmon With Bell Peppers

Preparation time: 15 minutes
Cooking time: 20 minutes
Servings: 6
Ingredients:
- 6 (3 oz) salmon fillets
- Pinch of salt
- Ground black pepper, as required
- 1 yellow bell pepper, seeded and cubed
- 1 red bell pepper, seeded and cubed
- 4 plum tomatoes, cubed
- 1 small onion, sliced thinly
- ½ cup fresh parsley, chopped
- ¼ cup olive oil
- 2 tbsp fresh lemon juice

Directions:
1. Preheat the oven to 400°F.
2. Flavor each salmon fillet with salt and black pepper lightly.
3. In a bowl, mix the bell peppers, tomato, and onion. Arrange 6 foil pieces onto a smooth surface. Place 1 salmon fillet over each foil paper and sprinkle with salt and black pepper.
4. Place veggie mixture over each fillet evenly and top with parsley and capers evenly. Drizzle with oil and lemon juice.
5. Fold each foil around the salmon mixture to seal it. Arrange the foil packets onto a large baking sheet in a single layer.
6. Bake for about 20 minutes.
7. Serve hot.

Nutrition:
- Calories: 220 Total fat: 14 g
- Saturated fat: 2 g Cholesterol: 38 mg
- Total carbs: 7.7 g Sugar: 4.8 g
- Fiber: 2 g Sodium: 74 mg
- Potassium: 647 mg Protein: 17.9 g

160. Shrimp Salad

Preparation time: 20 minutes
Cooking time: 4 minutes
Servings: 6
Ingredients:
For the salad:
- 1 lb shrimp, peeled and deveined
- Salt and ground black pepper, as required
- 1 tsp olive oil
- 1 ½ cup carrot, peeled and julienned
- 1 ½ cup red cabbage, shredded
- 1 ½ cup cucumber, julienned
- 5 cups fresh baby arugula
- ¼ cup fresh basil, chopped
- ¼ cup fresh cilantro, chopped
- 4 cups lettuce, torn
- ¼ cup almonds, chopped

For the dressing:
- 2 tbsp natural almond butter
- 1 garlic clove, crushed
- 1 tbsp fresh cilantro, chopped
- 1 tbsp fresh lime juice
- 1 tbsp unsweetened applesauce
- 2 tsp balsamic vinegar
- ½ tsp cayenne pepper
- Salt, as required
- 1 tbsp water
- ⅓ cup olive oil

Directions:
1. Slowly, add the oil, beating continuously until smooth.
2. For the salad: In a bowl, add shrimp, salt, black pepper, and oil and toss to coat well.
3. Warm a skillet over medium-high heat and cook the shrimp for about 2 minutes per side.
4. Detach from the heat and set aside to cool.
5. In a large bowl, add the shrimp, and vegetables and mix well.
6. For the dressing: in a bowl, add all ingredients except oil and beat until well combined.
7. Place the dressing over the shrimp mixture and gently, toss to coat well.
8. Serve immediately.

Nutrition:
- Calories: 274 Total fat: 17.7 g
- Saturated fat: 2.4 g
- Cholesterol: 159 mg
- Total carbs: 10 g Sugar: 3.8 g
- Fiber: 2.9 g Sodium: 242 mg
- Potassium: 481 mg
- Protein: 20.5 g

161. Shrimp and Veggies Curry

Preparation time: 20 minutes
Cooking time: 20 minutes
Servings: 6
Ingredients:
- 2 tsp olive oil
- 1 ½ medium white onions
- 2 medium green bell peppers
- 3 medium carrots, peeled and sliced thinly
- 3 garlic cloves, chopped finely
- 1 tbsp fresh ginger, chopped finely
- 2½ tsp curry powder
- 1 ½ lbs shrimp, peeled and deveined
- 1 cup of filtered water
- 2 tbsp fresh lime juice
- Salt and ground black pepper, as required
- 2 tbsp fresh cilantro, chopped

Directions:
1. In a large skillet, warm oil and sauté the onion for about 4–5 minutes.
2. Add the bell peppers and carrot and sauté for about 3–4 minutes.
3. Add the garlic, ginger, and curry powder and sauté for about 1 minute.
4. Add the shrimp and sauté for about 1 minute.
5. Stir in the water and cook for about 4–6 minutes, stirring occasionally.
6. Serve hot with the garnishing of cilantro.

Nutrition:
- Calories: 193 Total fat: 3.8 g
- Saturated fat: 0.9 g Cholesterol: 239 mg
- Total carbs: 12 g Sugar: 4.7 g
- Fiber: 2.3 g
- Sodium: 328 mg
- Potassium: 437 mg
- Protein: 27.1 g

162. Shrimp With Zucchini

Preparation time: 20 minutes
Cooking time: 8 minutes
Servings: 4
Ingredients:
- 3 tbsp olive oil
- 1 lb medium shrimp, peeled and deveined
- 1 shallot, minced
- 4 garlic cloves, minced
- ¼ tsp red pepper flakes, crushed
- Salt and ground black pepper, as required
- ¼ cup low-sodium chicken broth
- 2 tbsp fresh lemon juice
- 1 tsp fresh lemon zest, grated finely
- ½ lb zucchini, spiralized with Blade C

Directions:
1. In a large skillet, warm the oil and butter over medium-high heat and cook the shrimp, shallot, garlic, red pepper flakes, salt, and black pepper for about 2 minutes, stirring occasionally.
2. Stir in the broth, lemon juice, and lemon zest and bring to a gentle boil.
3. Set in zucchini noodles and cook for about 1–2 minutes.
4. Serve hot.

Nutrition:
- Calories: 245
- Total fat: 12.6 g
- Saturated fat: 2.2 g
- Cholesterol: 239 mg
- Total carbs: 5.8 g
- Sugar: 1.2 g
- Fiber: 08 g
- Sodium: 289 mg
- Potassium: 381 mg
- Protein: 27 g

163. Shrimp With Broccoli

Preparation time: 15 minutes
Cooking time: 12 minutes
Servings: 6
Ingredients:
- 2 tbsp olive oil, divided
- 4 cups broccoli, chopped
- 2–3 tbsp filtered water

- 1 ½lb large shrimp
- 2 garlic cloves, minced
- 1 (1-inch) piece fresh ginger, minced
- Salt and ground black pepper, as required

Directions:
1. In a large skillet, warm 1 tbsp oil over medium-high heat and cook the broccoli for about 1–2 minutes stirring continuously.
2. Stir in the water and cook, covered for about 3–4 minutes, stirring occasionally.
3. With a spoon, push the broccoli to the side of the pan.
4. Add the remaining oil and let it heat.
5. Add the shrimp and cook for about 1–2 minutes, tossing occasionally.
6. Add the remaining ingredients and sauté for about 2–3 minutes.
7. Serve hot.

Nutrition:
- Calories: 197 Total fat: 6.8 g
- Saturated fat: 1.3 g Cholesterol: 239 mg
- Total carbs: 6.1 g Sugar: 1.1 g Fiber: 1.6 g
- Sodium: 324 mg Potassium: 389 mg
- Protein: 27.6 g

164. Montreal Style Salmon

Preparation time: 20 minutes
Cooking time: 8 minutes
Servings: 4
Ingredients:
- ½tsp grated lemon peel
- ⅛tsp McCormick Dill Weed
- ½tsp McCormick Grill Mates Montreal Steak Seasoning
- ½lb salmon fillets (swordfish or mahi-mahi can also be used)

Directions:
1. Mix steak seasoning, dill weed, and lemon peel in a small bowl.
2. Rub mixture over salmon and let it stand for about 5 minutes.
3. Grill the salmon, skin side down, over medium heat until fish flakes easily with a fork, for about 10 minutes. Make sure you don't turn the salmon.
4. Serve immediately and enjoy it.

Nutrition:
- Calories: 122 Fat: 0.8 g
- Protein: 26.1 g Carbs: 2.9 g
- Fiber: 0.5 g Sugar: 1.3 g
- Sodium: 175 mg

165. Cracker Crusted Cod

Preparation time: 25 minutes
Cooking time: 0 minutes
Servings: 6
Ingredients:
- ¼tsp salt
- ⅛tsp pepper
- ¼ cup fat-free (skim) milk
- 2 tbsp canola oil
- 1 lb tilapia, cod, haddock, or other medium-firm fish fillets, about ¾-inch thick
- ½cup of graham cracker crumbs (about 8 squares) - 1 tsp grated lemon peel
- 2 tbsp chopped toasted pecans

Directions:
1. Place the oven rack in a position slightly just above the middle of the oven.
2. Heat the oven to 500°F.
3. Cut the fish files crosswise into 2-inch wide pieces. Mix cracker crumbs, salt, lemon peel, and pepper in a shallow dish.
4. Place milk in another shallow dish.
5. Dip fish into milk, then coat with the cracker mixture.
6. Place in the ungreased 13x9-inch pan.
7. Drizzle oil over the fish. Sprinkle with pecans. Bake for about 10 minutes.
8. Toasting nuts adds a lot of great flavors.
9. To toast nuts, bake uncovered in an ungreased shallow pan, for about 10 minutes, at 350°F occasionally stirring, until light brown. Serve and enjoy.

Nutrition:
- Calories: 306 Total fat: 1.8 g
- Saturated fat: 0 g
- Cholesterol: 63 mg
- Total carbs: 38 g Sugar: 26 g
- Fiber: 7.6 g Sodium: 324 mg
- Potassium: 602 mg
- Protein: 35.8 g

166. Phyllo Vegetable Triangles

Preparation time: 15 minutes
Cooking time: 6–11 minutes
Servings: 6
Ingredients:
- 3 tbsp minced onion
- 2 garlic cloves, minced
- 2 tbsp grated carrot
- 1 tsp olive oil
- 3 tbsp frozen baby peas, thawed
- 2 tbsp non-fat cream cheese, at room temperature
- 6 sheets of frozen phyllo dough, thawed
- Olive oil spray, for coating the dough

Directions:
1. In a baking pan, combine the onion, garlic, carrot, and olive oil. Air fry at 390°F (199°C) for 2–4 minutes, or until the vegetables are crisp-tender. Transfer to a bowl.
2. Stir in the peas and cream cheese to the vegetable mixture. Let it cool while you prepare the dough.
3. Set one sheet of phyllo and lightly spray with olive oil spray. Top with another sheet of phyllo.
4. Repeat with the remaining 4 phyllo sheets; you'll have 3 stacks with 2 layers each. Cut each stack lengthwise into 4 strips (12 strips total).
5. Place a scant 2 tsp of the filling near the bottom of each strip. Bring one corner up over the filling to make a triangle; continue folding the triangles over, as you would fold a flag Seal the edge with a bit of water. Repeat with the remaining strips and filling
6. Air fry the triangles, in 2 batches, for 4–7 minutes, or until golden brown. Serve.

Nutrition:
- Calories: 67
- Fat: 2 g
- Protein: 2 g
- Carbs: 11 g
- Fiber: 1 g
- Sugar: 1 g
- Sodium: 121 mg

167. Salmon Chowder

Preparation time: 20 minutes
Cooking time: 4 minutes
Servings: 6
Ingredients:
- ½ cup of cannellini beans, rinsed and drained
- ¼ tsp mustard powder
- 1 large garlic clove, finely chopped
- 2 tsp fresh lemon juice
- ¾ lb skinless salmon filet, cut into 1-inch cubes
- 1 (8 oz) bottle of clam juice
- ½ cup of non-fat evaporated milk
- Salt and ground black pepper, to taste
- 4 tsp chopped chives
- 2 tbsp light olive oil
- 1 onion, cut into ½-inch cubes
- 1 large yellow potato, peeled and diced
- 1 cup of frozen baby lima beans
- ⅔ cup of frozen yellow corn kernels

Directions:
1. In a small food processor, combine the mustard powder, beans, lemon juice, and garlic. Puree just until smooth, stopping as needed to scrape down the bowl.
2. Drizzle the oil with the motor running. The result will look like velvety mayonnaise; set this bean puree aside.
3. Combine potatoes, onion, and 1 ¼ cup water in a large deep saucepan. Seal and set the pot over medium-high heat.

4. Reduce the heat to medium when the water boils for about 7 minutes. Add the corn and lima beans; cook, covered, until the potatoes are tender, for about 3 minutes longer.
5. Add the calm juice, fish, bean puree, and ½ cup of water.
6. Mix until the bean puree dissolves.
7. Cook over medium heat, uncovered, until fish flakes easily and opaque in the center, for about 10 minutes.
8. Take the saucepan off the heat. Stir in the milk. Then season the chowder to taste with pepper and salt.
9. Divide the soup among 4 wide, shallow bowls, and garnish with chopped chives.
10. Serve and enjoy.

Nutrition:
- Calories: 223
- Fat: 12.2 g
- Protein: 25.7 g
- Carbs: 2.0 g
- Fiber: 0 g
- Sugar: 2.9 g
- Sodium: 203 mg

168. Mustard-Crusted Sole

Preparation time: 5 minutes
Cooking time: 8–11 minutes
Servings: 4
Ingredients:
- 5 tsp low-sodium yellow mustard
- 1 tbsp freshly squeezed lemon juice
- 4 (3½oz/99g) sole fillets
- ½ tsp dried thyme
- ½ tsp dried marjoram
- ⅛ tsp freshly ground black pepper
- 1 slice low-sodium whole-wheat bread, crumbled
- 2 tsp olive oil

Directions:
1. In a minor bowl, blend the mustard and lemon juice. Spread this evenly over the fillets. Place them in the air fryer basket.
2. In another small bowl, mix the thyme, marjoram, pepper, bread crumbs, and olive oil. Mix until combined.
3. Gently but firmly press the spice mixture onto each fish fillet's top.
4. Bake at 320°F (160°C) for 8–11 minutes, or until the fish grasps an inner temperature of at least 145°F (63°C) on a meat thermometer and the topping is browned and crisp. Serve immediately.

Nutrition:
- Calories: 143
- Fat: 4 g
- Protein: 20 g
- Carbs: 5 g
- Fiber: 1 g
- Sugar: 1 g
- Sodium: 140 mg

169. Lemony Salmon

Preparation time: 10 minutes
Cooking time: 3 minutes
Servings: 3
Ingredients:
- 1 lb salmon fillet, cut into 3 pieces
- 3 tsp fresh dill, chopped
- 5 tbsp fresh lemon juice, divided
- Salt and ground black pepper, as required

Directions:
1. Arrange a steamer trivet in Instant Pot and pour ¼ cup of lemon juice.
2. Season the salmon with salt and black pepper evenly.
3. Place the salmon pieces on top of the trivet, skin side down, and drizzle with the remaining lemon juice.
4. Now, sprinkle the salmon pieces with dill evenly.
5. Close the lid and place the pressure valve in the "Seal" position.
6. Press "Steam" and use the default time of 3 minutes.
7. Press "Cancel" and allow a "Natural" release.
8. Open the lid and serve hot.

Nutrition:
- Calories: 20 Fats: 9.6 g
- Carbs: 1.1 g Sugar: 0.5 g
- Protein: 29.7 g
- Sodium: 74 mg

170. Shrimp With Green Beans

Preparation time: 10 minutes
Cooking time: 2 minutes
Servings: 4
Ingredients:
- ¾ lb fresh green beans, trimmed
- 1 lb medium frozen shrimp, peeled and deveined
- 2 tbsp fresh lemon juice
- 2 tbsp olive oil
- Salt and ground black pepper, as required

Directions:
1. Arrange a steamer trivet in the Instant Pot and pour a cup of water.
2. Arrange the green beans on top of the trivet in a single layer and top with shrimp.
3. Drizzle with oil and lemon juice.
4. Sprinkle with salt and black pepper.
5. Close the lid and place the pressure valve in the "Seal" position.
6. Press "Steam" and just use the default time of 2 minutes.
7. Press "Cancel" and allow a "Natural" release.
8. Open the lid and serve.

Nutrition:
- Calories: 223 Fats: 1 g
- Carbs: 7.9 g
- Sugar: 1.4 g
- Protein: 27.4 g
- Sodium: 322 mg

171. Crab Curry

Preparation time: 10 minutes
Cooking time: 20 minutes
Servings: 2
Ingredients:
- ½ lb chopped crab
- 1 thinly sliced red onion
- ½ cup chopped tomato
- 3 tbsp curry paste
- 1 tbsp oil or ghee

Directions:
1. Set the Instant Pot to sauté and add the onion, oil, and curry paste.
2. When the onion is soft, add the remaining ingredients and seal.
3. Cook on "Stew" for 20 minutes.
4. Release the pressure naturally.

Nutrition:
- Calories: 2 Carbs: 11 g
- Sugar: 4 g
- Fat: 10 g
- Protein: 24 g
- GL: 9

172. Mixed Chowder

Preparation time: 10 minutes
Cooking time: 35 minutes
Servings: 2
Ingredients:
- 1lb fish stew mix
- 2 cups white sauce
- 3tbsp Old Bay seasoning

Directions:
1. Mix all the ingredients in your Instant Pot.
2. Cook on "Stew" for 35 minutes.
3. Release the pressure naturally.

Nutrition:
- Calories: 320
- Carbs: 9 g
- Sugar: 2 g
- Fat: 16 g
- Protein: 24 g
- GL: 4

173. Mussels in Tomato Sauce

Preparation time: 10 minutes
Cooking time: 3 minutes
Servings: 4
Ingredients:
- 2 tomatoes, seeded and chopped finely
- 2 lb mussels, scrubbed and de-bearded
- 1 cup low-sodium chicken broth
- 1 tbsp fresh lemon juice
- 2 garlic cloves, minced

Directions:
1. In the pot of Instant Pot, place tomatoes, garlic, wine, and bay leaf and stir to combine.
2. Arrange the mussels on top.

3. Close the lid and place the pressure valve in the "Seal" position.
4. Press "Manual" and cook under "High Pressure" for about 3 minutes.
5. Press "Cancel" and carefully allow a "Quick" release.
6. Open the lid and serve hot.

Nutrition:
- Calories: 213
- Fats: 25.2 g
- Carbs: 11 g
- Sugar: 1 g
- Protein: 28.2 g
- Sodium: 670 mg

174. Citrus Salmon

Preparation time: 10 minutes
Cooking time: 7 minutes
Servings: 4
Ingredients:
- 4 (4 oz) salmon fillets
- 1 cup low-sodium chicken broth
- 1 tsp fresh ginger, minced
- 2 tsp fresh orange zest, grated finely
- 3 tbsp fresh orange juice
- 1 tbsp olive oil
- Ground black pepper, as required

Directions:
1. In an Instant Pot, add all ingredients and mix.
2. Close the lid and place the pressure valve in the "Seal" position.
3. Press "Manual" and cook under "High Pressure" for about 7 minutes.
4. Press "Cancel" and allow a "Natural" release.
5. Open the lid and serve the salmon fillets with the topping of cooking sauce.

Nutrition:
- Calories: 190
- Fats: 10.5 g
- Carbs: 1.8 g
- Sugar: 1 g
- Protein: 22 g
- Sodium: 68 mg

175. Herbed Salmon

Preparation time: 10 minutes
Cooking time: 3 minutes
Servings: 4
Ingredients:
- 4 (4 oz) salmon fillets
- ¼ cup olive oil
- 2 tbsp fresh lemon juice
- 1 garlic clove, minced
- ¼ tsp dried oregano
- Salt and ground black pepper, as required
- 4 fresh rosemary sprigs
- 4 lemon slices

Directions:
1. For the dressing: In a large bowl, add oil, lemon juice, garlic, oregano, salt, and black pepper and beat until well co combined.
2. Arrange a steamer trivet in the Instant Pot and pour 1 ½ cups of water into the Instant Pot.
3. Place the salmon fillets on top of the trivet in a single layer and top with dressing
4. Arrange 1 rosemary sprig and 1 lemon slice over each fillet.
5. Close the lid and place the pressure valve in the "Seal" position.
6. Press "Steam" and just use the default time of 3 minutes.
7. Press "Cancel" and carefully allow a "Quick" release.
8. Open the lid and serve hot.

Nutrition:
- Calories: 262
- Fats: 17 g
- Carbs: 0.7 g
- Sugar: 0.2 g
- Protein: 22.1 g
- Sodium: 91 mg

176. Salmon in Green Sauce

Preparation time: 10 minutes
Cooking time: 12 minutes
Servings: 4
Ingredients:
- 4 (6 oz) salmon fillets

- 1 avocado, peeled, pitted, and chopped
- ½ cup fresh basil, chopped
- 3 garlic cloves, chopped
- 1 tbsp fresh lemon zest, grated finely

Directions:
1. Grease a large piece of foil.
2. In a large bowl, add all ingredients except salmon and water, and with a fork, mash completely.
3. Place fillets in the center of the foil and top with the avocado mixture evenly.
4. Fold the foil around fillets to seal them.
5. Arrange a steamer trivet in the Instant Pot and pour ½ cup of water.
6. Place the foil packet on top of the trivet.
7. Close the lid and place the pressure valve in the "Seal" position.
8. Press "Manual" and cook under "High Pressure" for about minutes.
9. Meanwhile, preheat the oven to the broiler.
10. Press "Cancel" and allow a "Natural" release.
11. Open the lid and transfer the salmon fillets onto a broiler pan.
12. Broil for about 3–4 minutes.
13. Serve warm.

Nutrition:
- Calories: 333 Fats: 20.3 g
- Carbs: 5.5 g Sugar: 0.4 g
- Protein: 34.2 g
- Sodium: 79 mg

177. Braised Shrimp

Preparation time: 10 minutes
Cooking time: 4 minutes
Servings: 4
Ingredients:
- 1 lb frozen large shrimp, peeled and deveined
- 2 shallots, chopped
- ¾ cup low-sodium chicken broth
- 2 tbsp fresh lemon juice
- 2 tbsp olive oil
- 1 tbsp garlic, crushed
- Ground black pepper, as required

Directions:
1. In the Instant Pot, place oil and press "Sauté." Now add the shallots and cook for about 2 minutes.
2. Add the garlic and cook for about 1 minute.
3. Press "Cancel" and stir in the shrimp, broth, lemon juice, and black pepper.
4. Close the lid and place the pressure valve in the "Seal" position.
5. Press "Manual" and cook under "High Pressure" for about 1 minute.
6. Press "Cancel" and carefully allow a "Quick" release.
7. Open the lid and serve hot.

Nutrition:
- Calories: 209
- Fats: 9 g
- Carbs: 4.3 g
- Sugar: 0.2 g
- Protein: 26.6 g
- Sodium: 293 mg

178. Shrimp Coconut Curry

Preparation time: 10 minutes
Cooking time: 20 minutes
Servings: 2
Ingredients:
- ½ lb cooked shrimp
- 1 thinly sliced onion
- 1 cup coconut yogurt
- 3 tbsp curry paste
- 1 tbsp oil or ghee

Directions:
1. Set the Instant Pot to sauté and add the onion, oil, and curry paste.
2. When the onion is soft, add the remaining ingredients and seal.
3. Cook on "Stew" for 20 minutes.
4. Release the pressure naturally.

Nutrition:
- Calories: 380 Carbs: 13 g
- Sugar: 4 g
- Fat: 22 g
- Protein: 40 g
- GL: 14

179. Trout Bake

Preparation time: 10 minutes
Cooking time: 35 minutes
Servings: 2
Ingredients:
- 1lb trout fillets, boneless
- 1lb chopped winter vegetables
- 1 cup low-sodium fish broth
- 1tbsp mixed herbs
- Sea salt as desired

Directions:
1. Mix all the ingredients except the broth in a foil pouch.
2. Place the pouch in the steamer basket in your Instant Pot.
3. Pour the broth into the Instant Pot.
4. Cook on Steam for 35 minutes.
5. Release the pressure naturally.

Nutrition:
- Calories: 310
- Carbs: 14 g
- Sugar: 2 g
- Fat: 12 g
- Protein: 40 g
- GL: 5

180. Sardine Curry

Preparation time: 10 minutes
Cooking time: 35 minutes
Servings: 2
Ingredients:
- 5 tins of sardines in tomato
- 1lb chopped vegetables
- 1 cup low-sodium fish broth
- 3tbsp curry paste

Directions:
1. Mix all the ingredients in your Instant Pot.
2. Cook on "Stew" for 35 minutes.
3. Release the pressure naturally.

Nutrition:
- Calories: 320
- Carbs: 8 g
- Sugar: 2 g
- Fat: 16 g
- Protein: 24 g GL: 3

181. Swordfish Steak

Preparation time: 10 minutes
Cooking time: 35 minutes
Servings: 2
Ingredients:
- 1lb swordfish steak, whole
- 1lb chopped Mediterranean vegetables
- 1 cup low-sodium fish broth
- 2tbsp soy sauce

Directions:
1. Mix all the ingredients except the broth in a foil pouch.
2. Place the pouch in the steamer basket for your Instant Pot.
3. Pour the broth into the Instant Pot. Lower the steamer basket into the Instant Pot.
4. Cook on "Steam" for 35 minutes.
5. Release the pressure naturally.

Nutrition:
- Calories: 270 Carbs: 5 g
- Sugar: 1 g Fat: 10 g
- Protein: 48 g
- GL: 1

182. Lemon Sole

Preparation time: 10 minutes
Cooking time: 5 minutes
Servings: 2
Ingredients:
- 1lb sole fillets, boned and skinned
- 1 cup low-sodium fish broth
- 2 shredded sweet onions
- Juice of ½ lemon
- 2tbsp dried cilantro

Directions:
1. Mix all the ingredients in your Instant Pot.
2. Cook on stew for 5 minutes.
3. Release the pressure naturally.

Nutrition:
- Calories: 230
- Carbs: 8 g
- Sugar: 1 g
- Fat: 6 g
- Protein: 46 g
- GL: 1

183. Grilled Tuna Steaks

Preparation time: 5 minutes
Cooking time: 10 minutes
Servings: 6
Ingredients:
- 6 (6 oz) tuna steaks
- 3 tbsp fresh basil, diced

From the store cupboard:
- 4 ½tsp olive oil
- ¾ tsp salt
- ¼ tsp pepper
- Nonstick cooking spray

Directions:
1. Heat grill to medium heat. Spray rack with cooking spray.
2. Drizzle both sides of the tuna with oil. Sprinkle with basil, salt, and pepper.
3. Place on grill and cook 5 minutes per side, tuna should be slightly pink in the center. Serve.

Nutrition:
- Calories: 343
- Total carbs: 0 g
- Protein: 51 g
- Fat: 14 g
- Sugar: 0 g Fiber: 0 g

184. Red Clam Sauce and Pasta

Preparation time: 10 minutes
Cooking time: 3 hours
Servings: 4
Ingredients:
- 1 onion, diced
- ¼ cup fresh parsley, diced

From the store cupboard:
- 2 (6 ½oz) cans of clams, chopped, undrained
- 14 ½oz tomatoes, diced, undrained
- 6 oz tomato paste
- 2 garlic cloves, diced
- 1 bay leaf
- 1 tbsp sunflower oil
- 1 tsp Splenda
- 1 tsp basil
- ½tsp thyme
- ½homemade pasta, cook and drain

Directions:
1. Heat oil in a small skillet over med-high heat. Add onion and cook until tender, add garlic and cook 1 minute more. Transfer to the crockpot.
2. Add remaining ingredients, except pasta, cover, and cook on low for 3–4 hours.
3. Discard bay leaf and serve over cooked pasta.

Nutrition:
- Calories: 223 Total carbs: 32 g
- Net carbs: 27 g Protein: 12 g
- Fat: 6 g Sugar: 15 g Fiber: 5 g

185. Salmon Milano

Preparation time: 10 minutes
Cooking time: 20 minutes
Servings: 6
Ingredients:
- 2 ½lb salmon filet
- 2 tomatoes, sliced
- ½cup margarine

From the store cupboard:
- ½cup basil pesto

Directions:
1. Heat the oven to 400°F. Line a 9x15-inch baking sheet with foil, making sure it covers the sides. Place another large piece of foil onto the baking sheet and place the salmon filet on top of it.
2. Place the pesto and margarine in a blender or food processor and pulse until smooth. Spread evenly over salmon. Place tomato slices on top.
3. Wrap the foil around the salmon, tenting around the top to prevent foil from touching the salmon as much as possible. Bake 15–25 minutes, or salmon flakes easily with a fork. Serve.

Nutrition:
- Calories: 444
- Total carbs: 2 g
- Protein: 55 g
- Fat: 24 g
- Sugar: 1 g
- Fiber: 0 g

186. Shrimp and Artichoke Skillet

Preparation time: 5 minutes
Cooking time: 10 minutes
Servings: 4
Ingredients:
- 1 ½ cup shrimp, peel and devein
- 2 shallots, diced
- 1 tbsp margarine

From the store cupboard:
- 2 (12 oz) jars of artichoke hearts, drain and rinse
- 2 cups white wine
- 2 garlic cloves, diced fine

Directions:
1. Melt margarine in a large skillet over med-high heat. Add shallot and garlic and cook until they start to brown, stirring frequently.
2. Add artichokes and cook for 5 minutes. Reduce heat and add wine. Cook for 3 minutes, stirring occasionally.
3. Add the shrimp and cook just until they turn pink. Serve.

Nutrition:
- Calories: 487
- Total carbs: 26 g
- Net carbs: 17 g
- Protein: 64 g
- Fat: 5 g
- Sugar: 3 g
- Fiber: 9 g

187. Tuna Carbonara

Preparation time: 5 minutes
Cooking time: 25 minutes
Servings: 4
Ingredients:
- ½ lb tuna fillet, cut into pieces
- 2 eggs
- 4 tbsp fresh parsley, diced

From the store cupboard:
- ½ homemade pasta, cook and drain
- ½ cup reduced-fat Parmesan cheese
- 2 garlic cloves, peeled
- 2 tbsp extra-virgin olive oil
- Salt and pepper, to taste

Directions:
1. In a small bowl, beat the eggs, Parmesan, and a dash of pepper.
2. Heat the oil in a large skillet over med-high heat. Add garlic and cook until browned. Add the tuna and cook for 2–3 minutes, or until the tuna is almost cooked through. Discard the garlic.
3. Add the pasta and reduce the heat. Stir in egg mixture and cook, stirring constantly, for about 2 minutes. If the sauce is too thick, thin with water, a little bit at a time until it has a creamy texture.
4. Salt and pepper to taste and serve garnished with parsley.

Nutrition:
- Calories: 409
- Total carbs: 7 g
- Net carbs: 6 g
- Protein: 25 g
- Fat: 30 g
- Sugar: 3 g
- Fiber: 1 g

188. Mediterranean Fish Fillets

Preparation time: 10 minutes
Cooking time: 3 minutes
Servings: 4
Ingredients:
- 4 cod fillets
- 1 lb grape tomatoes, halved
- 1 cup olives, pitted and sliced
- 2 tbsp capers
- 1 tsp dried thyme
- 2 tbsp olive oil
- 1 tsp garlic, minced
- Pepper
- Salt

Directions:
1. Pour 1 cup of water into the Instant Pot then place the steamer rack in the pot.
2. Spray heat-safe baking dish with cooking spray.
3. Add half grape tomatoes into the dish and season with pepper and salt.

4. Arrange fish fillets on top of cherry tomatoes. Drizzle with oil and season with garlic, thyme, capers, pepper, and salt.
5. Spread olives and remaining grape tomatoes on top of fish fillets.
6. Place dish on top of steamer rack in the pot.
7. Seal the pot with a lid and select manual and cook on high for 3 minutes.
8. Once done, release pressure using quick release. Remove lid.
9. Serve and enjoy.

Nutrition:
- Calories: 212
- Fat: 11.9 g
- Carbs: 7.1 g
- Sugar: 3 g
- Protein: 21.4 g
- Cholesterol: 55 mg

189. Alaskan Crab Omelette

Preparation time: 10 minutes
Cooking time: 1 minute
Servings: 1
Ingredients:
- ¼ cup cooked Alaskan crab meat
- 2 snow peas, trimmed, thinly sliced diagonally
- ½ shallot, finely sliced
- ½ chili, thinly sliced at an angle
- 1 tsp soy sauce
- A few drops of sesame oil
- 1 egg
- 1 tsp vegetable oil

Directions:
1. Start by tossing crab meat with snow peas, shallot, and chili in a small bowl.
2. Whisk egg with soy sauce and a tsp cold water in another bowl.
3. Stir in sesame oil and pepper then mix well.
4. Spray a non-stick skillet and place it over medium-high heat.
5. Pour this egg mixture into the skillet and spread it into a thin layer.
6. Cook for 30 seconds then spread the crab mixture over the egg

7. Fold the egg omelet over the crab mixture.
8. Serve warm.

Nutrition:
- Calories: 317 Total fat: 31.1 g
- Saturated fat: 7.6 g Cholesterol: 77 mg
- Sodium: 112 mg Total carbs: 9.7 g
- Fiber: 0 g Sugar: 7.4 g Protein: 1.4 g

190. Fish Pie

Preparation time: 10 minutes
Cooking time: 50 minutes
Servings: 4
Ingredients:
- 1 tbsp vegetable oil
- 1 large carrot, diced
- 2 medium leeks, thinly sliced
- 4 cups almond milk
- 1 ¼ cup thickened cream
- 1 medium onion, quartered and studded with 6 cloves
- 2.2 lb white fish fillets
- ¼ cup butter
- 3 tbsp almond flour
- ½ nutmeg, grated
- ½ cup chopped parsley
- Salt and pepper, to taste

Directions:
1. Take a non-stick pan and grease it with cooking oil.
2. Stir in carrots and leek then sauté for 3 minutes until soft.
3. Pour milk and cream into a large pot along with the onion studded with cloves.
4. Add fish to this mixture and let it simmer until the fish turns opaque.

5. Remove the fish and flake it into small pieces.
6. Spread the fish out on a baking dish along with leeks and carrots.
7. Strain the milk mixture then pour it into a saucepan.
8. Whisk butter with flour and pour it into the saucepan. Stir and cook until the sauce thickens.
9. Add salt, parsley, black pepper, and nutmeg for seasoning Pour this cream sauce over the fish and veggies.
10. Bake them for approximately 45 minutes at 320°F. Serve warm with a green leaf salad.

Nutrition:
- Calories: 317 Total fat: 31.1 g
- Saturated fat: 7.6 g Cholesterol: 77 mg
- Sodium: 112 mg Total carbs: 9.7 g
- Fiber: 0 g Sugar: 7.4 g Protein: 1.4 g

191. BBQ Prawn Gremolata

Preparation time: 10 minutes
Cooking time: 10 minutes
Servings: 8
Ingredients:
- Olive oil, to brush
- 8 green prawns, butterflied

For the gremolata:
- 2 garlic cloves, chopped
- 2 pieces lemon peel, chopped
- 1 tbsp parsley, chopped

Directions:
1. Start by cutting the heads of the prawns then remove the veins.
2. Thread the prawns onto wooden skewers then brush them with olive oil.
3. Preheat the grill and grill the prawns for 2 minutes per side.
4. Now, toss all the ingredients for the gremolata in a separate bowl.
5. Serve the prawn skewers with gremolata on top.
6. Serve.

Nutrition:
- Calories: 278
- Total fat: 6.3 g
- Saturated fat: 5.3 g
- Cholesterol: 141 mg
- Sodium: 603 mg
- Total carbs: 13.6 g
- Fiber: 2.5 g
- Sugar: 3.9 g
- Protein: 26.5 g

192. White Fish Kebabs

Preparation time: 10 minutes
Cooking time: 10 minutes
Servings: 4
Ingredients:
- 2.2 lb firm white fish, diced
- ¼ cup olive oil
- 1 lemon, juiced
- 1 tsp sea salt
- 1 large garlic clove, minced
- 1 tsp cumin ground
- 1 tsp smoked paprika
- ½ tsp turmeric
- ½ tsp cayenne pepper
- 3 tbsp coriander, chopped

Directions:
1. Dice the fish into cubes and set them aside.

2. Whisk lemon juice, oil, herbs, and spices in a small bowl.
3. Pour this mixture over the fish cubes and mix well to coat them.
4. Thread these cubes onto wooden skewers.
5. Grill these skewers for 2 minutes per side on a preheated grill.
6. Serve warm.

Nutrition:
- Calories: 577
- Total fat: 59.4 g
- Saturated fat: 37.4 g
- Cholesterol: 176 mg
- Sodium: 985 mg
- Total carbs: 2.2 g
- Fiber: 0.1 g
- Sugar: 0.1 g
- Protein: 10.9 g

193. Tuna Nicoise

Preparation time: 10 minutes
Cooking time: 0 minutes
Servings: 4
Ingredients:
- 1 can of John West tuna lemon and black pepper
- 1 cup baby spinach salad mix
- 3 green olives
- 3 cherry tomatoes, halved
- ¼ spring onion, sliced
- 1 anchovy, drained and diced
- 1 soft boiled egg
- Capers, to serve
- Cracked pepper, to taste
- 1 squeeze of lemon juice
- Feta cheese, to taste

Directions:
1. Slice the soft-boiled egg into slices.
2. Toss all the veggies in a large salad bowl.
3. Drain tuna and add it to the salad.
4. Top the salad with egg slices.
5. Garnish with Feta cheese
6. Serve fresh.

Nutrition:
- Calories: 242
- Total fat: 16.7 g
- Saturated fat: 11.5 g
- Cholesterol: 177 mg
- Sodium: 381 mg
- Total carbs: 4.1 g
- Fiber: 0.4 g
- Sugar: 0.2 g
- Protein: 13.6 g

194. Tuna-Stuffed Tomatoes

Preparation time: 10 minutes
Cooking time: 0 minutes
Servings: 1
Ingredients:
- 1 large tomato, cored
- 1 can of tuna
- 5 capers, preferably small ones
- 3 green olives, pitted and sliced
- ½ shallot, thinly sliced
- 1 squeeze of lemon juice
- Black pepper, to taste
- 1 slice of sourdough bread

Directions:
1. Chop the top of the tomato off and remove its core.
2. Whisk all the ingredients in a suitable bowl and mix well.

3. Scoop tuna mixture into the cored tomato.
4. Serve fresh.

Nutrition:
- Calories: 322 Total fat: 11.8 g
- Saturated fat: 6.3 g Cholesterol: 78 mg
- Sodium: 526 mg Total carbs: 6.7 g
- Fiber: 2.1 g Sugar: 6.7 g
- Protein: 12.2 g

195. Smoked Salmon Salad

Preparation time: 10 minutes
Cooking time: 0 minutes
Servings: 4
Ingredients:
- 5 ½ oz smoked salmon, skin removed and crumbled
- 1 handful of baby spinach leaves
- 1 handful baby rocket
- 6 cherry tomatoes, halved
- 1 shallot, sliced
- ¼ fennel, sliced
- 2 stalks of coriander leaves
- 1 squeeze of lemon juice
- 1 tsp olive oil, drizzled

Directions:
1. Start by throwing all the salad ingredients in a salad bowl.
2. Drizzle salt, black pepper, olive oil, and lemon juice on top. Serve.

Nutrition:
- Calories: 224
- Total fat: 19 g
- Saturated fat: 9.3 g
- Cholesterol: 53 mg
- Sodium: 869 mg Total carbs: 4.6 g
- Fiber: 0.1 g Sugar: 1.1 g Protein: 9.1 g

196. Baked Salmon With Zucchini Noodles

Preparation time: 10 minutes
Cooking time: 15 minutes
Servings: 2
Ingredients:
- 1 tsp dill
- 2 salmon fillets
- 2 tsp olive oil
- 1 tsp black sesame seeds
- 2 zucchini, spiralized into noodles
- 1 tsp sesame seeds, toasted
- ½ tsp oil - 8 cherry tomatoes, halved

For the sauce:
- ¼ cup soy sauce - 1 tbsp rice vinegar
- 1 tbsp sesame oil
- ½ tsp freshly grated ginger
- Toasted sesame seeds, for garnish

Directions:
1. Start by seasoning the salmon with oil, salt, black pepper, and dill.
2. Place the salmon on a baking sheet and spread the tomatoes around it.
3. Bake the fish for approximately 15 minutes at 300°F. Whisk soy sauce, sesame oil, ginger, and rice vinegar in a small bowl. Drizzle this sauce over the baked fish. Serve the salmon over zucchini noodles with baked tomatoes. Garnish with sesame seeds.
4. Serve.

Nutrition:
- Calories: 248 Total fat: 21.3 g
- Saturated fat: 11.5 g Cholesterol: 74 mg
- Sodium: 152 mg Total carbs: 2.2 g
- Fiber: 1.2 g Sugar: 1.1 g
- Protein: 13.8 g

197. Keralan Fish

Preparation time: 10 minutes
Cooking time: 13 minutes
Servings: 4
Ingredients:
- 1 tbsp vegetable oil
- 1 tsp mustard seeds
- 15 curry leaves
- 2 shallots, finely chopped
- 2 garlic cloves, thinly sliced
- 1 (2 ½ cm) piece ginger, thinly sliced
- 1 bird eye chili, chopped
- 1 heaping tsp of turmeric
- ½ tsp hot chili powder
- Splash of water
- 10 ½ oz firm white fish fillets, diced
- 1 cup low-fat coconut milk
- 3 ½ oz tinned chopped tomatoes
- 18 snow peas, trimmed
- Salt and black pepper, to taste
- 1 tbsp chopped coriander
- Zucchini noodles (optional)

Directions:
1. First, pour the oil into a wok and heat it until shimmering.
2. Stir in mustard and curry leaves then cook for 30 seconds.
3. Toss in chopped chili, shallots, garlic, and ginger.
4. Stir cook for 2 minutes until it releases the aroma.
5. Whisk chili powder and turmeric with a splash of water to make a paste.
6. Add this chili mixture to the wok and mix well.
7. Stir in fish, tomato, coconut milk, salt, and black pepper.
8. Cook it to a boil then stir in snow peas.
9. Let it cook for 10 minutes on a simmer.
10. Garnish with coriander then serve.

Nutrition:
- Calories: 374 Total fat: 26.9 g
- Saturated fat: 6.9 g Cholesterol: 133 mg
- Sodium: 393 mg Total carbs: 14.3 g
- Fiber: 4.7 g Sugar: 3.3 g
- Protein: 24 g Carbs: 16 g

198. Shrimp With Spinach

Preparation time: 15 minutes
Cooking time: 10 minutes
Servings: 4
Ingredients:
- 1 ½ cup fresh baby spinach
- 1 ½ tsp granulated garlic powder
- 20 frozen shrimp, thawed
- 1 tsp ground black pepper
- 1 tbsp olive oil, or as needed

Directions:
1. Place spinach in a large bowl; sprinkle with garlic powder, and toss. Place shrimp in a bowl; sprinkle with black pepper, and toss.
2. Heat oil in a skillet over medium-high heat. Add shrimp; cook and stir until bright pink on the outside and the meat is opaque about 5 minutes. Add spinach, cook, and stir until just wilted about 1 minute.

Nutrition:
- Calories: 240
- Fat: 12.3 g
- Carbs: 7.7 g
- Fiber: 3.1 g
- Sugar: 1.7 g
- Protein: 28.2 g

199. Scallops With Broccoli

Preparation time: 15 minutes
Cooking time: 9 minutes
Servings: 2
Ingredients:
- 1 tbsp olive oil
- 1 cup broccoli, cut into small pieces
- 1 garlic clove, crushed
- ½ lb scallops
- 1 tsp fresh lemon juice
- Salt, as required

Directions:
1. In a large non-stick pan, heat oil over medium heat and cook the broccoli and garlic for about 3–4 minutes, stirring occasionally.

2. Add in the scallops and cook for about 3–4 minutes, flipping occasionally.
3. Stir in the lemon juice and salt and remove from the heat.
4. Serve hot.

Nutrition:
- Calories: 178
- Fat: 8 g
- Carbs: 6.3 g
- Fiber: 1.2 g
- Sugar: 0.8 g
- Protein: 20.4 g

200. Salmon With Veggies

Preparation time: 15 minutes
Cooking time: 6 minutes
Servings: 4
Ingredients:
- 1 lb skin-on salmon fillets
- Salt and ground black pepper, as required
- 1 fresh parsley sprig
- 1 fresh dill sprig
- 3 tsp coconut oil, melted and divided
- ½ lemon, sliced thinly
- 1 carrot, peeled and julienned
- 1 zucchini, peeled and julienned
- 1 red bell pepper, seeded and julienned

Directions:
1. The salmon fillets are similarly seasoned with salt and black pepper.
2. Arrange a steamer trivet and put herb sprigs and 1 cup of water at the bottom of the Instant Pot.
3. Place the salmon fillets, skin side down, on top of the trivet.
4. Drizzle salmon fillets with 2 tsp coconut oil and top with lemon slices.
5. Secure the lid and turn to the "Seal" position.
6. Choose "Steam" and use the default time of 3 minutes only.
7. Press "Cancel" and do a "Natural" release.
8. Meanwhile, for the sauce: in a bowl, add the remaining ingredients and mix until well combined.
9. Remove the lid and transfer the salmon fillets onto a platter.
10. Remove the steamer trivet, herbs, and cooking water from the pot. With paper towels, pat dries the pot.
11. Place the remaining coconut oil in the Instant Pot and select "Sauté." Then add the veggies and cook for about 2–3 minutes.
12. Press "Cancel" and transfer the veggies onto a platter with salmon.

Nutrition:
- Calories: 204 Fat: 10.6 g
- Protein: 23.1 g Carbs: 5.7 g
- Net carbs: 4.3 g Fiber: 1.4 g

201. Shrimp and Endives

Preparation time: 5 minutes
Cooking time: 12 minutes
Servings: 2
Ingredients:
- 1 lb shrimp, peeled and deveined
- 2 tbsp avocado oil
- 2 spring onions, chopped
- 2 endives, shredded
- 1 tbsp balsamic vinegar
- 1 tbsp chives, minced
- A pinch of sea salt and black pepper

Directions:
1. Over medium-high heat, heat a pan with the oil, add the spring onions, endives, and chives, and stir and cook for 4 minutes.
2. Add the shrimp and remaining ingredients, toss, cook for 8 more minutes over medium heat, divide into bowls, and serve.

Nutrition:
- Calories: 378 Fat: 2 g
- Carbs: 6 g Protein: 6 g
- Sodium: 290 mg

202. Baked Fish Fillets

Preparation time: 5 minutes
Cooking time: 20 minutes
Servings: 2
Ingredients:
- 2 tbsp butter, melted

- A pinch of ground paprika
- 3 (5 oz) fish fillets
- Pepper to taste
- 1 tbsp lemon juice
- ½ tsp salt

Directions:
1. Ensure that your oven is preheated to 350°F.
2. By greasing it with some fat, prepare a pan for baking.
3. Sprinkle the fillets with salt and pepper and put them in the pan.
4. In a cup, add the butter, paprika, and lemon juice and stir.
5. Brush over the fillets with this mixture.
6. In the oven, put the baking pan and cook the fillets.

Nutrition:
- Calories: 245
- Fat: 12 g
- Carbs: 4 g
- Protein: 32 g
- Sodium: 455 mg

203. Salmon Cakes

Preparation time: 10 minutes
Cooking time: 10 minutes
Servings: 2
Ingredients:
- 2 (14.75 oz each) cans of salmon, drained
- 8 tbsp collagen
- 2 cups shredded Mozzarella cheese
- 1 tsp onion powder
- 4 large pastured egg
- 4 tsp dried dill
- 1 pink sea salt tsp or to taste
- 4 tbsp bacon grease

Directions:
1. Add salmon, collagen, Mozzarella, onion powder, eggs, dill, and salt into a bowl and mix well.
2. Make 8 patties from the mixture.
3. Place a large skillet with bacon grease over a medium-low flame.
4. Place the salmon cakes in the skillet once the fat is well heated and cook until it becomes golden brown on all sides.
5. Take off the pan from heat and let the patties remain in the cooked fat for 5 minutes. Serve.

Nutrition:
- Calories: 204 Fat: 10 g
- Carbs: 5 g
- Protein: 29 g
- Sodium: 643 mg

204. Grilled Split Lobster

Preparation time: 10 minutes
Cooking time: 15 minutes
Servings: 2
Ingredients:
- 4 tbsp olive oil or melted butter
- Kosher salt to taste
- 4 live lobsters (1 ½ lb each)
- Freshly ground pepper to taste
- Melted butter to serve
- Hot sauce like Frank's hot sauce, to serve
- Lemon wedges to serve

Directions:
1. For 15 minutes, put the live lobsters in the freezer.
2. Place them on your cutting board with the belly down on the cutting board. Hold the tail. Split the lobsters in half lengthwise. Start from the point where the tail joins the body and goes up to the head. Flip sides and cut it lengthwise via the tail.
3. Rub melted butter on the cut part immediately after cutting it. Sprinkle salt and pepper over it.
4. Set up your grill and preheat it to high heat for 5–10 minutes. Clean the grill grate and lower the heat to low heat.
5. Place the lobsters on the grill and press the claws on the grill until cooked—grill for 6–8 minutes.
6. Flip sides and cook until it is cooked through and lightly charred.
7. Transfer to a plate. Drizzle melted butter on top and serve.

Nutrition:
- Calories: 433 Fat: 4 g
- Carbs: 26 g Protein: 6 g
- Sodium: 455 mg

205. Fish Bone Broth

Preparation time: 10 minutes
Cooking time: 4 hrs.
Servings: 2
Ingredients:
- 2 lb fish head or carcass
- Salt to taste
- 7–8 quarts water, plus extra to blanch
- 2-inch ginger, sliced
- 2 tbsp lemon juice

Directions:
1. To blanch the fish: Add water and fish heads into a large pot. Place the pot over high heat.
2. Turn the heat off when it boils and discard the water.
3. Place the fish back in the pot. Pour 7–8 quarts of water.
4. Place the pot over high heat. Add ginger, salt, and lemon juice.
5. Reduce the heat as the mixture boils and cover it with a lid.
6. Remove from heat. When it cools down, strain it into a large jar with a wire mesh strainer.
7. Refrigerate for 5–6 days. Unused broth can be frozen.

Nutrition:
- Calories: 254 Fat: 4 g
- Carbs: 26 g
- Protein: 6 g
- Sodium: 455 mg

206. Garlic Butter Shrimp

Preparation time: 10 minutes
Cooking time: 10 minutes
Servings: 2
Ingredients:
- 1 cup unsalted butter, divided
- Kosher salt to taste
- ½ cup chicken stock
- Freshly ground pepper to taste
- ¼ cup chopped fresh parsley leaves
- 3 lb medium shrimp, peeled, deveined
- 2 garlic cloves
- Juice of 2 lemons

Directions:
1. Add 4 tbsp butter into a large skillet and place the skillet over medium-high flame. Once butter melts, stir in salt, shrimp, and pepper and cook for 2–3 minutes. Stir every minute or so. Remove the shrimp with a spoon and place it on a tray.
2. Add garlic into the pot and cook until you get a nice aroma. Pour lemon juice and stock and stir.
3. Lower the heat and cook until the stock falls to half its initial volume until it comes to a boil.
4. Add the rest of the butter, a tbs peach time, and stir until it melts each time.
5. Add shrimp and stir lightly until well coated.
6. Sprinkle parsley on top and serve.

Nutrition:
- Calories: 484
- Fat: 21 g
- Carbs: 4 g
- Protein: 33 g
- Sodium: 370 mg

207. Grilled Shrimp

Preparation time: 10 minutes
Cooking time: 5 minutes
Servings: 2
Ingredients:
For the shrimp seasoning:
- 2 tsp garlic powder
- 2 tsp Italian seasoning
- 2 tsp kosher salt
- ½–1 tsp cayenne pepper

For the grilling:
- 4 tbsp extra-virgin olive oil
- 2 lb shrimp, peeled, deveined
- 2 tbsp fresh lemon juice
- Oil to grease the grill grated

Directions:
1. You can grill the shrimp on a grill or boil it in an oven. Choose whatever method suits you and preheat the grill or oven to high heat.

2. In case you are broiling it in an oven, prepare a baking sheet by lining it with foil and greasing the foil as well, with some fat.
3. Add garlic powder, cayenne pepper, salt, and Italian seasoning into a large bowl and mix well.
4. Add lemon juice and oil and mix well.
5. Stir in the shrimp. Make sure that the shrimp are well coated with the mixture.
6. If using the grill, fix the shrimp on skewers; else, place them on the baking sheet.
7. Grease the grill grates with some oil. Grill the shrimp or broil them in an oven until they turn pink. It should take 180 seconds for each side.

Nutrition:
- Calories: 309
- Fat: 12 g
- Carbs: 8 g
- Protein: 16 g
- Sodium: 340 mg

208. Garlic Ghee Pan-Fried Cod

Preparation time: 5 minutes
Cooking time: 10 minutes
Servings: 2
Ingredients:
- 2 (4.8 oz each) cod fillets
- 3 garlic cloves, peeled, minced
- Salt to taste
- 1 ½ tbsp ghee
- ½ tbsp garlic powder (optional)

Directions:
1. Place a pan over medium-high flame. Add ghee.
2. Once ghee melts, stir in half the garlic and cook for about 6–10 seconds.
3. Add fillets and season with garlic powder and salt.
4. Soon the color of the fish will turn white. This color should be visible for about half the height of the fish.
5. Turn the fish over and cook, adding the remaining garlic.
6. When the entire fillet turns white, remove it from the pan.

Nutrition:
- Calories: 193 Fat: 16 g
- Carbs: 6 g Protein: 21 g
- Sodium: 521 mg

209. Mussel and Potato Stew

Preparation time: 10 minutes
Cooking time: 20 minutes
Servings: 2
Ingredients:
- 1 potato
- 1 broccoli
- 1 tbsp olive oil
- 2 rabe filets
- 2 garlic cloves
- ½ cup water

Directions:
1. Submerge potatoes in cold water in a medium saucepan. Put the salt, and boil. Allow cooling for 15 minutes till soft. Let drain.
2. Boil a saucepan of salted water. Put broccoli rabe, and allow to cook till just soft; it should turn bright green. Drain thoroughly, and slice into 2-inch lengths.
3. In a big, deep skillet, mix garlic, anchovies, and oil. Let cook over high heat for approximately a minute, crushing anchovies. In a skillet, scatter the mussels, and put chopped parsley, broccoli rabe, and potatoes on top. Put half a cup of water, and add salt to season. Place the cover, and allow to cook till mussels are open.

Nutrition:
- Calories: 254 Fat: 9 g
- Carbs: 12 g Protein: 11 g
- Sodium: 326 mg

210. Mustard Salmon With Herbs

Preparation time: 10 minutes
Cooking time: 30 minutes
Servings: 2
Ingredients:
- 1 tbsp mustard

- 1 tbsp mayonnaise
- 1 tbsp ranch dressing
- 1 tbsp Italian dressing
- Garlic powder to taste
- 1 lemon
- 2 salmon fillets

Directions:
1. In a bowl, combine garlic powder, ranch dressing, Italian dressing, mayonnaise, and mustard. Squeeze over the mixture with ½ of the lemon. Cut the leftover lemon halves
2. Put the preheated oven in and cook the fish for 30–45 minutes before the flesh can easily flake with a fork.

Nutrition:
- Calories: 277
- Fat: 11 g
- Carbs: 26 g
- Protein: 18 g
- Sodium: 520 mg

211. Nutty Coconut Fish

Preparation time: 10 minutes
Cooking time: 30 minutes
Servings: 2
Ingredients:
- 1 tbsp mayonnaise
- 1 tbsp mustard
- 1 cup breadcrumbs
- 1 cup shredded coconut
- ¼ cup mixed nuts
- 1 tsp granulated sugar
- 1 tsp salt
- ½ tsp cayenne pepper
- 1 lb white fish fillets

Directions:
1. The oven should be preheated to 190–195°C.
2. Blend brown mustard and mayonnaise in a small bowl. Mix cayenne pepper, salt, sugar, chopped mixed nuts, shredded coconut, and dry breadcrumbs in a medium bowl.
3. Dip fish in mayonnaise mixture, then dip in breadcrumb mixture. In a baking dish, put coated fish fillets.
4. Bake for 20–30 minutes in a preheated oven until the fish flakes easily with a fork.

Nutrition:
- Calories: 180 Fat: 2 g
- Carbs: 12 g
- Protein: 6 g
- Sodium: 426 mg

212. Olive Oil Poached Tuna

Preparation time: 10 minutes
Cooking time: 30 minutes
Servings: 2
Ingredients:
- 2 tuna steaks
- 2 garlic cloves
- ½ tsp thyme
- ¼ tsp pepper flakes
- 1 tbsp olive oil
- Sea salt to taste

Directions:
1. Set aside tuna for 10–15 minutes at room temperature.
2. In a heavy pan, mix red pepper flakes, garlic, and thyme. Pour in olive oil until 1-inch deep. On medium heat, heat for 5–10 minutes until the thyme and garlic sizzle.
3. Put the tuna lightly in the pan of hot oil, then turn the heat to low. Cook steaks for 5–7 minutes while constantly spooning oil on top until the tuna is hot and white. Take off the heat, move the steaks to a baking pan, and then pour hot oil and herbs on top. Let the fish cool down to temperature.
4. Use plastic wrap to tightly cover the baking dish and put the steaks in the refrigerator for 24 hours. Take the tuna out of the oil and top it with sea salt.

Nutrition:
- Calories: 208
- Fat: 21 g
- Carbs: 26 g
- Protein: 36 g
- Sodium: 543 mg

213. One-Pot Tuna Casserole

Preparation time: 10 minutes
Cooking time: 20 minutes
Servings: 2
Ingredients:
- 1 (16 oz) package of egg noodles
- 1 (10 oz) package of frozen green peas, thawed
- ¼ cup butter
- 1 (10.75 oz) can condense cream of mushroom soup
- 1 (5 oz) can tuna, drained
- ¼ cup milk
- 1 cup shredded Cheddar cheese

Directions:
1. Boil a big pot with lightly salted water. Cook pasta in boiling water, till "al dente"; add peas at 3 final minutes of cooking and drain.
2. Melt butter overheats in the same pot. Add Cheddar cheese, milk, tuna, and mushroom soup; mix till mixture is smooth and cheese melts. Mix peas and pasta in till evenly coated.

Nutrition:
- Calories: 398
- Fat: 16 g
- Carbs: 12 g
- Protein: 33 g
- Sodium: 455 mg

214. Bacon-Wrapped Salmon

Preparation time: 10 minutes
Cooking time: 30 minutes
Servings: 2
Ingredients:
- 4 (4 oz) skin-on salmon fillets
- 1 tsp garlic powder
- 1 tsp dried dill weed
- Salt and pepper to taste
- ½ lb bacon, cut in half
- Olive oil to grease

Directions:
1. Preheat the oven to 375°F. Generously brush olive oil on a cookie sheet.
2. Arrange salmon fillets skin-down on the cookie sheet. Season fillets with dill, salt, pepper, and garlic powder. Cover the fillets completely with bacon strips. Arrange the bacon, so they don't overlap each other.
3. Bake in the oven for 20–23 minutes, just until the fish's center is not translucent. To broil, change the oven setting and cook for another 1–2 minutes until the bacon becomes crispy.

Nutrition:
- Calories: 307
- Fat: 23 g
- Carbs: 8 g
- Protein: 16 g
- Sodium: 590 mg

215. Bagna Cauda

Preparation time: 10 minutes
Cooking time: 30 minutes
Servings: 2
Ingredients:
- ½ cup butter
- 10 garlic cloves, minced
- 3 pieces of anchovy fillets
- ¼ cup heavy cream

Directions:
1. Mix in garlic and cook until softened. Lower the heat to low. Mix in heavy cream and anchovy fillets.
2. Bring the mixture back to medium heat, stirring from time to time until bubbling Serve hot.

Nutrition:
- Calories: 670 Fat: 34 g
- Carbs: 26 g Protein: 28 g
- Sodium: 430 mg

216. Salmon Tikka

Preparation time: 10 minutes
Cooking time: 30 minutes
Servings: 2
Ingredients:
- Cayenne pepper to taste
- Turmeric to taste

- Salt to taste
- 1 salmon fillets
- 1 tbsp cornstarch
- 1 tbsp oil

Directions:
1. In a bowl, combine salt, turmeric, and cayenne pepper. Put salmon into the bowl; toss until evenly coated with seasoning mixture. Let fish rest for 15 minutes.
2. In a container, heat oil over medium heat. Meanwhile, sprinkle cornstarch all over salmon; toss to coat evenly.
3. Cook salmon in hot oil, about 1 minute on each side, until golden brown.

Nutrition:
- Calories: 254
- Fat: 24 g
- Carbs: 12 g
- Protein: 26 g
- Sodium: 765 mg

217. Almond and Parmesan Crusted Tilapia

Preparation time: 10 minutes
Cooking time: 30 minutes
Servings: 2
Ingredients:
- 1 tsp olive oil, or as needed
- 3 garlic cloves, minced
- ½ cup grated Parmesan cheese
- 2 tbsp almonds, crushed
- 1 tbsp mayonnaise
- ¼ cup breadcrumbs
- 2 tbsp fresh lemon juice
- ¼ tsp dried basil
- ¼ tsp ground black pepper
- ⅛ tsp onion powder
- ⅛ tsp celery salt
- 1 lb tilapia fillets

Directions:
1. Put the rack 6-inch away from the heat source and start preheating the oven's broiler. Use aluminum foil to line a broiling tray or use olive oil cooking spray to coat.
2. Heat olive oil in a frying container over medium heat, stir garlic while cooking for 3–5 minutes, or aromatic.
3. In a bowl, combine celery salt, onion powder, black pepper, basil, seafood seasoning, lemon juice, bread crumbs, mayonnaise, almonds, buttery spreads, garlic, and Parmesan cheese.
4. Set the tilapia fillets in a layer on top of the prepared pan, and use aluminum foil to cover it.
5. Put the container in the preheated oven and start boiling for about 2–3 minutes. Flip the fillets, cover the pan with aluminum foil, and restart the broiling for 2–3 more minutes. Remove aluminum foil and put the Parmesan cheese mixture on top to cover the fish. Broil in the oven for 2 more minutes until the topping gets browned; fish can be shredded easily with a fork.

Nutrition:
- Calories: 498
- Fat: 32 g
- Carbs: 26 g
- Protein: 8 g
- Sodium: 634 mg

218. Golden Turmeric Fish

Preparation time: 20 minutes
Cooking time: 30 minutes
Servings: 4
Ingredients:
- 2 tbsp unrefined coconut oil
- 2 tbsp fresh lime juice
- 1 tbsp grated fresh ginger
- 1 tsp ground coriander
- ½ tsp ground turmeric
- ⅛ tsp cayenne pepper
- 4 5 oz red snapper fish fillets
- ½ tsp salt
- ¼ tsp freshly ground black pepper
- Purchased mango chutney to serve

Directions:
1. Broiler with fire. In a shallow dish, mix the coconut oil, lime juice, ginger, coriander, turmeric, and cayenne pepper.

I was using black pepper and salt to season the cod. Add a paste of coconut oil to the skinless sides of the cod.
2. Place the fish in the broiler's greased pan. Broil for 10 minutes or before fish flakes easily, at 4-inch. Serve served with cilantro and chutney.

Tips: Coconut oil is strong, much like shortening, and liquefies when it's humid. If you stir it into the spices to make the rub, it does not matter whether it is solid or liquid.

Nutrition:
- Calories: 268
- Total fat: 9 g
- Cholesterol: 52 mg
- Sodium: 382 mg
- Potassium: 630 mg
- Carbs: 16 g
- Fiber: 0 g
- Sugar: 9 g
- Protein: 29 g
- Trans fatty acid: 0 g
- Thiamin: 0 mg
- Riboflavin: 0 mg
- Niacin equivalents: 0 mg
- Folate: 9 mcg
- Calcium: 51 mg
- Iron: 0 mg

CHAPTER 9:

Salad

The following are useful, easy, and delicious salad recipes that can help in your battle against type 2 diabetes.

219. Thai Quinoa Salad

Preparation time: 10 minutes
Cooking time: 0 minutes
Servings: 1–2
Ingredients:
For the dressing:
- 1 tbsp sesame seed
- 1 tsp chopped garlic
- 1 tsp lemon, fresh juice
- 3 tsp apple cider vinegar
- 2 tsp tamari, gluten-free.
- ¼ cup tahini (sesame butter)
- 1 pitted date
- ½ tsp salt
- ½ tsp toasted sesame oil

For the salad:
- 1 cup quinoa, steamed
- 1 big handful of arugula
- 1 tomato cut into pieces
- ¼ of 1 red onion, diced

Directions:
1. Add the following to a small blender: ¼ cup + 2 tbsp filtered water and the rest of the ingredients. Blend.
2. Steam 1 cup of quinoa in a steamer or a rice pan, then set aside.
3. Combine the quinoa, the arugula, the tomatoes sliced, the red onion diced on a serving plate or bowl, add the Thai dressing and serve with a spoon.

Nutrition:
- Calories: 100
- Carbs: 12 g

220. Green Goddess Bowl and Avocado Cumin Dressing

Preparation time: 10 minutes
Cooking time: 0 minutes
Servings: 1–2
Ingredients:
For the dressing of avocado cumin:
- 1 avocado
- 1 tbsp cumin powder
- 2 limes, freshly squeezed
- 1 cup filtered water
- ¼ tsp sea salt
- 1 tbsp extra-virgin olive oil
- Cayenne pepper dash
- Optional: ¼ tsp smoked pepper

For the tahini lemon dressing:
- ¼ cup of tahini (sesame butter)
- ½ cup of filtered water (more if you want thinner, less thick)
- ½ lemon, freshly squeezed
- 1 clove of minced garlic
- ¾ tsp sea salt (Celtic Gray, Himalayan, Redmond Real Salt)
- 1 tbsp olive extra-virgin olive oil
- Black pepper taste

For the salad:
- 3 cups kale, chopped
- ½ cup broccoli flowers, chopped
- ½ zucchini (make spiral noodles)
- ½ cup kelp noodles, soaked and drained
- ⅓ cup cherry tomatoes halved
- 2 tsp hemp seeds

Directions:
1. Gently steam the kale and the broccoli (flash the steam for 4 minutes), and set them aside.
2. Mix the zucchini noodles and kelp noodles and toss with a generous portion of the smoked avocado cumin dressing Add the cherry tomatoes and stir again.
3. Place the steamed kale and broccoli and drizzle with the lemon tahini dressing top the kale and the broccoli with the noodles and tomatoes and sprinkle the whole dish with the hemp seeds.

Nutrition:
- Calories: 89 Carbs: 11 g
- Fat: 1.2 g Protein: 4 g

221. Sweet and Savory Salad

Preparation time: 10 minutes
Cooking time: 0 minutes
Servings: 1–2
Ingredients:
- 1 big head of butter lettuce
- ½ of 1 cucumber, sliced
- 1 pomegranate seed or ⅓ cup seed
- 1 avocado, cubed
- ¼ cup shelled pistachio, chopped

For the dressing:
- ¼ cup apple cider vinegar
- ½ cup olive oil - 1 garlic clove, minced

Directions:
1. Put the butter lettuce in a salad bowl.
2. Add the remaining ingredients and toss with the salad dressing

Nutrition:
- Calories: 68
- Carbs: 8 g
- Fat: 1.2 g
- Protein: 2 g

222. Kale Pesto's Pasta

Preparation time: 10 minutes
Cooking time: 0 minutes
Servings: 1–2
Ingredients:
- 1 bunch of kale
- 2 cups fresh basil
- ¼ cup extra-virgin olive oil
- ½ cup walnuts
- 2 limes, freshly squeezed
- Sea salt and chili pepper
- 1 zucchini, noodle (spiralizer)
- Optional: garnish with chopped asparagus, spinach leaves, and tomato.

Directions:
1. The night before, soak the walnuts to improve absorption.
2. Put all the recipe ingredients in a blender and blend until the consistency of the cream is reached.
3. Add the zucchini noodles and enjoy.

Nutrition:
- Calories: 55
- Carbs: 9 g
- Fat: 1.2 g

223. Beet Salad With Basil Dressing

Preparation time: 10 minutes
Cooking time: 0 minutes
Servings: 4
Ingredients:
For the dressing:
- ¼ cup blackberries
- ¼ cup extra-virgin olive oil
- Juice of 1 lemon
- 2 tbsp minced fresh basil
- 1 tsp poppy seeds
- A pinch of sea salt

For the salad:
- 2 celery stalks, chopped
- 4 cooked beets, peeled and chopped
- 1 cup blackberries
- 4 cups spring mix

Directions:
1. To make the dressing, mash the blackberries in a bowl. Whisk in the oil, lemon juice, basil, poppy seeds, and sea salt.
2. To make the salad: Add the celery, beets, blackberries, and spring mix to the bowl with the dressing.

3. Combine and serve.

Nutrition:
- Calories: 192
- Fat: 15 g
- Carbs: 15 g
- Protein: 2 g

224. Basic Salad With Olive Oil Dressing

Preparation time: 10 minutes
Cooking time: 0 minute
Servings: 4
Ingredients:
- 1 cup coarsely chopped iceberg lettuce
- 1 cup coarsely chopped romaine lettuce
- 1 cup fresh baby spinach
- 1 large tomato, hulled and coarsely chopped
- 1 cup diced cucumber
- 2 tbsp extra-virgin olive oil
- ¼ tsp sea salt

Directions:
1. In a bowl, combine the spinach and the lettuce. Add the tomato and cucumber.
2. Drizzle with oil and sprinkle with sea salt.
3. Mix and serve.

Nutrition:
- Calories: 77
- Fat: 4 g
- Carbs: 3 g
- Protein: 1 g

225. Spinach and Orange Salad With Oil Drizzle

Preparation time: 10 minutes
Cooking time: 0 minute
Servings: 4
Ingredients:
- 4 cups fresh baby spinach
- 1 blood orange, coarsely chopped
- ½ red onion, thinly sliced
- ½ shallot, finely chopped
- 2 tbsp minced fennel fronds
- Juice of 1 lemon
- 1 tbsp extra-virgin olive oil
- Pinch sea salt

Directions:
1. In a bowl, toss together the spinach, orange, red onion, shallot, and fennel fronds.
2. Add the lemon juice, oil, and sea salt.
3. Mix and serve.

Nutrition:
- Calories: 79
- Fat: 2 g
- Carbs: 8 g
- Protein: 1 g

226. Fruit Salad With Coconut-Lime Dressing

Preparation time: 5 minutes
Cooking time: 0 minutes
Servings: 4
Ingredients:
For the dressing:
- ¼ cup full-fat canned coconut milk
- 1 tbsp raw honey
- Juice of ½ lime - Pinch sea salt

For the salad:
- 2 bananas, thinly sliced
- 2 mandarin oranges, segmented
- ½ cup strawberries, thinly sliced
- ½ cup raspberries
- ½ cup blueberries

Directions:
1. To make the dressing: Whisk all the dressing ingredients in a bowl.
2. To make the salad: Add the salad ingredients into a bowl and mix.
3. Drizzle with the dressing and serve.

Nutrition:
- Calories: 141 Fat: 3 g
- Carbs: 30 g Protein: 2 g

227. Cranberry and Brussels Sprouts With Dressing

Preparation time: 10 minutes
Cooking time: 0 minute
Servings: 4
Ingredients:
For the dressing:
- ⅓ cup extra-virgin olive oil

- 2 tbsp apple cider vinegar
- 1 tbsp pure maple syrup
- Juice of 1 orange
- ½ tbsp dried rosemary
- 1 tbsp scallion, whites only
- Pinch sea salt

For the salad:
- 1 bunch scallions, greens only, finely chopped
- 1 cup Brussels sprouts, stemmed, halved, and thinly sliced
- ½ cup fresh cranberries
- 4 cups fresh baby spinach

Directions:
1. To make the dressing: In a bowl, whisk the dressing ingredients.
2. To make the salad: Add the scallions, Brussels sprouts, cranberries, and spinach to the bowl with the dressing
3. Combine and serve.

Nutrition:
- Calories: 267
- Fat: 18 g
- Carbs: 26 g
- Protein: 2 g

228. Parsnip, Carrot, and Kale Salad With Dressing

Preparation time: 10 minutes
Cooking time: 0 minutes
Servings: 4
Ingredients:
For the dressing:
- ⅓ cup extra-virgin olive oil
- Juice of 1 lime
- 2 tbsp minced fresh mint leaves
- 1 tsp pure maple syrup
- Pinch sea salt

For the salad:
- 1 bunch kale, chopped
- ½ parsnip, grated
- ½ carrot, grated
- 2 tbsp sesame seeds

Directions:
1. To make the dressing, mix all the dressing ingredients in a bowl.
2. To make the salad, add the kale to the dressing and massage the dressing into the kale for 1 minute.
3. Add the parsnip, carrot, and sesame seeds.
4. Combine and serve.

Nutrition:
- Calories: 214
- Fat: 2 g
- Carbs: 12 g
- Protein: 2 g

229. Tomato Toasts

Preparation time: 5 minutes
Cooking time: 5 minutes
Servings: 4
Ingredients:
- 4 slices of sprouted bread toast
- 2 tomatoes, sliced
- 1 avocado, mashed
- 1 tsp olive oil
- 1 pinch of salt
- ¾ tsp ground black pepper

Directions:
1. Blend the olive oil, mashed avocado, salt, and ground black pepper.
2. When the mixture is homogenous—spread it over the sprouted bread.
3. Then place the sliced tomatoes over the toast.
4. Enjoy!

Nutrition:
- Calories: 125
- Fat: 11.1 g
- Carbs: 7.0 g
- Protein: 1.5 g

230. Every Day Salad

Preparation time: 10 minutes
Cooking time: 40 minutes
Servings: 6
Ingredients:
- 5 halved mushrooms
- 6 halved cherry (plum) tomatoes
- 6 rinsed lettuce leaves
- 10 olives

- ½ chopped cucumber
- Juice from ½ key lime
- 1 tsp olive oil
- Pure sea salt

Directions:
1. Tear rinsed lettuce leaves into medium pieces and put them in a medium salad bowl.
2. Add mushrooms halves, chopped cucumber, olives, and cherry tomato halves into the bowl. Mix well. Pour olive and key lime juice over the salad.
3. Add pure sea salt to taste. Mix it all till it is well combined.

Nutrition:
- Calories: 88
- Carbs: 11 g
- Fat: 5 g
- Protein: 8 g

231. Super-Seedy Salad With Tahini Dressing

Preparation time: 10 minutes
Cooking time: 0 minutes
Servings: 1–2
Ingredients:
- 1 slice of stale sourdough, torn into chunks
- 50 g mixed seeds
- 1 tsp cumin seeds
- 1 tsp coriander seeds
- 50 g baby kale
- 75 g long-stemmed broccoli, blanched for a few minutes then roughly chopped
- ½ red onion, thinly sliced
- 100 g cherry tomatoes, halved
- ½ small bunch of flat-leaf parsley, torn

For the dressing:
- 100ml natural yogurt
- 1 tbsp tahini
- 1 lemon, juiced

Directions:
1. Heat the oven to 200°C/fan 180°C/gas. Put the bread into a food processor and pulse into very rough breadcrumbs.
2. Put into a bowl with the mixed seeds and spices, season, and spray well with oil.
3. Tip onto a non-stick baking tray and roast for 15–20 minutes, stirring and tossing regularly, until deep golden brown.
4. Whisk together the dressing ingredients, some seasoning, and a splash of water in a large bowl.
5. Tip the baby kale, broccoli, red onion, cherry tomatoes, and flat-leaf parsley into the dressing, and mix well. Divide between 2 plates and top with the crispy breadcrumbs and seeds.

Nutrition:
- Calories: 78 Carbs: 6 g
- Fat: 2 g Protein: 1.5 g

232. Vegetable Salad

Preparation time: 10 minutes
Cooking time: 0 minutes
Servings: 1–2
Ingredients:
- 4 cups each of raw spinach and romaine lettuce
- 2 cups each of cherry tomatoes, sliced cucumber, chopped baby carrots, and chopped red, orange, and yellow bell pepper
- 1 cup each of chopped broccoli, sliced yellow squash, zucchini and cauliflower.

Directions:
1. Wash all these vegetables.
2. Mix in a large mixing bowl and top off with a non-fat or low-fat dressing of your choice.

Nutrition:
- Calories: 48
- Carbs: 11 g
- Protein: 3 g

233. Greek Salad

Preparation time: 10 minutes
Cooking time: 0 minutes
Servings: 1–2
Ingredients:
- 1 Romaine head, torn in bits
- 1 cucumber sliced

- 1 pint of cherry tomatoes, halved
- 1 green pepper, thinly sliced
- 1 onion sliced into rings
- 1 cup Kalamata olives
- 1 ½ cups Feta cheese, crumbled

For the dressing:
- 1 cup olive oil
- ¼ cup lemon juice
- 2 tsp oregano
- Salt and pepper

Directions:
1. Lay ingredients on a plate.
2. Drizzle dressing over salad

Nutrition:
- Calories: 107
- Carbs: 18 g
- Fat: 1.2 g
- Protein: 1 g

234. Alkaline Spring Salad

Preparation time: 10 minutes
Cooking time: 0 minutes
Servings: 1–2

Eating seasonal fruits and vegetables is a fabulous way of taking care of yourself and the environment at the same time. This alkaline-electric salad is delicious and nutritious.

Ingredients:
- 4 cups seasonal approved greens of your choice
- 1 cup cherry tomatoes
- ¼ cup walnuts
- ¼ cup herbs of your choice

For the dressing:
- 3–4 key limes
- 1 tbsp homemade raw sesame
- Sea salt and cayenne pepper

Directions:
1. First, get the juice of the key limes. In a small bowl, whisk the key lime juice with the homemade raw sesame "tahini" butter. Add sea salt and cayenne pepper, to taste.
2. Cut the cherry tomatoes in half.
3. In a large bowl, combine the greens, cherry tomatoes, and herbs. Pour the dressing on top and "massage" with your hands.
4. Let the greens soak up the dressing Add more sea salt, cayenne pepper, and herbs on top if you wish. Enjoy!

Nutrition:
- Calories: 77
- Carbs: 11 g

235. Fresh Tuna Salad

Preparation time: 10 minutes
Cooking time: none
Servings: 3
Ingredients:
- 1 (6 oz)can of tuna
- ⅓ cup fresh cucumber, chopped
- ⅓ cup fresh tomato, chopped
- ⅓ cup avocado, chopped
- ⅓ cup celery, chopped
- 2 garlic cloves, minced
- 4 tsp olive oil
- 2 tbsp lime juice
- Pinch of black pepper

Directions:
1. Prepare the dressing by combining olive oil, lime juice, minced garlic, and black pepper.
2. Mix the salad ingredients in a salad bowl and drizzle with the dressing.

Nutrition:
- Carbs: 4.8 g
- Protein: 14.3 g
- Total sugars: 1.1 g
- Calories: 212 g

236. Roasted Portobello Salad

Preparation time: 10 minutes
Cooking time: none
Servings: 4
Ingredients:
- 1 ½ lb Portobello mushrooms, stems trimmed
- 3 heads Belgian endive, sliced
- 1 small red onion, sliced
- 4 oz Blue cheese
- 8 oz mixed salad greens

For the dressing:
- 3 tbsp red wine vinegar
- 1 tbsp Dijon mustard
- ⅔ cup olive oil
- Salt and pepper to taste

Directions:
1. Preheat the oven to 450°F.
2. Prepare the dressing by whisking together vinegar, mustard, salt, and pepper. Slowly add olive oil while whisking.
3. Cut the mushrooms and arrange them on a baking sheet, stem-side up. Coat the mushrooms with some dressing and bake for 15 minutes.
4. In a salad bowl toss the salad greens with onion, endive, and cheese. Sprinkle with the dressing:
5. Add mushrooms to the salad bowl.
   - **Nutrition:**
   - Calories: 501
   - Carbs: 22.3 g
   - Protein: 14.9 g
   - Total sugars: 2.1 g

237. Shredded Chicken Salad

Preparation time: 5 minutes
Cooking time: 10 minutes
Servings: 6
Ingredients:
- 2 chicken breasts, boneless, skinless
- 1 head iceberg lettuce, cut into strips
- 2 bell peppers, cut into strips
- 1 fresh cucumber, quartered, sliced
- 3 scallions, sliced
- 2 tbsp chopped peanuts
- 1 tbsp peanut vinaigrette
- Salt to taste
- 1 cup water

Directions:
1. In a skillet simmer 1 cup of salted water.
2. Add the chicken breasts, cover, and cook on low for 5 minutes. Remove the cover. Then remove the chicken from the skillet and shred it with a fork.
3. In a salad bowl mix the vegetables with the cooled chicken, season with salt and sprinkle with peanut vinaigrette and chopped peanuts.

Nutrition:
- Calories: 117 Carbs: 9 g
- Protein: 11.6 g Total sugars: 4.2 g

238. Broccoli Salad

Preparation time: 10 minutes
Cooking time: none
Servings: 6
Ingredients:
- 1 medium head broccoli, raw, florets only
- ½ cup red onion, chopped
- 12 oz turkey bacon, chopped, fried until crisp
- ½ cup cherry tomatoes halved
- ¼ cup sunflower kernels
- ¾ cup raisins
- ¾ cup mayonnaise
- 2 tbsp white vinegar

Directions:
1. In a salad bowl combine the broccoli, tomatoes and onion.
2. Mix mayo with vinegar and sprinkle over the broccoli.
3. Add the sunflower kernels, raisins, and bacon, and toss well.

Nutrition:
- Calories: 220
- Carbs: 17.3 g
- Protein: 11 g
- Total sugars: 10 g

239. Cherry Tomato Salad

Preparation time: 10 minutes
Cooking time: none
Servings: 6
Ingredients:
- 40 cherry tomatoes halved
- 1 cup Mozzarella balls, halved
- 1 cup green olives, sliced
- 1 (6 oz) can of black olives, sliced
- 2 green onions, chopped
- 3 oz roasted pine nuts

For the dressing:
- ½ cup olive oil

- 2 tbs red wine vinegar
- 1 tsp dried oregano
- Salt and pepper to taste

Directions:
1. In a salad bowl, combine the tomatoes, olives and onions.
2. Prepare the dressing by combining olive oil with red wine vinegar, dried oregano, salt, and pepper.
3. Sprinkle with the dressing and add the nuts.
4. Let marinate in the fridge for 1 hour.

Nutrition:
- Carbs: 10.7 g
- Protein: 2.4 g
- Total sugars: 3.6 g

240. Ground Turkey Salad

Preparation time: 10 minutes
Cooking time: 35 minutes
Servings: 6
Ingredients:
- 1 lb lean ground turkey
- ½-inch ginger, minced
- 2 garlic cloves, minced
- 1 onion, chopped
- 1 tbsp olive oil
- 1 bag of lettuce leaves (for serving)
- ¼ cup fresh cilantro, chopped
- 2 tsp coriander powder
- 1 tsp red chili powder
- 1 tsp turmeric powder
- Salt to taste
- 4 cups water

For the dressing:
- 2 tbsp fat-free yogurt
- 1 tbsp sour cream, non-fat
- 1 tbsp low-fat mayonnaise
- 1 lemon, juiced
- 1 tsp red chili flakes
- Salt and pepper to taste

Directions:
1. In a skillet sauté the garlic and ginger in olive oil for 1 minute.
2. Add onion and season with salt.
3. Cook for 10 minutes over medium heat.
4. Add the ground turkey and sauté for 3 more minutes. Add the spices (turmeric, red chili powder, and coriander powder).
5. Add 4 cups of water and cook for 30 minutes, covered.
6. Prepare the dressing by combining yogurt, sour cream, mayo, lemon juice, chili flakes, salt, and pepper.
7. To serve arrange the salad leaves on serving plates and place the cooked ground turkey on them. Top with the dressing

Nutrition:
- Calories: 176 Carbs: 9.1 g
- Protein: 17.8 g
- Total sugars: 2.5 g

241. Asian Cucumber Salad

Preparation time: 10 minutes
Cooking time: none
Servings: 6
Ingredients:
- 1 lb cucumbers, sliced
- 2 scallions, sliced
- 2 tbsp sliced pickled ginger, chopped
- ¼ cup cilantro
- ½ red jalapeño, chopped
- 3 tbs rice wine vinegar
- 1 tbsp sesame oil
- 1 tbsp sesame seeds

Directions:
1. In a salad bowl combine all ingredients and toss together.

Nutrition:
- Calories: 52
- Carbs: 5.7 g
- Protein: 1 g
- Total sugars: 3.1 g

242. Cauliflower Tofu Salad

Preparation time: 10 minutes
Cooking time: 15 minutes
Servings: 4
Ingredients:
- 2 cups cauliflower florets, blended
- 1 fresh cucumber, diced

- ½ cup green olives, diced
- ⅓ cup red onion, diced
- 2 tbsp toasted pine nuts
- 2 tbsp raisins
- ⅓ cup Feta, crumbled
- ½ cup pomegranate seeds
- 2 lemons (juiced, zest grated)
- 8 oz tofu
- 2 tsp oregano
- 2 garlic cloves, minced
- ½ tsp red chili flakes
- 3 tbsp olive oil
- Salt and pepper to taste

Directions:
1. Season the processed cauliflower with salt and transfer it to a strainer to drain.
2. Prepare the marinade for the tofu by combining 2 tbsp lemon juice, 1.5 tbsp olive oil, minced garlic, chili flakes, oregano, salt, and pepper. Coat tofu in the marinade and set aside.
3. Preheat the oven to 450°F.
4. Bake tofu on a baking sheet for 12 minutes.
5. In a salad bowl mix the remaining marinade with onions, cucumber, cauliflower, olives and raisins. Add in the remaining olive oil and grated lemon zest.
6. Top with tofu, pine nuts, Feta, and pomegranate seeds.

Nutrition:
- Calories: 328 Carbs: 34.1 g
- Protein: 11.1 g Total sugars: 11.5 g

243. Scallop Caesar Salad

Preparation time: 5 minutes
Cooking time: 2 minutes
Servings: 2
Ingredients:
- 8 sea scallops
- 4 cups romaine lettuce
- 2 tsp olive oil
- 3 tbsp Caesar salad dressing
- 1 tsp lemon juice
- Salt and pepper to taste

Directions:
1. In a frying pan heat olive oil and cook the scallops in one layer for no longer than 2 minutes on both sides. Season with salt and pepper to taste.
2. Arrange lettuce on plates and place scallops on top.
3. Pour over the Caesar dressing and lemon juice.

Nutrition:
- Calories: 340
- Carbs: 14 g
- Protein: 30.7 g
- Total sugars: 2.2 g

244. Chicken Avocado Salad

Preparation time: 30 minutes
Cooking time: 15 minutes
Servings: 4
Ingredients:
- 1 lb chicken breast, cooked, shredded
- 1 avocado, pitted, peeled, sliced
- 2 tomatoes, diced
- 1 cucumber, peeled, sliced
- 1 head lettuce, chopped
- 3 tbsp olive oil
- 2 tbsp lime juice
- 1 tbsp cilantro, chopped
- Salt and pepper to taste

Directions:
1. In a bowl whisk together oil, lime juice, cilantro, salt, and a pinch of pepper.
2. Combine lettuce, tomatoes, and cucumber in a salad bowl and toss with half of the dressing.
3. Toss chicken with the remaining dressing and combine with the vegetable mixture.
4. Top with avocado.

Nutrition:
- Calories: 380
- Carbs: 10 g
- Protein: 38 g
- Total sugars: 11.5 g

245. California Wraps

Preparation time: 5 minutes
Cooking time: 15 minutes
Servings: 4
Ingredients:
- 4 slices of turkey breast, cooked
- 4 slices of ham, cooked
- 4 lettuce leaves
- 4 slices tomato
- 4 slices avocado
- 1 tsp lime juice
- A handful of watercress leaves
- 4 tbsp ranch dressing, sugar-free

Directions:
1. Top a lettuce leaf with a turkey slice, ham slice, and tomato.
2. In a bowl combine avocado and lime juice and place on top of tomatoes. Top with watercress and dressing.
3. Repeat with the remaining ingredients for
4. Topping each lettuce leaf with a turkey slice, ham slice, tomato and dressing

Nutrition:
- Calories: 140
- Carbs: 4 g
- Protein: 9 g
- Total sugars: 0.5 g

246. Chicken Salad in Cucumber Cups

Preparation time: 5 minutes
Cooking time: 15 minutes
Servings: 4
Ingredients:
- ½ chicken breast, skinless, boiled, and shredded
- 2 long cucumbers, cut into 8 thick rounds each, scooped out
- 1 tsp ginger, minced
- 1 tsp lime zest, grated
- 4 tsp olive oil
- 1 tsp sesame oil
- 1 tsp lime juice
- Salt and pepper to taste

Directions:
1. In a bowl combine lime zest, juice, olive and sesame oils, ginger, and season with salt.
2. Toss the chicken with the dressing and fill the cucumber cups with the salad.

Nutrition:
- Calories: 116
- Carbs: 4 g
- Protein: 12 g
- Total sugars: 0.5 g

247. Sunflower Seeds and Arugula Garden Salad

Preparation time: 5 minutes
Cooking time: 10 minutes
Servings: 6
Ingredients:
- ¼ tsp black pepper
- ¼ tsp salt
- 1 tsp fresh thyme, chopped
- 2 tbsp sunflower seeds, toasted
- 2 cups red grapes, halved
- 7 cups baby arugula, loosely packed
- 1 tbsp coconut oil
- 2 tsp honey
- 3 tbsp red wine vinegar
- ½ tsp stone-ground mustard

Directions:
1. In a small bowl, whisk together mustard, honey, and vinegar. Slowly pour oil as you whisk.
2. In a large salad bowl, mix thyme, seeds, grapes and arugula.
3. Drizzle with dressing and serve.

Nutrition:
- Calories: 86.7 Protein: 1.6 g
- Carbs: 13.1 g Fat: 3.1 g

248. Supreme Caesar Salad

Preparation time: 5 minutes
Cooking time: 10 minutes
Servings: 4
Ingredients:
- ¼ cup olive oil
- ¾ cup mayonnaise

- 1 head of Romaine lettuce, torn into bite-sized pieces
- 1 tbsp lemon juice
- 1 tsp Dijon mustard
- 1 tsp Worcestershire sauce
- 3 garlic cloves, peeled and minced
- 4 cups day-old bread cubed
- 5 anchovy filets, minced
- 6 tbsp grated Parmesan cheese, divided
- Ground black pepper to taste
- Salt to taste

Directions:
1. In a small bowl, whisk well lemon juice, mustard, Worcestershire sauce, 2 tbsp Parmesan cheese, anchovies, mayonnaise, and minced garlic. Season with pepper and salt to taste. Set aside in the ref.
2. On medium fire, place a large non-stick saucepan and heat oil.
3. Sauté quartered garlic until browned around a minute or two. Remove and discard.
4. Add bread cubes to the same pan, and sauté until lightly browned. Season with pepper and salt. Transfer to a plate.
5. In a large bowl, place lettuce and pour in the dressing Toss well to coat. Top with the remaining Parmesan cheese.
6. Garnish with bread cubes, serve, and enjoy.

Nutrition:
- Calories: 443.3
- Fat: 32.1 g
- Protein: 11.6 g
- Carbs: 27 g

249. Tabbouleh-Arabian Salad

Preparation time: 5 minutes
Cooking time: 10 minutes
Servings: 6
Ingredients:
- ¼ cup chopped fresh mint
- 1⅔ cup boiling water
- 1 cucumber, peeled, seeded and chopped
- 1 cup bulgur
- 1 cup chopped fresh parsley
- 1 cup chopped green onions
- 1 tsp salt
- ⅓ cup lemon juice
- ⅓ cup olive oil
- 3 tomatoes, chopped
- Ground black pepper to taste

Directions:
1. In a large bowl, mix boiling water and bulgur. Let soak and set aside for an hour while covered.
2. After one hour, toss in cucumber, tomatoes, mint, parsley, onions, lemon juice, and oil. Then season with black pepper and salt to taste. Toss well and refrigerate for another hour while covered before serving

Nutrition:
- Calories: 185.5
- Fat: 13.1 g
- Protein: 4.1 g
- Carbs: 12.8 g

CHAPTER 10:

Soup

The following are useful, easy, soup recipes that can help in your battle against type 2 diabetes.

250. Fresh Garden Vegetable Soup

Preparation time: 7 minutes
Cooking time: 20 minutes
Servings: 1–2
Ingredients:
- 2 huge carrots
- 1 little zucchini
- 1 celery stem
- 1 cup broccoli
- 3 stalks of asparagus
- 1 yellow onion
- 1 quart of (antacid) water
- 4–5tsp sans yeast vegetable stock
- 1 tsp new basil
- 2 tsp ocean salt to taste

Directions:
1. Put water in a pot, include the vegetable stock just like the onion, and bring to a boil.
2. In the meantime, mix the zucchini, the broccoli, and the asparagus, and shred the carrots and the celery stem in a food processor.
3. When the water is bubbling, it would be ideal if you turn off the oven as we would prefer not to heat up the vegetables. Simply put them all in the high temp water and hold up until the vegetables arrive at the wanted delicacy.
4. Permit to cool somewhat, at that point put all fixings into a blender and blend until you get a thick, smooth consistency.

Nutrition:
- Calories: 43 Carbs: 7 g
- Fat: 1 g

251. Raw Some Gazpacho Soup

Preparation time: 7 minutes
Cooking time: 3 hours
Servings: 3–4
Ingredients:
- 500 g tomatoes
- 1 small cucumber
- 1 red pepper
- 1 onion
- 2 garlic cloves
- 1 small chili
- 1 quart of water (preferably alkaline water)
- 4 tbsp cold-pressed olive oil
- Juice of 1 fresh lemon
- 1 dash of cayenne pepper
- Sea salt to taste

Directions:
1. Remove the skin of the cucumber and cut all vegetables into large pieces.
2. Put all ingredients except the olive oil in a blender and mix until smooth.
3. Add the olive oil and mix again until the oil is emulsified.
4. Put the soup in the fridge and chill for at least 2 hours (soup should be served ice cold).
5. Add some salt and pepper to taste, mix, place the soup in bowls, garnish with chopped scallions, cucumbers, tomatoes, and peppers and enjoy!

Nutrition:
- Calories: 39 Carbs: 8 g
- Fat: 0.5 g Protein: 0.2 g

252. Alkaline Carrot Soup With Fresh Mushrooms

Preparation time: 10 minutes
Cooking time: 20 minutes
Servings: 1–2
Ingredients:
- 4 mid-sized carrots
- 4 mid-sized potatoes
- 10 enormous new mushrooms (champignons or chanterelles)
- ½ white onion
- 2 tbsp olive oil (cold squeezed, additional virgin)
- 3 cups vegetable stock
- 2 tbsp parsley, new and cleaved
- Salt and new white pepper

Directions:
1. Wash and strip carrots and potatoes and dice them.
2. Warm-up vegetable stock in a pot on medium heat. Cook carrots and potatoes for around 15 minutes. Meanwhile finely shape onion and braise them in a container with olive oil for around 3 minutes.
3. Wash mushrooms, slice them to the wanted size, and add to the container, cooking approx. an additional 5 minutes, blending at times. Blend carrots, vegetable stock, and potatoes, and put the substance of the skillet into a pot.
4. When nearly done, season with parsley, salt, and pepper, and serve hot. Appreciate this alkalizing soup!

Nutrition:
- Calories: 75 Carbs: 13 g
- Fat: 1.8 g Protein: 1 g

253. Swiss Cauliflower-Emmenthal-Soup

Preparation time: 10 minutes
Cooking time: 15 minutes
Servings: 3–4
Ingredients:
- 2 cups cauliflower pieces
- 1 cup potatoes, cubed
- 2 cups vegetable stock (without yeast)
- 3 tbsp Swiss Emmenthal Cheddar, cubed
- 2 tbsp new chives
- 1 tbsp pumpkin seeds
- 1 touch of nutmeg and cayenne pepper

Directions:
1. Cook cauliflower and potato in vegetable stock until delicate and blend with a blender.
2. Season the soup with nutmeg and cayenne, and possibly somewhat salt and pepper.
3. Include Emmenthal Cheddar and chives and mix a couple of moments until the soup is smooth and prepared to serve.
4. Enhance it with pumpkin seeds.

Nutrition:
- Calories: 65
- Carbs: 13 g
- Fat: 2 g
- Protein: 1 g

254. Chilled Parsley-Gazpacho With Lime and Cucumber

Preparation time: 10 minutes
Cooking time: 2 hours
Servings: 1
Ingredients:
- 4–5 middle-sized tomatoes
- 2 tbsp extra-virgin olive oil, cold-pressed
- 2 cups fresh parsley
- 2 ripe avocados
- 2 garlic cloves, diced
- 2 limes, juiced
- 4 cups vegetable broth
- 1 middle-sized cucumber
- 2 small red onions, diced
- 1 tsp dried oregano
- 1½ tsp paprika powder
- ½ tsp cayenne pepper
- Sea salt and freshly ground pepper to taste

Directions:
1. In a pan, heat up olive oil and sauté onions and garlic until translucent. Set aside to cool down.

2. Use a large blender and blend parsley, avocado, tomatoes, cucumber, vegetable broth, lime juice, and onion-garlic mix until smooth. Add some water if desired, and season with cayenne pepper, paprika powder, oregano, salt, and pepper. Blend again and put in the fridge for at least 1, 5 hours.

Tip: Add chives or dill to the gazpacho. Enjoy this great alkaline (cold) soup!

Nutrition:
- Calories: 48 Carbs: 12 g
- Fat: 0.8 g

255. Chilled Avocado Tomato Soup

Preparation time: 7 minutes
Cooking time: 20 minutes
Servings: 1–2
Ingredients:
- 2 small avocados
- 2 large tomatoes - 1 stalk of celery
- 1 small onion - 1 garlic clove
- Juice of 1 fresh lemon
- 1 cup water (best: alkaline water)
- A handful of fresh lavage
- Parsley and sea salt to taste

Directions:
1. Scoop the avocados and cut all veggies into little pieces.
2. Spot all fixings in a blender and blend until smooth. Serve chilled and appreciate this nutritious and sound-soluble soup formula!

Nutrition:
- Calories: 68 Carbs: 15 g
- Fat: 2 g Protein: 8 g

256. Pumpkin and White Bean Soup With Sage

Preparation time: 10 minutes
Cooking time: 40 minutes
Servings: 3–4
Ingredients:
- 1 ½ lb pumpkin
- ½ lb yams
- ½ lb white beans
- 1 onion
- 2 garlic cloves
- 1 tbsp cold squeezed additional virgin olive oil
- 1 tbsp spices (your top picks)
- 1 tbsp sage
- 1 ½ quart water (best: antacid water)
- A spot of ocean salt and pepper

Directions:
1. Cut the pumpkin and potatoes into shapes, cut the onion, and cut the garlic, the spices, and the sage, into fine pieces.
2. Sauté the onion and also the garlic in olive oil for around two or three minutes.
3. Include the potatoes, pumpkin, spices, and sage, and fry for an additional 5 minutes.
4. At that point include the water and cook for around 30 minutes (spread the pot with a top) until the vegetables are soft.
5. At long last include the beans and some salt and pepper. Cook for an additional 5 minutes and serve right away. Prepared!! Appreciate this antacid soup. Alkalizing tasty!

Nutrition
- Calories: 78
- Carbs: 12 g

257. Alkaline Carrot Soup With Millet

Preparation time: 7 minutes
Cooking time: 40 minutes
Servings: 3–4
Ingredients:
- 2 cups cauliflower pieces
- 1 cup potatoes, cubed
- 2 cups vegetable stock (without yeast)
- 3 tbsp Swiss Emmenthal Cheddar, cubed
- 2 tbsp new chives
- 1 tbsp pumpkin seeds
- 1 touch of nutmeg and cayenne pepper

Directions:
1. Cook cauliflower and potato in vegetable stock until delicate and Blend with a blender.

2. Season the soup with nutmeg and cayenne, and possibly somewhat salt and pepper.
3. Include EmmenthalCheddar and chives and mix for a couple of minutes until the soup is smooth and prepared to serve. Can enhance with pumpkin seeds.

Nutrition:
- Calories: 65
- Carbs: 15 g
- Fat: 1 g
- Protein: 2 g

258. Alkaline Pumpkin Tomato Soup

Preparation time: 15 minutes
Cooking time: 30 minutes
Servings: 3–4
Ingredients:
- 1 quart of water (if accessible: soluble water)
- 400 g new tomatoes, stripped and diced
- 1 medium-sized sweet pumpkin
- 5 yellow onions
- 1 tbsp cold squeezed additional virgin olive oil
- 2 tsp ocean salt or natural salt
- Touch of cayenne pepper
- Your preferred spices (discretionary)
- Bunch of new parsley

Directions:
1. Cut onions into little pieces and sauté with some oil in a significant pot.
2. Cut the pumpkin down the middle, at that point remove the stem and scoop out the seeds.
3. At long last scoop out the fragile living creature and put it in the pot.
4. Include likewise the tomatoes and the water and cook for around 20 minutes.
5. At that point empty the soup into a food processor and blend well for a couple of moments. Sprinkle with salt pepper and other spices.
6. Fill bowls and trim with new parsley. Make the most of your alkalizing soup!

Nutrition:
- Calories: 78
- Carbs: 20 g
- Fat: 0.5 g
- Protein: 1.5 g

259. Alkaline Pumpkin Coconut Soup

Preparation time: 10 minutes
Cooking time: 15 minutes
Servings: 3–4
Ingredients:
- 2lb pumpkin
- 6 cups water (best: soluble water delivered with a water ionizer)
- 1 cup low-fat coconut milk
- 5 oz potatoes
- 2 large onions
- 3 oz leek
- 1 bunch of fresh parsley
- 1 touch of nutmeg
- 1 touch of cayenne pepper
- 1 tsp ocean salt or natural salt
- 4 tbsp cold squeezed additional virgin olive oil

Directions:
1. As a matter of first significance: cut the onions, the pumpkin, and the potatoes just as the hole into little pieces.
2. At that point, heat the olive oil in a significant pot and sauté the onions for a couple of moments.
3. At that point include the water and heat up the pumpkin, potatoes, and leek until delicate.
4. Include the coconut milk.
5. Presently utilize a hand blender and puree for around 1 moment. The soup should turn out to be extremely velvety.
6. Season with salt, pepper, and nutmeg lastly include the parsley. Appreciate this alkalizing pumpkin soup hot or cold!

Nutrition:
- Calories: 88 Carbs: 23 g
- Fat: 2.5 g
- Protein: 1.8 g

260. Cold Cauliflower-Coconut Soup

Preparation time: 7 minutes
Cooking time: 20 minutes
Servings: 3–4
Ingredients:
- 1 lb(450 g) new cauliflower
- 1 ¼ cup (300ml) unsweetened coconut milk
- 1 cup water (best: antacid water)
- 2 tbsp new lime juice
- ⅓cup cold squeezed additional virgin olive oil
- 1 cup new coriander leaves, slashed
- Spot of salt and cayenne pepper
- 1 bunch of unsweetened coconut chips

Directions:
1. Steam cauliflower for around 10 minutes.
2. At that point, set up the cauliflower with coconut milk and water in a food processor and procedure until extremely smooth.
3. Include new lime squeeze, salt and pepper, a large portion of the cleaved coriander, and the oil, and blend for an additional couple of moments.
4. Pour in soup bowls and embellishment with coriander and coconut chips. Appreciate!

Nutrition:
- Calories: 65
- Carbs: 11 g
- Fat: 0.3 g
- Protein: 1.5 g

261. Raw Avocado-Broccoli Soup With Cashew Nuts

Preparation time: 10 minutes
Cooking time: 30 minutes
Servings: 1–2
Ingredients:
- ½ cup water (if available: alkaline water)
- ½ avocado
- 1 cup chopped broccoli
- ½ cup cashew nuts
- ½ cup alfalfa sprouts
- 1 garlic clove
- 1 tbsp cold-pressed extra-virgin olive oil
- 1 pinch of sea salt and pepper
- Some parsley to garnish

Directions:
1. Put the cashew nuts in a blender or food processor, include some water, and puree for a moment.
2. Include the various fixings (except for the avocado) individually and puree each an ideal opportunity for a couple of moments.
3. Dispense the soup in a container and warm it up to normal room temperature. Enhance with salt and pepper. In the interim dice the avocado and slash the parsley.
4. Dispense the soup in a container or plate; include the diced avocado and embellishment with parsley.
5. That's it! Enjoy this excellent healthy soup!

Nutrition:
- Calories: 48 Carbs: 18 g
- Fat: 3 g
- Protein: 1.4 g

262. White Bean Soup

Preparation time: 10 minutes
Cooking time: 40 minutes
Servings: 6
Ingredients:
- 2 cups white beans, rinsed
- ¼ tsp cayenne pepper
- 1 tsp dried oregano
- ½ tsp fresh rosemary, chopped
- 3 cups filtered alkaline water
- 3 cups unsweetened almond milk
- 3 garlic cloves, minced
- 2 celery stalks, diced
- 1 onion, chopped
- 1 tbsp olive oil
- ½ tsp sea salt

Directions:
1. Add oil into the Instant Pot and set the pot on sauté mode.

2. Add carrots, celery, and onion in oil and sauté until softened, about 5 minutes.
3. Add garlic and sauté for a minute.
4. Add beans, seasonings, water, and almond milk and stir to combine.
5. Cover pot with lid and cook on high pressure for 35 minutes.
6. When finished, allow releasing pressure naturally then open the lid.
7. Stir well and serve.

Nutrition:
- Calories: 276
- Fat: 4.8 g
- Carbs: 44.2 g
- Sugar: 2.3 g
- Protein: 16.6 g
- Cholesterol: 0 mg

263. Kale Cauliflower Soup

Preparation time: 10 minutes
Cooking time: 25 minutes
Servings: 4
Ingredients:
- 2 cups baby kale
- ½ cup unsweetened coconut milk
- 4 cups water
- 1 large cauliflower head, chopped
- 3 garlic cloves, peeled
- 2 carrots, peeled and chopped
- 2 onions, chopped
- 3 tbsp olive oil
- Pepper
- Salt

Directions:
1. Add oil into the Instant Pot and set the pot on sauté mode.
2. Add carrot, garlic, and onion to the pot and sauté for 5–7 minutes.
3. Add water and cauliflower and stir well.
4. Cover pot with lid and cook on high pressure for 20 minutes.
5. When finished, release pressure using the quick release directions, then open the lid.
6. Add kale and coconut milk and stir well.
7. Blend the soup utilizing a submersion blender until smooth.
8. Season with pepper and salt.

Nutrition:
- Calories: 261
- Fat: 18.1 g
- Carbohydrates: 23.9 g
- Sugar: 9.9 g
- Protein: 6.6 g
- Cholesterol: 0 mg

264. Healthy Broccoli Asparagus Soup

Preparation time: 10 minutes
Cooking time: 20 minutes
Servings: 6
Ingredients:
- 2 cups broccoli florets, chopped
- 15 asparagus spears, ends trimmed and chopped
- 1 tsp dried oregano
- 1 tbsp fresh thyme leaves
- ½ cup unsweetened almond milk
- 3 ½ cup filtered alkaline water
- 2 cups cauliflower florets, chopped
- 2 tsp garlic, chopped
- 1 cup onion, chopped
- 2 tbsp olive oil
- Pepper
- Salt

Directions:
1. Add oil to the Instant Pot and set the pot on sauté mode.
2. Add onion to the olive oil and sauté until onion is softened.
3. Add garlic and sauté for 30 seconds.
4. Add all vegetables and water and stir well.
5. Cover pot with lid and cook on manual mode for 3 minutes.
6. When finished, allow releasing pressure naturally then open the lid.
7. Blend the soup utilizing a submersion blender until smooth.
8. Stir in almond milk, herbs, pepper, and salt. Serve and enjoy.

Nutrition:
- Calories: 85 Fat: 5.2 g
- Carbohydrates: 8.8 g Sugar: 3.3 g
- Protein: 3.3 g Cholesterol: 0 mg

265. Creamy Asparagus Soup

Preparation time: 10 minutes
Cooking time: 30 minutes
Servings: 6
Ingredients:
- 2 lb fresh asparagus cut off woody stems
- ¼ tsp lime zest
- 2 tbsp lime juice
- 14 oz coconut milk
- 1 tsp dried thyme
- ½ tsp oregano
- ½ tsp sage
- 1 ½ cups filtered alkaline water
- 1 cauliflower head, cut into florets
- 1 tbsp garlic, minced
- 1 leek, sliced
- 3 tbsp coconut oil
- Pinch of Himalayan salt

Directions:
1. Preheat the oven to 400°F/200°C.
2. Line a baking tray with parchment paper and set it aside.
3. Arrange asparagus spears on a baking tray. Drizzle with 2 tbsp coconut oil and sprinkle with salt, thyme, oregano, and sage. Bake in preheated oven for 20–25 minutes. Add remaining oil to the Instant Pot and set the pot on sauté mode.
4. Put some garlic and leek into the pot and sauté for 2–3 minutes.
5. Add cauliflower florets and water to the pot and stir well.
6. Cover pot with lid and select steam mode and set timer for 4 minutes.
7. When finished, release pressure using the quick release directions.
8. Add roasted asparagus, lime zest, lime juice, and coconut milk and stir well.
9. Blend the soup utilizing a submersion blender until smooth.
10. Serve and enjoy.

Nutrition:
- Calories: 265 Fat: 22.9 g
- Carbs: 14.7 g
- Sugar: 6.7 g Protein: 6.1 g
- Cholesterol: 0 mg

266. Quick Broccoli Soup

Preparation time: 5 minutes
Cooking time: 10 minutes
Servings: 6
Ingredients:
- 1 lb broccoli, chopped
- 6 cups filtered alkaline water
- 1 onion, diced
- 2 tbsp olive oil
- Pepper
- Salt

Directions:
1. Add oil into the Instant Pot and set the pot on sauté mode.
2. Add the onion to olive oil and sauté until softened.
3. Add broccoli and water and stir well.
4. Cover pot with top and cook on manual high pressure for 3 minutes.
5. When finished, release pressure using the quick release directions, then open the lid.
6. Blend the soup utilizing a submersion blender until smooth.
7. Season soup with pepper and salt.
8. Serve and enjoy.

Nutrition:
- Calories: 73 Fat: 4.9 g
- Carbohydrates 6.7 g
- Protein: 2.3 g Sugar: 2.1 g
- Cholesterol: 0 mg

267. Green Lentil Soup

Preparation time: 10 minutes
Cooking time: 30 minutes
Servings: 4
Ingredients:
- 1 ½ cup green lentils, rinsed
- 4 cups baby spinach
- 4 cups filtered alkaline water
- 1 tsp Italian seasoning
- 2 tsp fresh thyme
- 14 oz tomatoes, diced
- 3 garlic cloves, minced
- 2 celery stalks, chopped
- 1 carrot, chopped
- 1 onion, chopped

- Pepper
- Sea salt

Directions:
1. Add all ingredients except spinach into the direct pot and mix fine.
2. Cover pot with top and cook on manual high pressure for 18 minutes.
3. When finished, release pressure using the quick release directions, then open the lid.
4. Add spinach and stir well. Serve and enjoy.

Nutrition:
- Calories: 306 Fat: 1.5 g
- Carbohydrates: 53.7 g
- Sugar: 6.4 g Protein: 21 g
- Cholesterol: 1 mg

268. Squash Soup

Preparation time: 10 minutes
Cooking time: 40 minutes
Servings: 4
Ingredients:
- 3 lb butternut squash, peeled and cubed
- 1 tbsp curry powder
- ½ cup unsweetened coconut milk
- 3 cups filtered alkaline water
- 2 garlic cloves, minced
- 1 large onion, minced
- 1 tsp olive oil

Directions:
1. Add olive oil to the Instant Pot and set the pot on sauté mode.
2. Add onion and cook until tender, about 8 minutes.
3. Add curry powder and garlic and sauté for a minute.
4. Add butternut squash, water, and salt and stir well.
5. Cover pot with lid and cook on soup mode for 30 minutes.
6. When finished, allow releasing pressure naturally for 10 minutes then release using releasing directions, then open the lid. Blend the soup utilizing a submersion blender until smooth.
7. Add coconut milk and stir well.
8. Serve warm and enjoy.

Nutrition:
- Calories: 254
- Fat: 8.9 g
- Carbohydrates: 46.4 g
- Sugar: 10.1 g
- Protein: 4.8 g
- Cholesterol: 0 mg

269. Tomato Soup

Preparation time: 5 minutes
Cooking time: 20 minutes
Servings: 4
Ingredients:
- 6 tomatoes, chopped
- 1 onion, diced
- 14 oz coconut milk
- 1 tsp turmeric
- 1 tsp garlic, minced
- ¼ cup cilantro, chopped
- ½ tsp cayenne pepper
- 1 tsp ginger, minced
- ½ tsp sea salt

Directions:
1. Add all ingredients to the direct pot and mix fine.
2. Cover the Instant Pot with a lid and cook on manual high pressure for 5 minutes.
3. When finished, allow releasing pressure naturally for 10 minutes then release using the quick release directions.
4. Blend the soup utilizing a submersion blender until smooth.
5. Stir well and serve.

Nutrition:
- Calories: 81 Fat: 3.5 g
- Carbohydrates: 11.6 g
- Sugar: 6.1 g Protein: 2.5 g
- Cholesterol: 0 mg

270. Basil Zucchini Soup

Preparation time: 10 minutes
Cooking time: 20 minutes
Servings: 4
Ingredients:
- 3 medium zucchinis, peeled and chopped
- ¼ cup basil, chopped

- 1 large leek, chopped
- 3 cups filtered alkaline water
- 1 tbsp lemon juice
- 3 tbsp olive oil
- 2 tsp sea salt

Directions:
1. Add 2 tbsp oil into the pot and set the pot on sauté mode.
2. Add zucchini and sauté for 5 minutes.
3. Add basil and leeks and sauté for 2–3 minutes.
4. Add lemon juice, water, and salt. Stir well.
5. Cover pot with lid and cook on high pressure for 8 minutes.
6. When finished, allow releasing pressure naturally then open the lid.
7. Blend the soup utilizing a submersion blender until smooth.
8. Top with remaining olive oil and serve.

Nutrition:
- Calories: 157 Fat: 11.9 g
- Carbs: 8.9 g Protein: 5.8 g
- Sugar: 4 g Cholesterol: 0 mg

271. Summer Vegetable Soup

Preparation time: 5 minutes
Cooking time: 20 minutes
Servings: 10
Ingredients:
- ½ cup basil, chopped
- 2 bell peppers, seeded and sliced
- ½ cup green beans, trimmed and cut into pieces - 8 cups filtered alkaline water
- 1 medium summer squash, sliced
- 1 medium zucchini, sliced
- 2 large tomatoes, sliced
- 1 small eggplant, sliced
- 6 garlic cloves, smashed
- 1 medium onion, diced
- Pepper
- Salt

Directions:
1. Combine all elements into the direct pot and mix fine.
2. Cover pot with lid and cook on soup mode for 10 minutes.
3. Release pressure using quick-release directions, then open the lid.
4. Blend the soup utilizing a submersion blender until smooth.
5. Serve and enjoy.

Nutrition:
- Calories: 84
- Fat: 1.6 g
- Carbohydrates: 12.8 g
- Protein: 6.1 g
- Sugar: 6.1 g
- Cholesterol: 0 mg

272. Almond-Red Bell Pepper Dip

Preparation time: 14 minutes
Cooking time: 16 minutes
Servings: 3
Ingredients:
- 2–3 garlic cloves
- 1 pinch of sea salt, one
- 1 pinch of cayenne pepper
- 1 tbsp extra-virgin olive oil (cold-pressed)
- 60 g almonds
- 280 g red bell pepper

Directions:
1. First of all, cook garlic and pepper until they are soft.
2. Add all ingredients to a mixer and blend until the mix becomes smooth and creamy.
3. Finally, add pepper and salt to taste.
4. Serve.

Nutrition:
- Calories: 51
- Carbs: 10 g
- Fat: 1 g
- Protein: 2 g

273. Spicy Carrot Soup

Preparation time: 10 minutes
Cooking time: 20 minutes
Servings: 6
Ingredients:
- 8 large carrots, peeled and chopped
- 1 ½ cup filtered alkaline water
- 14 oz coconut milk

- 3 garlic cloves, peeled
- 1 tbsp red curry paste
- ¼ cup olive oil
- 1 onion, chopped
- Salt

Directions:
1. Combine all elements into the direct pot and mix fine.
2. Cover pot with lid and select manual and set timer for 15 minutes.
3. Allow releasing pressure naturally then open the lid.
4. Blend the soup utilizing a submersion blender until smooth.
5. Serve and enjoy.

Nutrition:
- Calories: 267 Fat: 22 g
- Carbs: 13 g Protein: 4 g
- Sugar: 5 g Cholesterol: 20 mg

274. Zucchini Soup

Preparation time: 10 minutes
Cooking time: 30 minutes
Servings: 10
Ingredients:
- 10 cups zucchini, chopped
- 32 oz filtered alkaline water
- 13 ½ oz coconut milk
- 1 tbsp Thai curry paste

Directions:
1. Combine all elements into the direct pot and mix fine.
2. Cover pot with lid and cook on manual high pressure for 10 minutes.
3. Release pressure using quick-release directions, then open the lid.
4. Using a blender blend the soup until smooth.
5. Serve and enjoy.

Nutrition:
- Calories: 122
- Fat: 9.8 g
- Carbs: 6.6 g
- Protein: 4.1 g
- Sugar: 3.6 g
- Cholesterol: 0 mg

275. Kidney Bean Stew

Preparation time: 15 minutes
Cooking time: 15 minutes
Servings: 2
Ingredients:
- 1lb cooked kidney beans
- 1 cup tomato passata
- 1 cup low-sodium beef broth
- 3tbsp Italian herbs

Directions:
1. Mix all the ingredients in your Instant Pot.
2. Cook on "Stew" for 15 minutes.
3. Release the pressure naturally.

Nutrition:
- Calories: 270
- Carbs: 16 g
- Sugar: 3 g
- Fat: 10 g
- Protein: 23 g
- GL: 8

276. Cabbage Soup

Preparation time: 15 minutes
Cooking time: 35 minutes
Servings: 2
Ingredients:
- 1lb shredded cabbage
- 1 cup low-sodium vegetable broth
- 1 shredded onion
- 2tbsp mixed herbs
- 1tbsp black pepper

Directions:
1. Mix all the ingredients in your Instant Pot.
2. Cook on "Stew" for 35 minutes.
3. Release the pressure naturally.

Nutrition:
- Calories: 60 Carbs: 2 g
- Sugar: 0 g Fat: 2 g
- Protein: 4 g GL: 1

277. Pumpkin Spice Soup

Preparation time: 10 minutes
Cooking time: 35 minutes
Servings: 2
Ingredients:
- 1lb cubed pumpkin

- 1 cup low-sodium vegetable broth
- 2tbsp mixed spice

Directions:
1. Mix all the ingredients in your Instant Pot.
2. Cook on "Stew" for 35 minutes.
3. Release the pressure naturally.
4. Blend the soup.

Nutrition:
- Calories: 100
- Carbs: 7 g
- Sugar: 1 g
- Fat: 2 g
- Protein: 3 g
- GL: 1

278. Cream of Tomato Soup

Preparation time: 15 minutes
Cooking time: 15 minutes
Servings: 2
Ingredients:
- 1lb fresh tomatoes, chopped
- 1 ½ cup low-sodium tomato puree
- 1tbsp black pepper

Directions:
1. Mix all the ingredients in your Instant Pot.
2. Cook on "Stew" for 15 minutes.
3. Release the pressure naturally.
4. Blend.

Nutrition
- Calories: 20
- Carbs: 2 g
- Sugar: 1 g
- Fat: 0 g
- Protein: 3 g
- GL: 1

279. Shiitake Soup

Preparation time: 15 minutes
Cooking time: 35 minutes
Servings: 2
Ingredients:
- 1 cup shiitake mushrooms
- 1 cup diced vegetables
- 1 cup low-sodium vegetable broth
- 2tbsp 5 spice seasoning

Directions:
1. Mix all the ingredients in your Instant Pot.
2. Cook on "Stew" for 35 minutes.
3. Release the pressure naturally.

Nutrition:
- Calories: 70 Carbs: 5 g Sugar: 1 g
- Fat: 2 g Protein: 2 g GL: 1

280. Spicy Pepper Soup

Preparation time: 15 minutes
Cooking time: 15 minutes
Servings: 2
Ingredients:
- 1lb chopped mixed sweet peppers
- 1 cup low-sodium vegetable broth
- 3tbsp chopped chili peppers
- 1tbsp black pepper

Directions:
1. Mix all the ingredients in your Instant Pot.
2. Cook on "Stew" for 15 minutes.
3. Release the pressure naturally. Blend.

Nutrition:
- Calories: 100 Carbs: 11 g
- Sugar: 4 g Fat: 2 g Protein: 3 g GL: 6

281. Zoodle Won-Ton Soup

Preparation time: 15 minutes
Cooking time: 5 minutes
Servings: 2
Ingredients:
- 1lb spiralized zucchini
- 1 pack of unfried won-tons
- 1 cup low-sodium beef broth
- 2tbsp soy sauce

Directions:
1. Mix all the ingredients in your Instant Pot.
2. Cook on "Stew" for 5 minutes.
3. Release the pressure naturally.

Nutrition:
- Calories: 300
- Carbs: 6 g
- Sugar: 1 g
- Fat: 9 g
- Protein: 43 g
- GL: 2

CHAPTER 11:

Dessert

The following are useful, easy, and sweet dessert recipes that can help in your battle against type 2 diabetes.

282. Chocolate Crunch Bars

Preparation time: 5 minutes
Cooking time: 5 minutes
Servings: 4
Ingredients:
- 1 ½ cup sugar-free chocolate chips
- 1 cup almond butter
- Stevia to taste
- ¼ cup coconut oil
- 3 cups pecans, chopped

Directions:
1. Layer an 8-inch baking pan with parchment paper.
2. Mix chocolate chips with butter, coconut oil, and sweetener in a bowl.
3. Melt it by heating in a microwave for 2–3 minutes until well mixed.
4. Stir in nuts and seeds. Mix gently.
5. Pour this batter carefully into the baking pan and spread evenly.
6. Refrigerate for 2–3 hours.
7. Slice and serve.

Nutrition:
- Calories: 316 Total fat: 30.9 g
- Saturated fat: 8.1 g Cholesterol: 0 mg
- Total carbs: 8.3 g
- Sugar: 1.8 g Fiber: 3.8 g
- Sodium: 8 mg Protein: 6.4 g

283. Homemade Protein Bar

Preparation time: 5 minutes
Cooking time: 10 minutes
Servings: 4
Ingredients:
- 1 cup nut butter
- 4 tbsp coconut oil
- 2 scoops of vanilla protein
- Stevia, to taste
- ½ tsp sea salt
- 1 cup chocolate chips
- Optional: 1 tsp cinnamon

Directions:
1. Mix coconut oil with butter, protein, Stevia, and salt in a dish.
2. Stir in cinnamon and chocolate chip.
3. Press the mixture firmly and freeze until firm.
4. Cut the crust into small bars.
5. Serve and enjoy.

Nutrition:
- Calories: 179 Total fat: 15.7 g
- Saturated fat: 8 g
- Cholesterol: 0 mg
- Total carbs: 4.8 g Sugar: 3.6 g
- Fiber: 0.8 g Sodium: 43 mg
- Protein: 5.6 g

284. Shortbread Cookies

Preparation time: 10 minutes
Cooking time: 70 minutes
Servings: 6
Ingredients:
- 2 ½ cup almond flour
- 6 tbsp nut butter
- ½ cup Erythritol
- 1 tsp vanilla essence

Directions:
1. Preheat your oven to 350°F.
2. Layer a cookie sheet with parchment paper.
3. Beat butter with Erythritol until fluffy.

4. Stir in vanilla essence and almond flour. Mix well until becomes crumbly.
5. Spoon out a tbsp cookie dough onto the cookie sheet.
6. Add more dough to make as many cookies.
7. Bake for 15 minutes until brown.
8. Serve.

Nutrition:
- Calories: 288 Total fat: 25.3 g
- Saturated fat: 6.7 g
- Cholesterol: 23 mg
- Total carbs: 9.6 g Sugar: 0.1 g
- Fiber: 3.8 g Sodium: 74 mg
- Potassium: 3 mg
- Protein: 7.6 g

285. Coconut Chip Cookies

Preparation time: 10 minutes
Cooking time: 15 minutes
Servings: 4
Ingredients:
- 1 cup almond flour
- ½ cup cacao nibs
- ½ cup coconut flakes, unsweetened
- ⅓ cup Erythritol
- ½ cup almond butter
- ¼ cup nut butter, melted
- ¼ cup almond milk
- Stevia, to taste
- ¼ tsp sea salt

Directions:
1. Preheat your oven to 350°F.
2. Layer a cookie sheet with parchment paper.
3. Add and then combine all the dry ingredients in a glass bowl.
4. Whisk in butter, almond milk, vanilla essence, Stevia, and almond butter.
5. Beat well then stir in dry mixture. Mix well.
6. Spoon out a tbsp cookie dough on the cookie sheet.
7. Add more dough to make as many as 16 cookies.
8. Flatten each cookie using your fingers.
9. Bake for 25 minutes until golden brown.
10. Let them sit for 15 minutes.
11. Serve.

Nutrition:
- Calories: 192
- Total fat: 17.44 g
- Saturated fat: 11.5 g
- Cholesterol: 125 mg
- Total carbs: 2.2 g
- Sugar: 1.4 g
- Fiber: 2.1 g
- Sodium: 135 mg
- Protein: 4.7 g

286. Peanut Butter Bars

Preparation time: 10 minutes
Cooking time: 10 minutes
Servings: 6
Ingredients:
- ¾ cup almond flour
- 2 oz almond butter
- ¼ cup swerve
- ½ cup peanut butter
- ½ tsp vanilla

Directions:
1. Combine all the ingredients for bars.
2. Transfer this mixture to a 6-inch small pan. Press it firmly.
3. Refrigerate for 30 minutes.
4. Slice and serve.

Nutrition:
- Calories: 214
- Total fat: 19 g
- Saturated fat: 5.8 g
- Cholesterol: 15 mg
- Total carbs: 6.5 g
- Sugar: 1.9 g
- Fiber: 2.1 g
- Sodium: 123 mg
- Protein: 6.5 g

287. Zucchini Bread Pancakes

Preparation time: 15 minutes
Cooking time: 35 minutes
Servings: 3
Ingredients:
- 1 tbsp grapeseed oil

- ½ cup chopped walnuts
- 2 cups walnut milk
- 1 cup shredded zucchini
- ¼ cup mashed burro banana
- 2 tbsp date sugar
- 2 cups Kamut flour or spelt

Directions:
1. Place the date sugar and flour into a bowl. Whisk together.
2. Add in the mashed banana and walnut milk. Stir until combined. Remember to scrape the bowl to get all the dry mixture. Add in walnuts and zucchini. Stir well until combined.
3. Place the grapeseed oil onto a griddle and warm.
4. Pour 25 cups of batter on the hot griddle. Leave it along until bubbles begin forming on to surface. Carefully turn over the pancake and cook another four minutes until cooked through.
5. Place the pancakes onto a serving plate and enjoy with some agave syrup.

Nutrition:
- Calories: 246 Carbs: 49.2 g
- Fiber: 4.6 g Protein: 7.8 g

288. Berry Sorbet

Preparation time: 10 minutes
Cooking time: 20 minutes
Servings: 6
Ingredients:
- 2 cups water
- 2 cups blend strawberries
- 1 ½ tsp spelt flour
- ½ cup date sugar

Directions:
1. Add the water into a large pot and let the water begin to warm. Add the flour and date sugar and stir until dissolved. Allow this mixture to start boiling and continue to cook for around ten minutes. It should have started to thicken. Take off the heat and set it to the side to cool.
2. Once the syrup has cooled off, add in the strawberries, and stir well to combine.
3. Pour into a container that is freezer safe and put it into the freezer until frozen.
4. Take sorbet out of the freezer, cut into chunks, and put it either into a blender or a food processor. Hit the pulse button until the mixture is creamy.
5. Pour this into the same freezer-safe container and put it back into the freezer for four hours.

Nutrition:
- Calories: 99 Carbs: 8 g

289. Quinoa Porridge

Preparation time: 5 minutes
Cooking time: 15 minutes
Servings: 4
Ingredients:
- Zest of 1 lime
- ½ cup coconut milk
- ½ tsp cloves
- 1 ½ tsp ground ginger
- 2 cups spring water
- 1 cup quinoa
- 1 grated apple

Directions:
1. Cook the quinoa. Follow the instructions on the package. When the quinoa has been cooked, drain well. Place it back into the pot and stir in spices.
2. Add coconut milk and stir well to combine.
3. Grate the apple now and stir well.
4. Divide equally into bowls and add the lime zest on top. Sprinkle with nuts and seeds of choice.

Nutrition:
- Calories: 180 Fat: 3 g
- Carbs: 40 g
- Protein: 10 g

290. Apple Quinoa

Preparation time: 15 minutes
Cooking time: 30 minutes
Servings: 4
Ingredients:
- 1 tbsp coconut oil
- Ginger

- ½ key lime
- 1 apple
- ½ cup quinoa

Optional toppings:
- Seeds
- Nuts
- Berries

Directions:
1. Fix the quinoa according to the instructions on the package. When you are getting close to the end of the cooking time, grate in the apple and cook for 30 seconds.
2. Zest the lime into the quinoa and squeeze the juice in. Stir in the coconut oil.
3. Divide evenly into bowls and sprinkle with some ginger.
4. You can add in some berries, nuts, and seeds right before you eat.

Nutrition:
- Calories: 146
- Fiber: 2.3 g
- Fat: 8.3 g

291. Kamut Porridge

Preparation time: 10 minutes
Cooking time: 25 minutes
Servings: 4
Ingredients:
- 4 tbsp agave syrup
- 1 tbsp coconut oil
- ½ tsp sea salt
- 3 ¾ cups coconut milk
- 1 cup Kamut berries

Optional toppings:
- Berries
- Coconut chips
- Ground nutmeg
- Ground cloves

Directions:
1. You need to "crack" the Kamut berries. You can try this by placing the berries into a food processor and pulsing until you have 1.25 cup of Kamut.
2. Place the cracked Kamut in a pot with salt and coconut milk.
3. Give it a good stir to combine everything.

4. Allow this mixture to come to a full rolling boil and then turn the heat down until the mixture is simmering.
5. Stir now and then until the Kamut has thickened to your likeness.
6. This normally takes about ten minutes.
7. Take off heat, stir in agave syrup and coconut oil.
8. Garnish with toppings of choice and enjoy.

Nutrition:
- Calories: 114 Protein: 5 g
- Carbs: 24 g Fiber: 4 g

292. Hot Kamut With Peaches, Walnuts, and Coconut

Preparation time: 10 minutes
Cooking time: 35 minutes
Servings: 4
Ingredients:
- 4 tbsp toasted coconut
- ½ cup toasted and chopped walnuts
- 8 chopped dried peaches
- 3 cups coconut milk
- 1 cup Kamut cereal

Directions:
1. Mix the coconut milk into a saucepan and allow it to warm up. When it begins simmering, add in the Kamut. Let this cook for about 15 minutes, while stirring now and then.
2. When done, divide evenly into bowls and top with the toasted coconut, walnuts, and peaches.
3. You could even go one more and add some fresh berries.

Nutrition:
- Calories: 156 Protein: 5.8 g
- Carbs: 25 g Fiber: 6 g

293. Overnight "Oats"

Preparation time: 5 minutes
Cooking time: 0 minutes
Servings: 4
Ingredients:
- ½ cup berry of choice
- ½ tbsp walnut butter

- ½ burro banana
- ½ tsp ginger
- ½ cup coconut milk
- ½ cup hemp seeds

Directions:
1. Put the hemp seeds, salt, and coconut milk into a glass jar. Mix well.
2. Place the lid on the jar then put it in the refrigerator to sit overnight.
3. The next morning, add the ginger, berries, and banana.
4. Stir well and enjoy.

Nutrition:
- Calories: 139 Fat: 4.1 g
- Protein: 9 g Sugar: 7 g

294. Blueberry Cupcakes

Preparation time: 15 minutes
Cooking time: 40 minutes
Servings: 4
Ingredients:
- Grapeseed oil
- ½ tsp sea salt
- ¼ cup sea moss gel
- ⅓ cup agave
- ½ cup blueberries
- ¾ cup teff flour
- ¾ cup spelt flour
- 1 cup coconut milk

Directions:
1. Warm your oven to 365°F. Place paper liners into a muffin tin.
2. Place sea moss gel, sea salt, agave, flour, and milk in a large bowl. Mix well to combine. Gently fold in blueberries.
3. Gently pour batter into paper liners. Place in oven and bake for 30 minutes.
4. They are done if they have turned a nice golden color, and they spring back when you touch them.

Nutrition:
- Calories: 85
- Fat: 0.7 g
- Carbs: 12 g
- Protein: 1.4 g
- Fiber: 5 g

295. Brazil Nut Cheese

Preparation time: 2 hours
Cooking time: 0 minutes
Servings: 4
Ingredients:
- 2 tsp grapeseed oil
- 1 ½ cup water
- 1 ½ cup hemp milk
- ½ tsp cayenne
- 1 tsp onion powder
- ½ lime juice
- 2 tsp sea salt
- 1 lb Brazil nuts
- 1 tsp onion powder

Directions:
1. You will need to start the process by soaking the Brazil nuts in some water. You just put the nuts into a bowl and make sure the water covers them. Soak no less than two hours or overnight. Overnight would be best.
2. Now you need to put everything except water into a food processor or blender.
3. Add just ½ cup water and blend for two minutes.
4. Continue adding ½ cup water and blending until you have the consistency you want.
5. Scrape into an airtight container and enjoy.

Nutrition:
- Calories: 187
- Protein: 4.1 g
- Fat: 19 g
- Carbs: 3.3 g
- Fiber: 2.1 g

296. Slow Cooker Peaches

Preparation time: 10 minutes
Cooking time: 4 hours 20 minutes
Servings: 4–6
Ingredients:
- 4 cups peaches, sliced
- ⅔ cup rolled oats
- ⅓ cup bisques
- ¼ tsp cinnamon

- ½ cup brown sugar
- ½ cup granulated sugar

Directions:
1. Spray the Slow Cooker pot with a cooking spray.
2. Mix oats, bisques, cinnamon, and all the sugars in the pot.
3. Add peaches and stir well to combine. Cook on low for 4–6 hours.

Nutrition:
- Calories: 617
- Fat: 3.6 g
- Total carbs: 13 g
- Protein: 9 g

297. Pumpkin Custard

Preparation time: 10 minutes
Cooking time: 2 hours 30 minutes
Servings: 6
Ingredients:
- ½ cup almond flour
- 4 eggs
- 1 cup pumpkin puree
- ½ cup Stevia Erythritol blend granulated
- ⅛ tsp sea salt
- 1 tsp vanilla extractor maple flavoring
- 4 tbsp butter, ghee, or coconut oil melted
- 1 tsp pumpkin pie spice

Directions:
1. Grease or spray a Slow Cooker with butter or coconut oil spray.
2. In a medium mixing bowl, beat the eggs until smooth. Then add in the sweetener.
3. To the egg mixture, add the pumpkin puree along with vanilla or maple extract.
4. Then add almond flour to the mixture along with the pumpkin pie spice and salt.
5. Add melted butter, coconut oil, or ghee.
6. Transfer the mixture into a Slow Cooker.
7. Close the lid and cook for 2–2 ¾ hours on low.
8. When through, serve with whipped cream, and then sprinkle with little nutmeg if need be. Enjoy!
9. Set the slow-cooker to the low setting Cook for 2–2.45 hours, and begin checking at the two-hour mark. Serve warm with Stevia-sweetened whipped cream and a sprinkle of nutmeg

Nutrition:
- Calories: 147 Fat: 12 g
- Total carbs: 4 g Protein: 5 g

298. Blueberry Lemon Custard Cake

Preparation time: 10 minutes
Cooking time: 3 hours
Servings: 12
Ingredients:
- 6 eggs separated
- 2 cups light cream
- ½ cup coconut flour
- ½ tsp salt
- 2 tsp lemon zest
- ½ cup granulated sugar substitute
- ⅓ cup lemon juice
- ½ cup blueberries fresh
- 1 tsp lemon liquid Stevia

Directions:
1. Into a stand mixer, add the egg whites and whip them well until stiff peaks have formed; set aside.
2. Whisk the yolks together with the remaining ingredients except for blueberries, to form the batter.
3. When done, fold egg whites into the formed batter a little at a time until slightly combined.
4. Grease the crockpot and then pour in the mixture. Then sprinkle the batter with the blueberries.
5. Close the lid then cook for 3 hours on low. When the cooking time is over, open the lid and let cool for an hour, and then let chill in the refrigerator for at least 2 hours or overnight.
6. Serve cold with little sugar-free whipped cream and enjoy!

Nutrition:
- Calories: 165 Fat: 10 g
- Total carbs: 14 g
- Protein: 4 g

299. Sugar-Free Carrot Cake

Cooking time: 4 hours
Servings: 8
Ingredients:
For the carrot cake:
- 2 eggs
- 1 ½ almond flour
- ½ cup butter, melted
- ¼ cup heavy cream
- 1 tsp baking powder
- 1 tsp vanilla extract or almond extract, optional
- 1 cup sugar substitute
- 1 cup carrots, finely shredded
- 1 tsp cinnamon
- ¼ tsp nutmeg
- ⅛ tsp allspice - 1 tsp ginger
- ½ tsp baking soda

For the cream cheese frosting:
- 1 cup confectioner's sugar substitute
- ¼ cup butter softened
- 1 tsp almond extract
- 4 oz cream cheese, softened

Directions:
1. Grease a loaf pan well and then set it aside.
2. Using a mixer, combine butter with eggs, vanilla, sugar substitute, and heavy cream in a mixing bowl, until well blended.
3. Combine almond flour with baking powder, spices, and baking soda in another bowl until well blended.
4. When done, combine the wet ingredients with the dry ingredients until well blended, and then stir in carrots. Pour the mixer into the prepared loaf pan, and then place the pan into a Slow Cooker on a trivet. Add 1 cup of water inside.
5. Cook for about 4–5 hours on low. Be aware that the cake will be very moist.
6. When the cooking time is over, let the cake cool completely. To prepare the cream cheese frosting: blend the cream cheese with extract, butter, and powdered sugar substitute until frosting is formed.
7. Top the cake with the frosting

Nutrition:
- Calories: 299
- Fat: 25.4 g
- Total carbs: 15 g
- Protein: 4 g

300. Sugar-Free Chocolate Molten Lava Cake

Preparation time: 10 minutes
Cooking time: 3 hours
Servings: 12
Ingredients:
- 3 egg yolks
- 1 ½ cup swerve sweetener divided
- 1 tsp baking powder
- ½ cup flour, gluten-free
- 3 whole eggs
- 5 tbsp cocoa powder, unsweetened, divided
- 4 oz chocolate chips, sugar-free
- ½ tsp salt
- ½ tsp vanilla liquid Stevia
- ½ cup butter melted cooled
- 2 cups hot water
- 1 tsp vanilla extract

Directions:
1. Grease the crockpot well with cooking spray.
2. Whisk 1 ¼ cup swerve together with flour, salt, baking powder, and 3 tbsp cocoa powder in a bowl.
3. Stir the cooled melted butter together with eggs, yolks, liquid Stevia, and the vanilla extract in a separate bowl.
4. When done, add the wet ingredients to the dry ingredient until nicely combined, and then pour the mixture into the prepared crockpot.
5. Then top the mixture in the crockpot with chocolate chips.
6. Whisk the rest of the swerve sweetener and the remaining cocoa powder with the hot water, and then pour this mixture over the chocolate chips top.

7. Close the lid and cook for 3 hours on low. When the cooking time is over, let cool a bit and then serve. Enjoy!

Nutrition:
- Calories: 157
- Fat: 13 g
- Total carbs: 10.5 g
- Protein: 3.9 g

CHAPTER 12:

Meal Plan

1-Week Fast Easy Diet Plan

DAYS	BREAKFAST	LUNCH	DINNER	DESSERT
1	Whole-grain breakfast cookies	Fried pork chops	Baked salmon with garlic parmesan topping	Chocolate crunch bars
2	Blueberry breakfast cake	Pork on a blanket	Baked seafood casserole	Homemade protein bar
3	Whole-grain pancakes	Chicken thighs	Bbq oysters with bacon	Shortbread cookies
4	Buckwheat grouts breakfast bowl	Tasty harissa chicken	Pork rind	Coconut chip cookies
5	Peach muesli bake	Cheesy salmon fillets	Ginger chili broccoli	Peanut butter bars
6	Steel-cut oatmeal bowl with fruit and nuts	Salmon with asparagus	Pork tenderloin	Zucchini bread pancakes
7	Whole-grain dutch baby pancake	Shrimp in garlic butter	Chicken soup	Berry sorbet

4-Week Diet Plan

DAYS	BREAKFAST	LUNCH	DINNER	DESSERT
1	Mushroom, zucchini, and onion frittata	Roasted pork	Basic salad with olive oil dressing	Quinoa porridge
2	Spinach and cheese quiche	Marinated loin potatoes	Spinach and orange salad with oil drizzle	Apple quinoa
3	Spicy jalapeno popper deviled eggs	Homemade flamingos	Fruit salad with coconut-lime dressing	Kamut porridge

4	Lovely porridge	Meatloaf reboot	Cranberry and brussels sprouts with dressing	Hot kamut with peaches, walnuts, and coconut
5	Salty macadamia chocolate smoothie	Tasty chicken tenders	Parsnip, carrot, and kale salad with dressing	Overnight "oats"
6	Basil and tomato baked eggs	Blackened shrimp	Chilled avocado tomato soup	Blueberry cupcakes
7	Cinnamon and coconut porridge	Cajun catfish	Pumpkin and white bean soup with sage	Brazil nut cheese
8	An omelet of swiss chard	Cajun flounder and tomatoes	Alkaline carrot soup with millet	Slow cooker peaches
9	Cheesy low-carb omelet	Cajun shrimp and roasted vegetables	Alkaline pumpkin tomato soup	Pumpkin custard
10	Yogurt and kale smoothie	Cilantro lime grilled shrimp	Alkaline pumpkin coconut soup	Blueberry lemon custard cake
11	Bacon and chicken garlic wrap	Thai quinoa salad	Lemon pepper salmon	Sugar-free chocolate molten lava cake
12	Grilled chicken platter	Green goddess bowl and avocado cumin dressing	Green salmon florentine	Chocolate quinoa brownies
13	Parsley chicken breast	7 sweet and savory salad	Seared scallops with orange sauce	Blueberry crisp
14	Mustard chicken	Kale pesto's pasta	Cod fillet with quinoa and asparagus	Maple custard
15	Balsamic chicken	Beet salad with basil dressing	Red cabbage and mushroom potstickers	Raspberry cream cheese coffee cake
16	Greek chicken breast	Fresh garden vegetable soup	Greek chicken lettuce wraps	Pumpkin pie bars
17	Chipotle lettuce chicken	Raw some gazpacho soup	Lemon chicken with kale	Dark chocolate cake
18	Stylish chicken-bacon wrap	Alkaline carrot soup with fresh mushrooms	Pumpkin, bean, and chicken enchiladas	Lemon custard
19	Healthy cottage cheese pancakes	Swiss cauliflower-omental-soup	Mu shu chicken	Quinoa porridge

20	Avocado lemon toast	Chilled parsley-gazpacho with lime and cucumber	Stove-top chicken, macaroni, and cheese	Apple quinoa
21	Healthy baked eggs	Chicken and tofu	Coconut shrimp	Kamut porridge
22	Quick low-carb oatmeal	Chicken and peanut stir-fry	Crab cakes	Hot kamut with peaches, walnuts, and coconut
23	Tofu and vegetable scramble	Honey mustard chicken	Crab frittata	Overnight "oats"
24	Breakfast smoothie bowl with fresh berries	Lemon garlic turkey	Crispy baked flounder with green beans	Blueberry cupcakes
25	Chia and coconut pudding	Chicken and spinach	Crock pot fish and tomatoes	Brazil nut cheese
26	Tomato and zucchini sauté	Crunchy lemon shrimp	Creamy mushroom pork chops	Slow cooker peaches
27	Steamed kale with mediterranean dressing	Dill smoked salmon over noodles	Pork and sweet potato mash	Pumpkin custard
28	Healthy carrot muffins	Fisherman's pie	Lamb roast	Blueberry lemon custard cake
29	Mushroom, zucchini, and onion frittata	Garlic shrimp with sun-dried tomatoes	Burgundy lamb shanks	Sugar-free chocolate molten lava cake
30	Spinach and cheese quiche	Tuna sweet corn casserole	Fruity pork roast	Chocolate quinoa brownies

Conclusion

With the knowledge I have shared, you now know why you may have developed diabetes, you know what this means, and what to do with it. You are armed with resources, apps, and recipes to help you along this lifelong journey. Food is not your enemy; it's your friend.

Cook your way to vitality and health with these recipes and tips. Good things are made for sharing, so please help a friend find out about this way of life. Call them over for a meal, talk about diabetes, and let's help create awareness as we feast on every delectable spoonful of diabetic cooking made easy.

The warning symptoms of diabetes type 1 are the same as type 2. However, in type 1, these signs and symptoms tend to occur slowly over months or years, making them harder to spot and recognize. Some of these symptoms can even occur after the disease has progressed.

Each disorder has risk factors that, when found in an individual, favor the development of the disease. Diabetes is no different.

Usually, having a family member, especially first-degree relatives, could indicate that you are at risk of developing diabetes. Your risk of diabetes is about 15% if you have one parent with diabetes, while it is 75% if both your parents have diabetes.

Being pre-diabetic means that you have higher than normal blood glucose levels. However, they are not high enough to be diagnosed with type 2 diabetes. Having pre-diabetes is also a risk factor for developing type 2 diabetes as well as other conditions such as cardiac conditions. Since there are no symptoms or signs of pre-diabetes, it is often a latent condition that is discovered accidentally during routine investigations of blood glucose levels or when investigating other conditions.

Your metabolism, fat stores, and eating habits when you are overweight or above the healthy weight range contribute to abnormal metabolism pathways that put you at risk for developing diabetes type 2. There have been consistent research results on the obvious link between developing diabetes and being obese.

Having a lifestyle where you are most physically inactive predisposes you to a lot of conditions, including diabetes type 2. That is because being physically inactive causes you to develop obesity or become overweight. Moreover, you don't burn any excess sugars that you ingest, which can lead you to become prediabetic and eventually diabetic.

Developing gestational diabetes, which is diabetes that occurred due to pregnancy (and often disappears after pregnancy) is a risk factor for developing diabetes at some point.

Belonging to certain ethnic groups such as Middle Eastern, South Asian, or Indian backgrounds. Studies of statistics have revealed that the prevalence of diabetes type 2 in these ethnic groups is high. If you come from any of these ethnicities, this puts you at risk of developing diabetes type 2 yourself.

Studies have shown an association between having hypertension and having an increased risk of developing diabetes. If you have hypertension, you should not leave it uncontrolled.

Diabetes can occur at any age. However, being too young or too old means your body is not in its best form, and therefore, this increases the risk of developing diabetes.

When your body is low on sugars, it will be forced to use a subsequent molecule to burn for energy. In that case, this will be fat. The burning of fat will lead you to lose weight.

I hope you have learned something and… Good luck!

Appendix Measurement Conversion Chart

Volume

Imperial	Metric	Imperial	Metric
1 tbsp	15ml	1 pint	570 ml
2 fl oz	55 ml	1 ¼ pints	725 ml
3 fl oz	75 ml	1 ¾ pints	1 litre
5 fl oz (¼ pint)	150 ml	2 pints	1.2 litres
10 fl oz (½ pint)	275 ml	2½ pints	1.5 litres
		4 pints	2.25 litres

Weight

Imperial	Metric	Imperial	Metric	Imperial	Metric
½ oz	10 g	4 oz	110 g	10 oz	275 g
¾ oz	20 g	4½ oz	125 g	12 oz	350 g
1 oz	25 g	5 oz	150 g	1 lb	450 g
1½ oz	40 g	6 oz	175 g	1 lb 8 oz	700 g
2 oz	50 g	7 oz	200 g	2 lb	900 g
2½ oz	60 g	8 oz	225 g	3 lb	1.35 kg
3 oz	75 g	9 oz	250 g		

Metric Cups Conversion

Cups	Imperial	Metric
1 cup flour	5oz	150 g
1 cup caster or granulated sugar	8oz	225 g
1 cup soft brown sugar	6oz	175 g
1 cup soft butter/margarine	8oz	225 g
1 cup sultanas/raisins	7oz	200 g
1 cup currants	5oz	150 g
1 cup ground almonds	4oz	110 g
1 cup oats	4oz	110 g
1 cup golden syrup/honey	12oz	350 g

1 cup uncooked rice	7oz	200 g
1 cup grated cheese	4oz	110 g
1 stick butter	4oz	110 g
¼ cup liquid (water, milk, oil, etc.)	4 tbsp	60ml
½ cup liquid (water, milk, oil, etc.)	¼ pint	125ml
1 cup liquid (water, milk, oil, etc.)	½ pint	250ml

Oven Temperatures

Gas Mark	Fahrenheit	Celsius	Gas Mark	Fahrenheit	Celsius
¼	225	110	4	350	180
½	250	130	5	375	190
1	275	140	6	400	200
2	300	150	7	425	220
3	325	170	8	450	230
			9	475	240

Weight

Imperial	Metric	Imperial	Metric
½ oz	10 g	6 oz	175 g
¾ oz	20 g	7 oz	200 g
1 oz	25 g	8 oz	225 g
1½ oz	40 g	9 oz	250 g
2 oz	50 g	10 oz	275 g
2½ oz	60 g	12 oz	350 g
3 oz	75 g	1 lb	450 g
4 oz	110 g	1 lb 8 oz	700 g
4½ oz	125 g	2 lb	900 g
5 oz	150 g	3 lb	1.35 kg

Printed in Great Britain
by Amazon